AFFIRMATIVE ACTION

Contemporary Issues

Series Editors: Robert M. Baird
Stuart E. Rosenbaum

All volumes have been edited by the series editors, except where otherwise noted.

Other titles in this series:

AFFIRMATIVE ACTION

Social Justice or Reverse Discrimination?

Edited by
Francis J. Beckwith and Todd E. Jones

Prometheus Books

59 John Glenn Drive
Amherst, NewYork 14228-2197

Published 1997 by Prometheus Books

Inquiries should be addressed to
Prometheus Books, 59 John Glenn Drive, Amherst, New York 14228–2197.
VOICE: 716–691–0133, ext. 207. FAX: 716–564–2711.
WWW.PROMETHEUSBOOKS.COM

03 02 01 00 99   7 6 5 4 3 2

Library of Congress Cataloging-in-Publication Data

Affirmative action : social justice or reverse discrimination? / edited by Francis
      J. Beckwith and Todd E. Jones.
            p.   cm. — Contemporary issues (Amherst, N.Y.)
      Includes bibliographical references (p.   ).
      ISBN 1–57392–157-2 (paper : alk. paper)
      1. Race discrimination—United States—History—20th century. 2. United
States—Race relations. 3. Afro-Americans—Civil rights—History—20th century 4. Affirmative action programs—Law and legislation—United States. I.
Beckwith, Francis. II. Jones, Todd E. III. Series
E185.615.A592   1997
305.8'00973—dc21   97-25098
                                                                          CIP

Printed in Canada on acid-free paper

To my parents, William and Elaine, who taught me that we should strive continually to leave the world a better place than when we enter it.

—TEJ

To my nephews and nieces, who as adults will be citizens of the twenty-first century: Jordan Wiegand, Tyler Wiegand, Dean Beckwith, Dylan Beckwith, Riley Beckwith, Devin Beckwith, and Darby Beckwith. May the world you occupy be more just, more good, and more true than the one in which we now live, and may your lives contribute to that achievement.

—FJB

CONTENTS

PART II: PHILOSOPHICAL DISCUSSIONS OF AFFIRMATIVE ACTION

WHAT IS AFFIRMATIVE ACTION AND WHAT IS THE CONTROVERSY ABOUT?

On November 5, 1996 the people of the state of California passed one of the most important ballot questions pertaining to the question of affirmative action, the California Civil Rights Initiative (CCRI). Intended to eliminate most, though not all, forms of California state-sponsored affirmative action, a portion of the initiative reads:

> Neither the State of California nor any of its political subdivisions or agents shall use race, sex, color, ethnicity, or national origin as a criterion for either discriminating against, or granting preferential treatment to, any individual or group in the operation of the State's system of public employment, public education or public contracting.

To its supporters the initiative is consistent with the primary goal of the American Civil Rights movement, equal opportunity for all regardless of race or gender. They cite in their defense a portion of the Civil Rights Act of 1964, which states that no employer is required to "grant preferential treatment to any individual or group on account of any imbalance which may exist" between the number of employees in such groups and "the total number or percentage of persons of such race, color, religion, sex, or national origin in any community, State, section, or other area" (from provision 703(j) of Title VII of the Civil Rights Act of 1964).

9

Supporters of the initiative also point out that in order to achieve its primary goal the civil rights leadership did not propose preferential treatment but rather fought to eliminate barriers to advancement, such as segregation, laws which discriminated against blacks and other minorities, discrimination in employment, and policies which prevented blacks and other minorities from attending a number of educational institutions including universities and colleges. The idea of preferential treatment apparently was out of the question. In fact, Roy Wilkins, then Executive Director of the NAACP (National Association for the Advancement of Colored People), testified before a congressional committee considering the 1964 Civil Rights Act: "Our association has never been in favor of a quota system. We believe the quota system is unfair whether it is used for [blacks] or against [blacks]. . . . [We] feel people ought to be hired because of their ability, irrespective of their color. . . . We want equality, equality of opportunity and employment on the basis of ability."[1]

On the other hand, opponents of the California initiative defend preferential treatment by pointing out that it became apparent in the mid to late 1960s that eradication of discriminatory laws did not result in the Civil Rights movement's vision of a completely unsegregated society. In pursuit of this vision, President Lyndon Baines Johnson in 1965 issued Executive Order 11246 in which the Department of Labor was required to award on the basis of race government contracts with construction companies. This was justified by maintaining that it was necessary in order to make up for the centuries of the loathsome practice of racial discrimination which resulted in oppression. President Johnson, in a speech inaugurating Executive Order 11246, used an analogy to make his point:

> Imagine a hundred yard dash in which one of the two runners has his legs shackled together. He has progressed 10 yds., while the unshackled runner has gone 50 yds. How do they rectify the situation? Do they merely remove the shackles and allow the race to proceed? Then they could say that "equal opportunity" now prevailed. But one of the runners would still be forty yards ahead of the other. Would it not be the better part of justice to allow the previously shackled runner to make-up the forty yard gap; or to start the race all over again? That would be affirmative action towards equality.

Supporters of affirmative action argue that the history of discrimination against women and minorities in America has resulted in white males dominating and controlling the network of social institutions which is the focus of power and authority in our society; these institutions include banks, universities, corporations, and governments (federal, state, and local). Thus, in order to truly achieve justice and fairness there must be a shift in the power base in these institutions. According to the supporters of affirmative action, this can be achieved only by preferential treatment programs with goals and timetables.

II. Two Forms of Affirmative Action

The California initiative will no doubt set in motion a nationwide debate over affirmative action. Because there is a tendency in the American media to portray the partisans in this debate as polarized opposites, the fact that there are different definitions of affirmative action is rarely, if ever, clearly articulated.

Affirmative action policies take a large variety of forms, ranging from making recruiting efforts in ethnic communities to mandating a specific number of positions be set aside for minorities. The different types of affirmative action are sometimes thought of as occupying one of two rough categories. The first can be termed *weak affirmative action.* Louis P. Pojman defines weak affirmative action as the employment of "such measures as the elimination of segregation, widespread advertisement to groups not previously represented in certain privileged positions, special scholarships for the disadvantaged classes (e.g., all the poor), using underrepresentation or a history of past discrimination as a tie breaker when candidates are relatively equal, and the like."[2] This view stresses *equal opportunity,* an opportunity to compete without irrelevant characteristics being taken into consideration. The stress is *not* on equal results. For example, an employer or a college admissions officer should in every case, except perhaps in the case of a tie, ignore the race or gender of the candidate; the candidate should be judged on the basis of his or her qualifications. If this results in a particular profession having a disproportionate number of a certain group in comparison to the percentage of the general population (e.g., 95 percent of the employees are white while only 78 percent of the general population is white), the result is not unfair since everyone was given an equal opportunity to excel.

On the other hand, *strong affirmative action* "involves more positive steps to eliminate past injustice, such as reverse discrimination, hiring candidates on the basis of race or gender in order to reach equal or near equal results, proportionate representation in each area of society."[3] This view stresses *equal results* (or at least some goal or pattern which ought to be achieved) by using timetables, goals, or quotas as criteria by which to judge whether one has achieved fairness. Rather than stressing fair process, the proponents of this position see fairness as result, which is why they can ignore what their opponents think are ordinary canons of fair play as well as maintain that it is permissible (if not obligatory in some cases) to hire a less though adequately qualified candidate for a position because such a hiring results in equality or fairness. Proponents often defend this notion of fairness by appealing to ethnic and gender diversity, proportional representation, and/or some form of reparations for past injustice (e.g., whites must pay blacks for slavery and segregation as well as their unjust results).

It would be wrong, however, to say that the proponent of this approach is arguing that unqualified minorities and women should receive scarce educational and employment positions over qualified white males. Qualifications and merit do matter, but they are not the only criteria when allocating scarce resources. Some proponents of this perspective put forth what has come to be called *the threshold argument.* According to this argument, universities, employment, etc. are forms for the distribution of goods. Some goods are things like socially necessary skills (e.g., becoming a doctor), but in addition, they distribute wealth, status, power, and so forth. Society has an interest in making sure that these latter goods do not line up with divisions along ethnic and gender lines. In this case we would think in terms of thresholds, not in terms of an absolute hierarchy of merit.

The threshold argument seems to be saying that at above some level of competence in certain positions greater qualifications are unnecessary and for that reason it would not be unjust for an employer, manager, or admissions officer to select a person on the basis of other factors, such as race or gender, since society has an interest in the diverse distribution of its goods. In other words, race and gender membership should trump better qualifications when they are important to the position but not necessary for minimal competence. Some of the contributors to this book hold to some version of the threshold argument.

An example of strong affirmative action that many find controversial, if not disturbing, is the widely practiced but little known policy of *race norming* (a practice that was ultimately banned by the Civil Rights Act of 1991 for any employer subject to federal regulation)[4]

> Imagine that four men came into a state employment office in order to apply for a job. One is black, one Hispanic, one Asian and one white. They take the standard test (a version of the General Aptitude Test Battery or VG-GATB). All get a composite score of 300. None of them will ever see that score. Instead the numbers will be fed into a computer and the applicants' percentile ranking emerges. The scores are group-weighted. Blacks are measured against blacks, whites against whites, Hispanics against Hispanics. Since blacks characteristically do less well than other groups, the effect is to favor blacks. For example, a score of 300 as an accountant will give the black a percentile of 87, an Hispanic a percentile of 74 and a white or Oriental a score of 47. The black will get the job as the accountant.[5]

Numerous other examples of strong affirmative action policies practiced in many different venues, such as education, public employment, and the private sector, are found in some of the essays in this volume

There is little doubt that strong affirmative action is much more controversial than weak affirmative action. In fact, one could say that weak affirmative action is not controversial at all and that most forms of it are consistent with CCRI. This is why some people refer to strong affirmative action as preferential treatment.

III. DIFFERENT APPROACHES TO AFFIRMATIVE ACTION.

In this book we divide the debate over affirmative action into two general categories: Part One: The Public Policy Debate Over Affirmative Action, and Part Two: Philosophical Discussions Of Affirmative Action. Although the issues discussed in the essays in each category certainly overlap, there is a difference between the public policy debate and the philosophical debate.

First, the philosophical justification of affirmative action is logically prior to the public policy justification, though the defense of a public policy proposal may appeal to as well as employ philosophical argument (which is true of most of the essays in Part One). By logical priority we mean that any public policy recommendation needs to be given a grounding in one philosophical moral principle or another. To give a clear cut example, suppose person Y proposed that as a matter of public policy we ought to reinstitute the practice of human slavery. Suppose he defended this proposal by arguing that it would lead to economic growth which would significantly benefit nearly 80 percent of the population. Even if Y's prediction were true, his proposal would be dismissed on a philosophical basis, namely, the well-grounded moral intuition that treating human persons as property violates their fundamental rights. Although Part One deals with the public policy debate, the authors in that section understand that philosophical and moral considerations are fundamentally important. These considerations are taken up with greater rigor and care by the authors in Part Two.

Second, even though philosophical justification is logically prior to public policy justification, inquiry into philosophical justification may lead to one of three conclusions about the policy in question: (1) the policy is impermissible, (2) the policy is permissible (but not obligatory), or (3) the policy is obligatory. If a policy, such as the one proposed by Y, is impermissible, then we need not go any further. It seems that authors Ward Connerly (chapter 3), Louis P. Pojman (chapter 11), and Michael E. Levin (chapter 13) are arguing that, with the exception of rare cases, affirmative action is morally impermissible. That is to say, as a matter of policy, the state is obligated not to engage in virtually any affirmative action program. (The question of whether the private sector should be permitted to practice affirmative action is a different matter which none of these authors explicitly addresses.) However, if a policy is permissible or obligatory, numerous considerations must come into play.

If a policy is permissible, then questions of prudence and pragmatism must be considered. For example, suppose that some strong forms of affirmative action are morally permissible, but we discover that employing such policies in some institutions, such as higher education, leads to either greater harm than the policies were supposed to eradicate or less benefit than the policies were supposed to produce. Then we have good reasons why we ought not to put those policies in place. However, if such policies result in more benefit than harm, then we have good reason to institute these forms of strong affirmative action. When policies are merely permissible, then considerations of cost-benefit analysis are legitimate. And the cost-benefit need not be financial; it may include benefits such as cultural diversity, excellence, institutional integrity, a society free of prejudice, etc. As long as the policy is not morally impermissible, one may consider certain good ends as part of one's policy analysis. Authors Ronald Dworkin (chapter 4), Frederick R. Lynch (chapter 5), Thomas Sowell (chapter 6), Shelby Steele (chapter 8), William Julius Wilson (chapter 10), Richard Wasserstrom (chapter 12), Tom L. Beauchamp (chapter 14), and George Sher (chapter 15) all seem to be arguing their cases, either for or against certain affirmative action policies, primarily on the basis of cost-benefit analysis, though each does take into consideration moral argument. On the other hand, when policies are impermissible (see above), such cost-benefit considerations are not legitimate.

If a policy is obligatory, then the recipient of the policy's benefit is entitled to and/or deserves that benefit. For example, if person X steals a car from person Y, the latter is owed the value of the car (or the car itself) plus the financial rewards she would have received if not for the absence of the car (e.g., she uses her car for business). That is to say, Y is entitled to as well as deserves what was taken from her by X. Arguments for affirmative action based on reparations for slavery and segregation as well as compensation for past injustice typically appeal to these notions. It seems that authors Lyndon Baines Johnson (chapter 2), Cornel West (chapter 7), and Stanley Fish (chapter 9) are trying to justify affirmative action by arguing that the policy, if instituted correctly, is morally obligatory.

In addition to the distinctions between impermissible, permissible, and obligatory policies, there are different features of the cases put forth by those who support weak and/or strong affirmative action policies. One aspect of their cases is the *forward-looking feature*.[6] When this feature is employed by a proponent of affirmative action, she is maintaining that affirmative action is good because it results in something worthwhile and beneficial. For example, an executive from Wal-Mart while speaking in a Whittier College business class (April 4, 1997) said that his company wants to hire a culturally diverse workforce because it wants to have employees who look like its customers. And this, it hopes, will result in a greater sense of community, and hence, greater profits for Wal-Mart. This argument is not based on "reparations for slavery and/or segregation" or "compensation for past discrimination," which would be backward-looking reasons, but rather, it is an argument based on achieving some good to which no one is either owed or entitled. Many universities and colleges hire employees from underrepresented groups in order to have a more diverse environment so that their students and faculty may have role models as well as achieve a better understanding of those from different backgrounds. This diversity, the argument goes, helps intellectually and socially enrich the institution. Arguments for affirmative action based on cost-benefit analysis are typically forward-looking arguments. Moreover, forward-looking arguments are usually both utilitarian and deontological. That is to say, proponents of such arguments attempt to justify their cases by appealing both to considerations of consequences (e.g., the policies result in the greatest happiness for the greatest number) and to suggestions that such policies result in a society that is more just, more good, and/or more fair, irrespective of increases or decreases in happiness, etc.

Another aspect of cases put forth to defend both weak and strong affirmative action is *the backward-looking feature*. Those who appeal to this feature attempt to justify affirmative action by arguing that it is necessary in order to compensate for and/or correct past injustice. Those who maintain that some affirmative action programs are morally obligatory typically emphasize the backward-looking feature of their cases. Moreover, backward-looking arguments are strictly deontological, since they typically appeal to such moral notions as just compensation and rectifying past wrongs. It should be noted, however, that most proponents of any form of affirmative action usually present a mixed case for their position in which both forward-looking and backward-looking arguments are employed.

IV. A CALL TO CIVILITY

The editors of this text each take different positions on the issue of affirmative action. Although we disagree, we are friends who have respect for each other. Unfortunately, the popular debate often results in name-calling, race-baiting, and political incivility. For this reason, we believe this collection of essays satisfies a real need for a book which deals with the more serious philosophical and public policy defenses and critiques of affirmative action as well as providing a hearing for nuanced positions which don't fit very well into the two polarized camps often portrayed in the popular media. In order to help the reader better understand the essays in this book as well as study this issue more deeply, we have provided detailed introductions to both parts of this text as well as a lengthy bibliography at the end.

Although our views differ, we both take to heart, and we hope the reader does as well, the words of Martin Luther King Jr., "We will not be satisfied until justice rolls down like waters and righteousness like a mighty stream."[7]

I hate Liverpool librarians

Francis J. Beckwith
Anaheim Hills, California

Todd E. Jones
Las Vegas, Nevada

NOTES

1. Quoted by William Bradford Reynolds in his article, "Affirmative Action is Unjust," in *Social Justice*, ed. D. Bender and B. Leone (St. Paul, Minn., 1984), 23.

2. Louis P. Pojman, "The Moral Status of Affirmative Action," *Public Affairs Quarterly* 6 (April 1992): 183. A large portion of this article is republished as chapter 11 of this book.

3. Ibid.

4. Richard J. Herrnstein and Charles Murray, *The Bell Curve: Intelligence and Class Structure in American Life* (New York: The Free Press, 1994), 504

5. Pojman, "The Moral Status of Affirmative Action," 188.

6. Pojman makes this distinction between forward-looking and backward-looking features in ibid., 183.

7. From a speech delivered in Washington, D.C., on June 15, 1963. King is quoting the biblical passage Amos 5:24.

PART ONE

THE PUBLIC POLICY DEBATE
OVER AFFIRMATIVE ACTION

INTRODUCTION TO PART I

America is known as "the land of opportunity." But it has also long been clear that some Americans seem to lack the opportunities that others have, or seem less able to take advantage of these opportunities. In our universities for example, tenured male professors outnumber tenured female professors by a factor of 10 to 1 (see Beauchamp, chapter 14). In this day and age, almost no one would attribute such a disparity to an inherent male intellectual superiority. In terms of *preparation* for a university education, we find Americans of African descent lagging a long way behind their white counterparts. In 1983 for example, only 600 blacks in America scored over 1200 on the SAT, compared with 60,000 whites.[1] The statistics for black Americans outside of the academic realm, however, are far more grim, More college-age black males are in jail or are clients of the correctional system than are in school (see Steele, chapter 8).

Such disparities in "the land of opportunity" have prompted compassionate people to take a variety of measures to try to make things more fair and equal for members of disadvantaged groups. Collectively, these measures have come to be known as "affirmative action." They range from efforts like widespread job advertising to groups that are underrepresented in privileged positions, to outright quotas mandating that a certain number of positions must be set aside for minorities. Since these programs began in the mid 1960s, a number of minority achievements and success stories

21

can, in part, be attributed to these affirmative action efforts. As Wilson (chapter 10) points out, many more black students are attending college than in years past. There are many more blacks in professional and administrative positions than there were decades ago, as well.

But such achievements have not come without a cost, and many feel that the costs have been far too high for relatively meager gains. "[I]n a tight labor market," writes Frederick R. Lynch, "affirmative action must necessarily operate in a zero sum context: when one person was hired because of race, ethnicity or gender, others were thereby excluded on the same discriminatory grounds." If black males and women were helped by affirmative action, white males, often having superior qualifications, were directly harmed by it. Paradoxically, many black people, too, suffered harms as many white people began to automatically assume that any black person in a position of prestige had not earned his or her position, but had merely been awarded it in an affirmative action program.

Affirmative action programs also come with the cost of seeming to force us to violate our deeply held ideals in order to satisfy those same ideals. Affirmative action programs seek to create a society in which people were not barred from opportunities because of their color or gender. To do this, however, many programs were put in place in which people with superior qualifications were disqualified from certain positions *because* of their color or gender. Such dissonance has been too much for many people to live comfortably with. Indeed, the very legality of such programs under our Constitution has been repeatedly questioned. Over the last several decades, in a series of cases, such as *Griggs, DeFunis, Bakke,* and *Pena,* the Supreme Court has struggled with the question of whether our Constitution encourages such equalizing measures, or forbids them as race- or gender-based discrimination.

In this first section of this book we will look at the public policy debate about affirmative action. As the public debate about affirmative action covers a wider range of concerns, so do the essays in this section. The first article, by Lemann, gives a brief history of affirmative action policies and the debates surrounding them. He points out that many of our current affirmative action policies had their origins in executive orders and in obscure executive branch agencies during the Johnson administration. The origins and subsequent development of these policies in the executive branch of government kept them from having to go through legislative scrutiny and debate. The result has been policies that have taken root without the sort of thorough public hearing normally accorded to policies of this magnitude. Lemann ends up arguing that there is a legitimate case to be made for affirmative action policies, but that that case has not been thoroughly made, and until it is, affirmative action policies will lack public support.

The next essay, the text of a speech made by President Lyndon Baines Johnson at Howard University in 1965, takes us back to the days when historic civil rights legislation was being passed and affirmative action programs were defended with soaring rhetoric. Johnson's speech is an early, impassioned defense of the very sorts of affirmative action programs so commonly attacked in more recent times. Johnson argues that affirmative action is part of our basic American ideals of justice and fairness. Laws like the Civil Rights Act of 1964 and the Voting Rights Act were seen as making sure that our ideals of freedom and justice were extended to every American. But in a memorable passage, Johnson argues that it is not enough just to guarantee equal basic freedoms:

> You do not wipe away the scars of centuries by saying: Now you are free to go where you want, and do as you desire, and choose the leaders as you please. You do not take a person who for years has been hobbled by chains and liberate him, bring him up to the starting line of a race and then say, "you are free to compete with all the others," and still justly believe you have been completely fair.

Johnson believed that to guarantee everyone the right to full participation in the American dream, we must implement policies that give previously disadvantaged black people preferential treatment in education and employment.

In the next essay, Ward Connerly gives an equally impassioned and eloquent defense of the ideal that is often invoked by opponents of affirmative action—that of a truly color-blind, nondiscriminatory society. Connerly was chairman of the "Yes on Proposition 209" campaign, which supported the 1996 California Civil Rights Initiative (CCRI) that we discussed earlier (see Introduction). Connerly's essay is the text of the Victory Speech he gave on the Evening of November 5, 1996. Speaking over a quarter century after exsegregationist Johnson's affirmative action call to arms, this black businessman argues that it is only when we ignore color completely that all Americans will be free and equal. He writes that affirmative action only allows people to blame failings on others, rather than look inwardly and strive to improve. He quotes numerous popular icons to make clear how deep and widespread our commitment to color-blind self-reliance is. Even Disney's Jimminy Cricket is pressed into service, reminding people "when you wish upon a star, it makes no difference who you are . . ."

With ideals so heartfelt and so conflicting, it was inevitable that the question of which feelings represented our true ideal as embodied in the Constitution would be taken up by the courts, and eventually reach the Supreme Court. One of the most celebrated cases considered by the court was that of *DeFunis* v. *Washington State.* At issue in that case was whether the constitutional rights to equal protection of Marco DeFunis, a white student, had been violated when black students with lower test scores had been admitted to Washington State's Law School while DeFunis had originally been refused admission. That case turned out to be more famous for what it couldn't decide than what it could decide. As Lemann describes in the first chapter, the court was split down the middle in its opinions about whether the ideals embodied in our Constitution were those that receive such eloquent voice in President Johnson's Howard University Speech, or in those conflicting ones that receive voice in Ward Connerly's Victory Speech. In "The DeFunis Case" Ronald Dworkin painstakingly goes through the moral and legal considerations both sides brought to the table in arguing their cases. The article is long and complicated, but full of very important moral and legal considerations and distinctions which need to be made, but are often overlooked in everyday discourse. Dworkin ultimately argues that Washington State had a legal right to refuse DeFunis admission to its Law School. He begins with the elementary claim that DeFunis had no constitutional *right* to any kind of legal education. If Washington State did not have a law school, no one's constitutional rights would have been violated. What DeFunis may have been unfairly denied, however, was the right to *equal treatment,* which the Constitution does prescribe. Just what equal treatment amounts to, however, is vague, and was precisely what was at issue for the court to decide. Dworkin points out that this cannot mean that we should indiscriminately try to make things more equal as a general policy, for that would justify measures like having a lottery and selecting some wealthy students to be charged double to make sure more poorer students could attend some school. At the same time equal treatment cannot mean merely treating everyone the same, for that would mandate, say, giving the same amount of medicine to a dying person as to a person who was merely uncomfortable. We must sometimes allow some people to be treated with less favor if this increases the benefits to the group overall. Dworkin argues that, indeed, numerous utilitarian benefits for the society overall can be achieved by increasing the number of black students in law school. And the process by which they were selected, in Washington State, was neither arbitrary or unfair, nor violated any individual's rights.

The central worry for many, however, is that the same utilitarian arguments used to justify DeFunis's inadmittance could be used to argue against disadvantaged groups. Indeed, such arguments had once had been used to claim that that society's interests were better served if Harvard admitted more WASPS (White Anglo-Saxon Protestants), people more likely to be senators and captains of industries, and fewer more overtly intellectual Jews. Dworkin argues that such worries can be blocked, however, by making a distinction between personal preferences (ones' own wants) and external preferences (the desires that *other people's* preferences be fulfilled or unfulfilled). He argues that when external preferences, such as racial prejudice against minority groups, are excluded, as they should be if we are to respect equal treatment, such discrimination against oppressed groups would not be allowed. However, some affirmative action policies employed to help disadvantaged minorities would be permissible, since such policies are based on the personal preferences of minorities (e.g., to be treated equally), and not on external preferences such as racial preference against others. (What this does not clearly establish, however, is that there could not, *in principle*, be *some* utilitarian grounding for some types of discrimination against minorities— and this is what opponents of discrimination of any sort want to *assure* one avoids). Washington State's policy, according to Dworkin, was thus a legitimate one on moral and constitutional grounds.

Outside of the lofty and moral and constitutional ideals we find in the rhetoric of the jurists and politicians, there also continue to be numerous straightforward practical worries concerning who affirmative action programs help, and who they hurt. In "Casualties and More Casualties: Surviving Affirmative Action (More or

Less)," Frederick R. Lynch discusses the point of view of those who often feel harmed by affirmative action: white males. Numerous white males feel that they have had severe career set-backs because of affirmative action programs. While these men may have never discriminated against anyone, they nevertheless find themselves being denied positions they are clearly qualified for, while less-qualified members of minority groups are offered the positions. These men feel that *they* are being made to pay the price of for the discriminating practices of people in the past. The result is resentment, both against minority group members seen as taking jobs they are less qualified for, and of government programs in general. Such resentment, it should be noted, cannot be helpful in a establishing a more racially harmonious society.

Furthermore, besides causing disappointment and resentment among whites, it is not clear that affirmative action has been that helpful to black Americans. In "From Equal Opportunity to 'Affirmative Action,' " Thomas Sowell points out such surprising facts as the number of blacks in technical and professional occupations being less in the two years following the civil rights act of 1964 than in the years before it. In 1969, before the imposition of numerical affirmative action goals, Puerto Rican family income was 63 percent of the national average. But it was down to 50 percent by 1977. Sowell argues that it's not merely *in spite* of affirmative action that minorities are not advancing, but *because* of it. Affirmative action, he contends, has made it very difficult to fire minority workers who don't work out—therefore there is a heavy demand to hire *only* the very most qualified minorities. This leaves less qualified minorities even worse off than before. Sowell also argues that we needn't make any assumption that massive discrimination is the cause of some groups doing better than others. Some groups are doing better because their members are older, on average, than members of other groups. In other cases groups do better by living primarily in more high-income areas of the country. Sometimes groups can easily be underrepresented because of mere statistical fluctuations. While some minority groups are not doing well, Sowell argues, we need assume neither that there is massive discrimination, nor that affirmative action is an effective way of curing it.

In "Nihilism in Black America," Cornel West concurs that things are indeed bleak for African Americans. Indeed, he argues, things are far worse in the black community than economic and demographic indicators suggest. There are not merely problems of unemployment, teen pregnancy, and violent crime, but also deeper problems of a "monumental eclipse of hope, the unprecedented collapse of meaning, the incredible disregard for human (especially black) life and property in black America. . . ." Because of this deep-seated despair, West believes that "liberal" solutions to racial problems bases on such things as full employment, child-care programs, and affirmative action will be inadequate by themselves. Nihilism is a "disease of the soul" that must be cured by affirmations of one's worth fueled by the mutual concern of others. He speaks of the need for a grass-roots, locally based "politics of conversion" based in self-affirmation, and directly confronting self-destructive and inhumane behaviors.

At the same time, the problems of poverty must not be overlooked. "The fundamental crisis in black America," he writes, "is twofold: too much poverty and too little self-love." Indeed, it is a continuing poverty, in the face of the continual march of the media preaching that one's potential for market consumption is the only measure of worth, that has largely led to the ensuing nihilism in the black communities. For this reason, rigorous affirmative action programs, which help redistribute wealth and opportunities, are still essential. West believes that however limited the success of these programs may be (and it's possible that *contra* Sowell the success has been limited because they are not pursued vigorously *enough* to make such programs bear fruit), without affirmative action programs, the problems would be much worse. "Given the history of this country, it is a virtual certainty that without affirmative action racial and sexual discrimination would return with a vengeance," writes West. With affirmative action, blacks are given at least some hope of success, even if they haven't previously been among society's winners; and that hope provides some safeguards against the nihilism that is the worst enemy of the black community. "For as long as hope and meaning is preserved," writes West, "the possibility of overcoming oppression stays alive."

In "Affirmative Action: The Price of Preference," however, Shelby Steele argues that despair and lack of hope may be actually made worse by affirmative action. "Under affirmative action the quality that earns us preferential treatment is an implied inferiority," writes Steele. The rationale for affirmative action is that, for whatever reason, blacks and whites are currently unable to compete for positions of prestige on equal terms, so that black people need to be given extra advantages. Both black and white people end up focusing on this implied expected inferiority. The result, writes Steele, is that "Preferential treatment, no matter how it is justified in the light of day, subjects blacks to a midnight of self doubt."

Affirmative action also ends up hurting black people by encouraging them to focus on the sufferings of the past, rather than to achieve excellence in the future. As Steele puts it:

> Victimization, like implied inferiority, is what justifies preference, so that to receive the benefits of preferential treatment one must, to some extent, become invested in the view of one's self as a victim. In this way, affirmative action nurtures a victim-focused identity in blacks. The obvious irony here is that we become inadvertently invested in the very condition we are trying to overcome. Racial preferences send us the message that there is more power in our past sufferings than in our present achievements—none of which could bring us preference over others.

Affirmative action also hurts black people, Steele argues, by the effect it has on white peoples' perception of them. As long as their exist policies of affirmative action, in which less qualified people can be selected over more qualified people when the less qualified people are of the proper race, then white people will usually tend to subtly assume that black people in positions of prestige always got there, not on their own merits, but through government mandates. Black people who achieve excellence will not be recognized as having done so. "[I]t may be that at a certain level employers impose a glass ceiling, but this may not be against the race so much as against the race's reputation for having advanced by color as much as by competence," writes Steele. Thus even the most competent black people are tainted and stigmatized as a direct result of the presence of affirmative action programs.

For Steele, the underlying problem with affirmative action is that it is a cosmetic bandage that treats the symptoms rather than the disease. What we truly want is to teach the skills and instill the motivation in black people that would give them truly equal qualifications with white people. Instead, with affirmative action, what we get "on campuses (for example) has been a democracy of colors rather than of people, an artificial diversity that gives the appearance of educational parity between black and white students that has not yet been achieved in reality. Here again, racial preferences allow society to leapfrog over the difficult position of developing blacks to parity with whites and into a cosmetic diversity that covers the blemish of disparity. . . ."

While Steele does not discuss this in much detail, he implies that such "cosmetic bandaging" can do further damage to black people in at least two ways. First, the existence of such programs makes it look as if something is being done to achieve parity, when the real necessary developmental work is not being done at all. With the affirmative action-aided appearance that things are all right, people do not see the true need for such developmental efforts. Secondly, if black people are awarded positions of prestige that they are less qualified for than nonminority workers or students who would otherwise have gotten the positions, then the black people with whom whites will be interacting will indeed be ones who are less well-prepared for these positions. White myths and stereotypes of black inferiority, then, will actually be paradoxically *reinforced* by affirmative action.

Steele's suggestion is that we abandon affirmative action as it now exists. Instead we should concentrate on fighting actual documented discrimination. This, of course, will not be enough to eliminate disparities. But for that we should pursue "the educational and economic development of disadvantaged people— regardless of race." It is this developmental work that will truly uplift people, and not artificially put people on top where they are artificially stigmatized.

The idea that our deep moral obligations are to do things to help disadvantaged people of any sort, and not to give preferential treatment to any racial group, is one that strikes a chord in many people. Even Dinesh D'Souza, a fierce opponent of affirmative action, urges that universities should "retain their policies of preferential treatment, but alter their criteria of application from race to socioeconomic disadvantage" (as cited by Fish, this volume). Even Cornel West says that what he supports "in principle" is a class-based affirmative action. In "Reverse Racism, or How the Pot Got to Call the Kettle Black," however, Stanley Fish argues that we still have a strong need in this country for race-based affirmative action policies.

To begin with, most raced-based affirmative action actually *is* socioeconomic class-based affirmative action, as so many black people helped by affirmative action are from the lower economic sphere. But racism is still so prevalent in this country that special aid also needs to be given to upper- and middle-class black people if they are to enjoy the same privileges and opportunities higher class whites have. Fish discusses a dramatic presentation of this point depicted on ABC's "Prime Time Live," when a sophisticated young black man and a sophisticated young white man were followed by camera crews as they did a variety of tasks in St. Louis. As Fish describes it:

> But that small difference turned out to mean everything. In a series of encounters with shoe salesmen, record store employees, rental agents, landlords, employment agencies, taxicab drivers and ordinary citizens, the black member of the pair was either ignored or given a special and suspicious attention. He was asked to pay more for the same goods or come up with a larger down payment for the same car, was turned away as a prospective tenant, was rejected as a prospective taxicab fare, was treated with contempt and irritation by clerks and bureaucrats, and in every way possible was made to feel inferior and unwanted.

In a country where such experiences happen routinely, writes Fish, it is silly to speak about a "level playing field" where everyone has a fair chance to succeed on his or her own merits. "The playing field is already tilted, and resistance to altering it by the mechanisms of affirmative action is in fact a determination to make sure the present imbalances persist as long as possible." We should not, argues Fish, be led astray by surface similarities. Programs that have the effect of making it harder for whites to enter certain positions are not the same sort of "discrimination" as programs that deliberately made it harder for blacks to enter certain positions. To see them as the same is to ignore history.

William Julius Wilson, on the other hand, argues that if we really want to help black people, a large percentage of whom are poor, the most effective way to do so is with a race-neutral affirmative action. As it stands now, Wilson argues, affirmative action most benefits those blacks who are already well off to begin with, as they are the ones best equipped and trained for the prestige positions sought through affirmative action. These people, however, are the ones who need aid the least. Furthermore, affirmative action, as it now stands, has lost the support of vast numbers of white voters—voters whose support is needed to sustain aid programs of any sort. While such programs had a lot of support among whites in the 1960s, when the economy was expanding, this support waned as average incomes stagnated in the 1970s and beyond, and people became more interested in protecting their own declining resources than in helping others. Many white people also came to believe in the 1980s that their living standards had declined *because* of "expensive and wasteful programs for the poor (and implicitly for minorities)."

Wilson believes, however, that large numbers of people would support government aid programs if they didn't see them as explicitly targeted for blacks. "Americans across racial and class lines continue to be concerned about unemployment and job security, declining real wages, escalating medical costs, the sharp decline in the quality of public education, the lack of good child care and crime and drug trafficking in neighborhoods," writes Wilson. Programs to combat these problems, including some sort of nonracial affirmative action could enjoy wide public support. And while they would not be targeted specifically at blacks, the black population would benefit tremendously from such programs, aimed at improving the lives of disadvantaged people. "For those who came of age in the 1970s, it seems paradoxical that this goal is now best achieved via race neutral approaches," writes Wilson. "Yet a society without racial preference has, of course, always been the long-term goal of the civil rights movement."

In the public policy debates over affirmative action as they are reflected in these essays, people often speak as though our only choices are to have strong race-based affirmative action policies or not to have any. When considering these issues, however, we should also keep in mind that other options might also be possible. There are a number of "mixed" strategies one could consider. One might, for example, take up the suggestion of Wilson and Steele that affirmative action policies be set up to give preferential treatment and aid to "disadvantaged" Americans, rather than to Americans of African descent, but *add* to their suggestion the idea that *black Americans should automatically qualify as disadvantaged.* This would take into consideration the fact that, as Fish points out, having black skin still tends to unfairly puts one at a huge disadvantage for profiting from a large number of opportunities, regardless of that person's socioeconomic status. Not reserving the "disadvantaged" category for black people alone might well remove much of the white resentment that Wilson and others speak of. If the government adopted policies of giving aid to "the disadvantaged" in which many whites qualified as disadvantaged, poor whites might stop feeling like their hard-earned tax dollars were going to pay for programs that benefitted only minorities at their expense—even if disadvantaged minorities were also extensively aided by these programs as well. Another possible mixed strategy would be to support raced-based affirmative action programs in some areas but not in others. An obvious candidate would be to support it in education but not in employment. Education could be viewed as the arena where everyone is given the opportunity to acquire the skills, knowledge, and motivation needed for positions in the work force. Since all Americans do not currently enjoy the same skill levels etc., education is the place where some people are given the opportunity to "catch up" with others. Vigorous affirmative action could be pursued here to make sure blacks were able to have equal access to quality education and training. After college, however, everyone would be required to "make it on his or her own merits." This sort of "mixed" affirmative action might entirely remove all too prevalent beliefs that any black person in a prestige position only got that position through affirmative action.

Yet another option would be to support Steele's call for increased specialized developmental assistance, rather than any sort of affirmative action program. People who advocate this solution to the inequalities existing in America, however, need to realize that such programs would require a much higher degree of expenditures and effort toward improving the lives of the disadvantaged than the American people heretofore have shown the political will to support. In an era of budget cuts and government downsizing, could such non-affirmative action-based aid ever get off the ground? It is this sort of consideration that leads people like Cornell West to ultimately support race-based affirmative action, even though it is a "second choice" to an in principle preferred class-based affirmative action, because "in the heat of the battle in American politics, a redistributive measure in principle with no power and pressure behind it means no redistributive measure at all." Seeing the difficulties in this alternative solution to the problem makes clear that there is probably no way to achieve the superior equality we seek without incurring serious costs somewhere. Whether the right place to pay the costs is to pay for more aid to the downtrodden, to pay the costs of giving up the dream of color-blind equality, or to give up the benefits of preferential treatment, is something we, as a society, will have to decide.

That there are a number of costs and benefits to affirmative action, or for any other way of aiding the downtrodden in our society, is something that these essays in this section make amply clear. Because there are so many benefits and so many costs, as well as so many fundamental ideals involved in the positions of both sides of the debate, neither side has been able to fully prevail in the court of public opinion. Thus, an uneasy stalemate about the propriety of affirmative action prevails—a stalemate with which no one is completely comfortable. We should not rule out, however, the possibility that by carefully considering all of the costs and benefits discussed in essays such as these, we will eventually come upon a consensus solution in which a satisfactory combination of costs and benefits is achieved. The hope is that such a solution can be found, and in so finding it, America will become more fully "the land of opportunity."

NOTE

1. Thomas Sowell, *Race and Culture* (New York: Basic Books, 1994), 176.

TAKING AFFIRMATIVE ACTION APART

Nicholas Lemann

Compton is a mostly black and Hispanic, down-at-the-heels, inner-ring suburb of Los Angeles known to the outside world mainly as the home of rap groups like N.W.A. (Niggas With Attitude—its first album was *Straight Outta Compton*). On a quiet blue-collar street of tract houses with lawns that need mowing stands, incongruously, a fancy new house with a BMW parked in its bricked front courtyard. There's a touch of Graceland about it, the poor boy's mansion. Inside the front door is a large, round, marble-floored entrance foyer overlooked by a balcony. There is a swimming pool in the backyard.

The house belongs to Dr. Patrick Chavis, a forty-three-year-old obstetrician-gynecologist with an enormous practice comprising entirely poor people on Medicaid. Chavis is where he is because he was swept up in a historical tide. He is a beneficiary of affirmative action. In 1973, he and four other African Americans were admitted, under a special minorities-only program, to the University of California Medical School at Davis. Although all of the five were good students, medical-school admission is extremely competitive and none would have been admitted purely on the basis of undergraduate records. They got in because they were black, and therefore took the places of five white applicants with better grades and test scores.

This article originally appeared in the *New York Times Magazine* (June 11, 1995): 36–43. Reprinted by permission of International Creative Management, Inc. Copyright © 1995 by Nicholas Lemann.

One of these was a young engineer named Allan Bakke. He sued the medical school for discriminating against him on the basis of his race. The case went to the Supreme Court, resulting in its best-known decision to date on affirmative action: In June 1978, Bakke was ordered admitted (he too is a doctor today) and the special program was abolished. The Court also ruled, however, that universities could make being a minority a plus factor in their admissions decisions. *Bakke* v. *Regents of the University of California* was, then, an endorsement of affirmative action, but an extremely limited one. In the years following the decision, U.C.-Davis medical school admitted fewer blacks. Post-*Bakke*, Patrick Chavis couldn't have become a poor-folks' doctor.

Four hundred miles north of Compton lies Berkeley, a beautiful small city that is home to what is probably the finest institution of public education in the United States, the University of California at Berkeley. In a drowsy neighborhood of graduate-student housing and organic grocery stores there is a shabby-genteel bungalow owned by one of those left-liberal cause organizations that spring up in university towns, the World Without War Council. The address is 1730 Martin Luther King Jr. Way. Improbably, the California chapter of the National Association of Scholars, an anti-P.C. organization, has its office upstairs in a tiny sublet space.

This year, the bungalow has been the site of occasional media stakeouts because it is the unofficial headquarters of a citizen initiative that would abolish in California precisely what the *Bakke* decision let stand—giving some measure of preference to black (and other minority) applicants in the name of promoting diversity. The fathers of the initiative, Tom Wood and Glynn Custred, are middle-aged white academics. Wood, a philosopher by training, has spent most of his career moving from short-term job to short-term job; he is now executive director of the California Association of Scholars. Custred is a tenured professor of anthropology at California State University at Hayward, down the road from Berkeley.

Custred is a friendly man with a fringe of white hair, a broad open face, and searchlight blue eyes—a true believer. He was born in Birmingham, Alabama, during the Jim Crow era. His father was a steelworker who became a white-collar employee at the local gas company. When he was fourteen, the family moved to Vincennes, Indiana, and his father got a job as a sales manager for a gas company there.

Over the last few years, Custred told me recently, he began to feel that affirmative action was causing California to go through a process that reversed the journey of his youth: he saw it abandoning the amicable, everyone's-the-same racial climate that he believes characterized Indiana in the '50s and becoming as obsessed with racial classification as the pre-civil-rights South. In 1991, the legislature passed a bill (quickly vetoed by Governor Pete Wilson) that encouraged the state universities to strive for graduating classes that would reflect the state's ethnic makeup. Worse, there seemed to be no venue for complaints about such things. The press, it seemed to Custred, barely covered affirmative action. Five years ago, Custred came to the conclusion that an initiative would be the only way to get the issue on the public agenda. He began toying with wording he'd lifted straight from Lyndon B. Johnson's monument, the 1964 Civil Rights Act, and finally came up with this:

"Neither the State of California nor any of its political subdivisions or agents shall use race, sex, color,'ethnicity, or national origin as a criterion for either discriminating against, or granting preferential treatment to, any individual or group in the operation of the state's system of public employment, public education or public contracting." That's almost an exact quote from the Civil Rights Act, except for the one little phrase about preferential treatment.

SUDDENLY, AN ISSUE

To Glynn Custred, racial preference is a great injustice, the most significant departure from the principle of fairness in American social policy. To Patrick Chavis, affirmative action is the one opening into the system for people like him, generally consigned at birth to exist in a poor, self-enclosed black world. For Chavis, that feeling of race as destiny is the great unfairness in American life. Such perceptual stalemates can go on for many years, taking on an odd stability. But in 1995 that is no longer the case with regard to affirmative action. Mainly because of Custred and Wood's initiative, it has abruptly emerged as an issue that could decide the 1996 presidential election. The country has to figure out who's right.

Custred and Wood were introduced by a mutual friend in 1991. For their first couple of years as a team, they had almost no luck in promoting their cause. Then, while driving home one day, Custred happened to hear William Rusher, the former publisher of *National Review,* on the radio. He gave Rusher a call and told him about the initiative, and Rusher wrote about it enthusiastically in his syndicated column. This led to the initiative's being taken up by the conservative press: William F. Buckley and Pat Buchanan praised it.

What changed everything, though, was the 1994 elections, which overnight transformed the abolition of affirmative action from a conservative-movement cause into a mainstream one. Three of the leading Republican presidential candidates, Bob Dole, Phil Gramm, and Pete Wilson, all made statements opposing racial preference. (Earlier this month [June 1995], Wilson issued an executive order dismantling some of California's affirmative-action programs.) President Clinton publicly ordered up an internal review of affirmative action, something no previous President has done—which, at the very least, sent a signal of less-than-total commitment to affirmative action. A . . . report prepared for the President . . . seemed to be groping for some middle ground— backing the principle of affirmative action, criticizing some particular programs and expressing empathy for "bystanders," that is, white men. . . .

THE LONG, LIBERAL SILENCE

. . . [T]here is an enormous well of pent-up hostility to affirmative action. The morally elegant vision of a color-blind society that Glynn Custred wrote into the initiative has the same animating power today that it did when used by the Reverend Dr. Martin Luther King Jr. in the 1960s. In addition, there is by now a vast trove of affirmative-action horror stories. Is there a white person who has never been told that the reason some desirable billet or other is unavailable is that it has been reserved for minorities under an affiliative-action program? Or who hasn't been privy to sorrowful, head-shaking conversation about this or that shockingly poor performance of black beneficiaries of affirmative action?

The opponents of affirmative action have been honing their arguments for a good thirty years. While the term and the programs associated with it embrace women and Hispanics, in politics and in the public mind affirmative action remains essentially a black-and-white issue. The opponents have learned not to make the argument too forcefully that affirmative action is unfair to white people. Instead, the anti-affirmative-action position now has prominent black spokesmen like Shelby Steele, the writer, and, in

California, Ward Connerly, a member of the University of California Board of Regents. And the case is now built to a great extent on a rhetoric of what's good for blacks: affirmative action, opponents insist, does nothing to alleviate the worst problem in black America, the state of the poor ghettos. Instead, their argument goes, its beneficiaries are the best-off blacks, who, by being put above their academic or career level by affirmative action, are set up for failure in a way that damages their self-confidence and reinforces white prejudices about black inferiority.

A second essential anti-affirmative-action point that has come to the fore in recent years is that affirmative action is the opening wedge of a comprehensive ideology that threatens the basic American creed. If multiculturalism is given full sway, according to this argument, we'll find ourselves living in a society in which all decisions are made on the principle of apportionment to oppressed groups. "A lot of people use the word *Balkanization*," Glynn Custred says.

Arrayed against these compelling arguments is a very loud silence, especially from white liberals. Either opponents of affirmative action are patronizingly dismissed, as they were by President Clinton recently, as "angry white males" or they're told that they want to "turn back the clock" to the days before affirmative action, which opponents freely admit. The level of feeling among supporters of affirmative action, especially black ones, is obviously high, but the case for it is rarely laid out. It looks to the opponents as if there is some secret reason for affirmative action that liberals will not reveal—or no reason for it at all, in which case the supporters are merely people who are afraid of being yelled at by minorities.

As far as the public discourse goes, the next move is affirmative action's supporters to make. They need to acknowledge and confront the other side's position and then to explain why, nonetheless, America should still support affirmative-action programs.

BIRTH OF A CONCEPT

How did we get to this peculiar point? Whose idea was affirmative action in the first place? How did it spread? What does it actually consist of? And does it do any good?

The affirmative action trail begins faintly at the time of the Presidential inauguration of John F. Kennedy. At the Texas State Society's inaugural ball, Lyndon Johnson, the incoming Vice President, was pressing flesh in the receiving line. When a young black lawyer from Detroit named Hobart Taylor Jr.—known to Johnson because Hobart Taylor Sr., a businessman in Houston and an active Democrat, was a close friend—came through the line, Johnson pulled him aside and said he needed something. An executive order banning discriminatory hiring by Federal contractors was being drafted for President Kennedy's signature; could Taylor help work on it?

The next day, Taylor holed up in a room at the Willard Hotel with two future Supreme Court justices, Arthur Goldberg and Abe Fortas, to prepare a document with the not-very-catchy title of Executive Order 10925. "I put the word *affirmative* in there at that time," Taylor later told an interviewer for the archives of the Lyndon Baines Johnson Library. "I was searching for something that would give a sense of positiveness to performance under that executive order, and I was torn between the words *positive action* and the words *affirmative action*. . . . And I took *affirmative action* because it was alliterative."

The key point about the inception of affirmative action is that it went virtually unnoticed. Executive Order 10925 merged two obscure Eisenhower administration committees that were supposed to prevent discriminatory hiring—one aimed at the civil service and the other at federal contractors—under the name of the President's Committee on Equal Employment Opportunity. The committee met twelve times. Its main activity was a program called "Plans for Progress," in which big federal contractors were persuaded to adopt voluntary efforts to increase their black employment.

Although the committee did not exercise much direct power and was not in the news, its basic mission clearly would offend present-day critics of affirmative action, since it was to promote race-conscious hiring. There wasn't any conservative backlash against the committee, because practically no one knew it existed. But as soon as President Kennedy proposed a civil rights bill in 1963, opponents began attacking it as one that would impose racial-quota hiring schemes. During the titanic congressional debate that followed Johnson's proposing the Civil Rights Act in 1964, quotas were a frequent theme. "The bill would discriminate against white people," said Senator James Eastland of Mississippi. ". . . I know what will happen if the bill is passed. I know what will happen if there is a choice between hiring a white man or hiring a Negro both having equal qualifications. I know who will get the job. It will not be the white man."

The Civil Rights Act, therefore, contained a sentence explicitly disavowing quotas. And, although the law created an Equal Employment Opportunity Commission (EEOC) to prevent job discrimination, the commission was given no powers of enforcement whatsoever, so that it could not promote quota hiring; it was taking away the EEOC's enforcement power that prevented a Senate filibuster against the bill and so made its passage possible.

The passage of the Civil Rights Act set in motion a series of events that ended with President Johnson's issuing what is now regarded as the originating document of affirmative action: Executive Order 11246. Bear in mind what was on the minds of liberals at that time. Simply abolishing the South's legal apartheid system—the thrust of the Civil Rights Act—wasn't going to solve America's racial problems. There were small urban race riots in the summers of 1963 and 1964 and a large one in Watts in 1965. The gap between black and white was shockingly large. At the time, blacks were almost twice as likely as whites to be poor, twice as likely to be unemployed, and more than four times as likely to be illiterate. The voices warning against quotas and reverse discrimination all seemed to belong to Southern segregationists, like Senators Eastland, Sam Ervin of North Carolina, Lister Hill of Alabama, J. William Fulbright of Arkansas, and John Tower of Texas. So the anti-quota argument looked like merely a cover for something less legitimate.

THE INVISIBLE MILESTONE

The fullest expression of the liberal mood was a commencement address that President Johnson gave at Howard University on June 4, 1965. The key phrase (supplied by the young Daniel Patrick Moynihan) was, "We seek . . . not just equality as a right and a theory but equality as a fact and equality as a result." "Equality of result" has long been used by the opponents of affirmative action as the perfect distillation of the principle they find odious, but Johnson's speech was regarded within the White House as a great political triumph and the phrase generated no objections from the public.

Affirmative action specifically, however—the originating document, Executive Order 11246, issued on Sept. 24, 1965—appears to have been a kind of accident. The Civil Rights Act made the President's Committee on Equal Employment Opportunity, traditionally headed by the Vice President, potentially irrelevant, because it created several new government agencies to make sure blacks weren't being discriminated against. In February 1965, Johnson created a new President's Council on Equal Opportunity, to be headed by his vice president, Hubert Humphrey, a lifelong crusader for civil rights; this made Humphrey chairman of a White House committee and a White House council on the same thing.

Johnson ordered Humphrey to come up with a reorganization plan for all the government's civil rights organizations. Humphrey responded by proposing to abolish the equal opportunity committee but to keep alive the equal opportunity council. The council would be in charge of "community relations" (one of the new functions created by the Civil Rights Act) and of making sure federal contractors didn't discriminate against black job applicants—that is, affirmative action.

On June 21, 1965, shortly after his speech at Howard, Johnson approved this plan of Humphrey's. As late as mid-August, it was still on track. Then, in September, Johnson changed his mind. The reason is unknown, but it may have had to do with Humphrey's having made a hard-charging black lawyer named Wiley Branton the director of the equal opportunity council, which raised the possibility of controversial and high-profile civil rights enforcement actions emanating from the White House. A memo from a White House lawyer to Johnson, dated Sept. 20, 1965, lays out a scheme to abolish Humphrey's council entirely rather than give it more power. Community relations would be given to the Justice Department and affirmative action to a new Office of Federal Contract Compliance Programs in the Labor Department. "Humphrey can show his bigness by recommending the dissolution of a group that he heads which has performed its assignment and no longer needs to remain in existence," the memo said.

Humphrey's staff obediently drew up a memo to Johnson designed to make the official record reflect that the whole thing had been Humphrey's idea; Johnson's staff drew up a memo to Humphrey commending him for his statesmanship, and Executive Order 11246, which abolished the two White House equal opportunity groups and is now considered the opening bell for affirmative action, was drawn up and signed. There seemed to be two salient points about the executive order: it wasn't very important and it represented a setback for Hubert Humphrey and the civil rights cause because it did away with everything he headed. The *Times* first mentioned Executive Order 11246 three weeks after the fact, under the headline "Rights Groups Fear Easing of U.S. Enforcement Role." (By the way, Executive Order 11246 did not call for affirmative action to combat gender discrimination; that was added a few years later after prodding by feminist groups. The original concept of affirmative action was exclusively racial.)

The reason that Executive Order 11246 did, in fact, turn out to be a milestone is that it took affirmative action out of the White House, which is under intense perpetual scrutiny and has a small staff with high turnover, and made it the raison d'être of a division of the Labor Department. This meant there would be a much larger and more permanent staff devoted to carrying out affirmative action—a staff with the power to write federal regulations and with the maneuvering room that comes from the press not reporting on your every move.

Because the end of segregation came in the form of a bill being passed, the country realized it was making a momentous change. The Civil Rights Act of 1964 was furiously debated and examined. Compromises were struck. The result was that by the time the act became law, Americans had consciously made up their minds to take this great step. Executive Order 11246 had exactly the opposite dynamic: it was an invisible milestone that was not debated at all (or noticed, even) before the fact. Given its significance, it was inevitable that it would be publicly debated with Civil Rights Act-like intensity at some point after the fact—and now we are at that point.

The Meritocracy as a Racial Barrier

The original, executive-order definition of affirmative action is that it requires employers only to search aggressively for qualified minority applicants—through advertising, for instance, or special recruitment efforts. Once found, these new minority applicants would go into the same pool with everybody else and the final selection would be made on a color-blind basis. Almost everybody, including the leading critics of affirmative action and the majority of respondents in polls, claims to support affirmative action if we could stick to the original definition, and most defenders of affirmative action say that it's only the official definition that they're defending.

But there's an enormous problem with putting the official definition into practice. The civil rights revolution occurred at the same time that an even more important change in American society was taking place: the construction—by liberals, it should be noted—of a formal meritocracy based on education and standardized testing. This country has always been obsessed with individual opportunity, but before the 1950s there was no system in place that could evaluate and assign a numerical value to every American. At the time that affirmative action began, there was such a system and it judged people mainly on a single criterion, their ability to get good grades in school. (Most standardized tests are designed to predict school grades.)

In a way, the construction of this meritocratic system was good for the civil rights movement because it provided a target to aim at. It's no accident that the string of landmark cases leading to *Brown* v. *Board of Education* involved schools; it was the argument that education equals opportunity that dealt the death blow to legal segregation. But in a crucial sense, the numerical, education-based meritocracy was bad news for blacks. It rendered the key affirmative-action concept of creating biracial pools of equally qualified applicants meaningless, because now everybody was ranked serially. And it apportioned opportunity on the basis of performance in the one area where blacks were most disadvantaged: education. For as long as there have been standardized tests, blacks have on average scored lower than whites. As education for blacks has improved, the gap has closed substantially and is now at an all-time low, but it is still large enough that for institutions, hiring and admitting purely on the basis of educational credentials would produce extremely low counts of blacks, and also of Latinos and American Indians. To cite just one example, in 1992 only 1,493 African Americans had SAT verbal scores of 600 or above—and 55,224 whites.

The history of affirmative action can be seen as a struggle over the fairness of the modern meritocracy, with minorities arguing that educational measures shouldn't be the deciding factor in who gets ahead and opponents of affirmative action saying that to bend the criteria for blacks is to discriminate unfairly against more deserving whites. The 1964 Civil Rights Act contained an amendment put in by John Tower explicitly permitting the use of standardized tests in hiring. However, the first few important Supreme Court cases on affirmative action—in particular *Griggs* v. *Duke Power Company* in 1971—went in the opposite, prominority, direction by restricting the use of test scores as screens for employment. (The Court has swung the other way more recently.) Either way, the trade-off is stark and will remain so until black America and white America are on the same educational and cultural footing—in other words, for generations. If hiring and admission are done purely on the basis of test scores, the black presence will be a fraction of what it is in the population, and bringing it higher requires rejecting some whites who scored better than the blacks who were hired or admitted.

What present-day opponents of affirmative action, smelling victory, don't like to admit is that these are issues capable of generating real confusion in the minds of people of good will. An education-based meritocracy makes its judgments about people before they've ever really done anything, based on a measure, school performance, that depends heavily on who their parents are and what kind of environment they create. People tend to shy away from meritocracy in pure form, or at least to want to sand off its rough edges, because the definition of merit seems too narrow and because it doesn't seem genuinely to offer equal opportunity to everyone. No American institution of higher education is willing to select solely on the basis of (as opposed to mainly on the basis of) merit as defined by grades and test scores.

THE JUSTICE WHO COULDN'T MAKE UP HIS MIND

The Supreme Court's *Griggs* decision left a perfect opening for a case filed by a white student who felt he'd been discriminated against in higher-education admissions. It was one thing to limit the use of educational credentials in hiring, but it would seem absurd to do so in admission to a school—even though it was precisely by departing from strict adherence to educational credentials that majority-white schools were able to register a large increase in black students during the late 1960s and early 1970s.

Robert Klitgaard, a social scientist, calculated that in one year in the 1970s, if affirmative action had been eliminated, the total number of blacks in law school in America would have dropped from 1,539 to 285—which presumably meant that the total number of whites would have risen by the same number. In 1971, one of these discriminated-against whites sued: Marco DeFunis, who had been rejected by the University of Washington law school even though his grades and test scores put him ahead of virtually all the black students who were accepted.

DeFunis won his case and entered the law school under a court order. The Washington State Supreme Court reversed the decision and ordered him out. DeFunis appealed to the United States Supreme Court, which stayed the lower-court decision, permitting him to remain, and agreed to hear the case. The justice who wrote the order keeping DeFunis in law school was William O. Douglas, the longest-serving member of the Supreme Court in American history. Douglas's papers, which have been opened, provide an extraordinary (and heretofore unknown) look at a strong mind blowing its fuses over affirmative action.

Douglas, then seventy-five years old and the last of Franklin Roosevelt's appointees remaining on the Court, was himself the product of humble origins in the state of Washington; his own meteoric rise had been set off by admission to law school. He had every reason to empathize with Marco DeFunis At the same time, he was a fiery liberal and champion of the downtrodden who had come down on the side of blacks in every landmark civil rights case.

One of Douglas's clerks, Ira Ellman, wrote him a memo recommending that he vote for the Court to take up the case because "there really was some kind of quota here," which he thought was a wrong that ought to be corrected. The Court did grant DeFunis a hearing and then recessed; in March 1974, with DeFunis only weeks away from his law-school graduation, the justices began working on their opinions again. It quickly became apparent that Douglas would be the swing vote: four justices wanted to kick DeFunis out of law school while four wanted to order his admission.

Douglas was known within the Supreme Court building as someone who made up his mind about every case instantly and then quickly dashed off an opinion. He had little use for lengthy colloquy or deliberation with his clerks, who barely saw him. But in the case of DeFunis, uncharacteristically, he seemed genuinely torn. Ellman, sensing that Douglas couldn't make up his mind, hesitantly offered to draft an opinion himself—something Douglas's clerks never did. Douglas told Ellman to go ahead, as long as he didn't circulate the draft to the other justices.

"I don't know about these tests," Douglas told Ellman by way of instruction—meaning the Law School Aptitude Test (LSAT). What he was getting at was that perhaps the way to a liberal opinion lay through pointing out that the test (which hadn't existed back in Douglas's law-student days) was biased against blacks. Before putting Ellman in charge of the opinion, Douglas had dashed off some wording, dated March 8, 1974, that said the LSAT was "by no means objective" and might contain "hidden bias." Ellman obtained data from the Educational Testing Service, however, showing that the LSAT did not inaccurately predict blacks' grades.

Douglas's early wording strongly opposed reverse discrimination. "The democratic ideal as I read the Constitution and Bill of Rights presupposes an aristocracy of talent, and all races must be permitted to compete for a position in that hierarchy," it said. How, then, to square the circle? Douglas proposed that the law school first admit "those clearly qualified" purely on academic merit and then fill the rest of its places by a lottery.

On March 11, the justices decided privately to declare the case moot. The stated reason was that DeFunis was about to graduate (today he's practicing law in Seattle) and the underlying reason was that no clear majority position on the issue was emerging. But Douglas decided to steam ahead and produce a dissent that would address the merits of the case; as he told Ellman, "I might not be around next time this issue comes up."

On March 21, there was another draft of Douglas's opinion. This one argued that the school should be allowed to admit minorities with lower test scores than whites who were rejected. But the very next day, there was another draft taking a different position: that while "racial classifications cannot be used," universities should discriminate in favor of people from disadvantaged backgrounds.

The following draft, printed up a few days later, showed that Douglas's opposition to racial preferences was becoming firmer. But Douglas still couldn't accept the idea of the law school's admitting people purely on the basis of academic credentials. Another draft was produced, which said, "The presence of an LSAT test is sufficient warrant for a school to separate minorities into a class in order better to probe their capacities and potentials." Douglas ordered Ellman to circulate this draft to the other justices. But the next morning, he called Ellman into his office and said, matter-of-factly rather than accusingly, that he actually hadn't wanted the draft circulated, so Ellman should go and retrieve all the copies from the justices' offices. When Ellman came back with them, Douglas told him that from now on he would work on the opinion without any help.

He then wrote one last draft: this time, rather than coming down on one or another side of the case, he came down on both at the same time. He was strongly against reverse discrimination, but insisted that DeFunis had not been discriminated against on the basis of his race when he was denied admission. So, for the first time in all the drafts, he did not order DeFunis admitted to law school. When the Supreme Court printer delivered the opinion to Ira Ellman he said, with a quizzical look, "He changed the bottom line."

The way Douglas got to this final position was by returning to his attack on the LSAT, with greater fury than ever before. It is racially biased, he wrote; its bias justifies reverse bias by the law school; in fact, the LSAT should be abolished entirely. That Douglas decided to declare the LSAT biased although he had no evidence that it was is mainly a demonstration that he was intellectually trapped and couldn't find any other way out. He couldn't reconcile his passionate belief in meritocracy with the actual meritocracy's mechanical feeling and its tendency to reward some ethnic cultures far more than others. So he went through every possible feeling one can have about affirmative action in sequence and wound up in effect throwing up his hands.

A year later, Justice Douglas had a stroke and retired from the Court. In 1977, a case almost exactly like that of DeFunis presented itself to the Court: *Bakke* v. *Regents of the University of California*. The University of California-Davis Medical School had created a separate admissions pool for minority applicants and rejected higher-ranked white applicants to make room for them. One of these was Allan Bakke.

Douglas's seat on the Court had been taken by John Paul Stevens, but his position as swing vote had been assumed by Lewis F. Powell, a gentlemanly former corporate lawyer with none of Douglas's Whitmanesque pretensions. Powell, unlike Douglas, found a logical route to a decision, but it would be difficult to find a less resounding one on a major issue in the history of the Supreme Court. By a 5–4 majority, the Court struck down U.C.-Davis's racial-quota admissions system and ordered Bakke admitted. Also by a 5–4 majority, however, with Powell on the other side this time, the Court approved the idea of taking race into account as a positive factor in admissions decisions, in order to achieve a diverse student body. The decision may have been a statesmanlike piece of jurisprudence, but in admissions-office circles it is widely viewed as meaning that it's OK to reverse discriminate as long as you're not really obvious about it.

THE ESTABLISHMENT EMBRACES AFFIRMATIVE ACTION

Much of what is now most unpopular about affirmative action occurred well after the heyday of civil rights. The two small federal affirmative-action bureaucracies established in 1965—the Equal Employment Opportunity Commission and the Office of Federal Contract Compliance—both defined their mission as being to promote affirmative action aggressively. They quickly began to deal with companies in terms of numerical racial hiring "goals."

"The average business guy wants to know what to do," Edward Sylvester, who was the first head of the contract compliance office, told me recently. "You've got to give him numbers. They'd say, 'Tell me what you want and when.' "

Richard Nixon and George Shultz, when he was Secretary of Labor, imposed the government's harshest, most explicit quota plan ever on building contractors in Philadelphia in 1969; we now know from the diaries and notes of John Ehrlichman and H. R. Haldeman that Nixon thought of the Philadelphia Plan as a wonderful way to pit two key Democratic constituencies, blacks and labor, against each other and endorsed it partly for that reason.

... Last year's [1995] poster child in reverse for affirmative action is Frank Washington, the black millionaire who tried to use the Federal Communications Commission's (FCC) minority tax certificate program (known in the trade as "Section 1071") in order to make a quick killing for himself and a white billionaire, Sumner Redstone of Viacom. Section 1071 began during the Carter Administration and was expanded during the Reagan administration. The contract office's current regulations—41 Code of Federal Regulations 60.2—contain such notorious provisions as a requirement that "effective affirmative-action programs" must include "active support of local and national community action programs and community service programs"—that is, mandated charity. They were promulgated in 1978 under Jimmy Carter. So were federal minority set-asides for federal contractors. "Race-norming," the practice (later outlawed) of not directly comparing the test scores of white and black applicants for federal employment, was begun in 1980.

Through the years, states and localities by the dozens were creating affirmative-action laws of their own. And even more significant than whatever government has done has been the massive and largely voluntary adoption of affirmative-action plans by virtually all big institutions. The current conversational meaning of affirmative action is something like "stuff that's done explicitly to help black people"—the stuff being everything from preferential college admissions to the way news is covered to what's hung in museums to corporate promotion practices. All of this followed from the civil rights movement and President Johnson's embrace of it, but it isn't explicitly attributable to the exercise of federal power.

Part of what was propelling affirmative action was that it had an interest group behind it, namely minority organizations. Much of their support of affirmative action is standard political behavior. Black people don't control America, though. All along, the overwhelmingly white establishment has supported affirmative action and that is what accounts for its durability. The establishment's reasoning, never openly stated, would have gone something like this: Sure, affirmative action, generates white victims of reverse discrimination, but there aren't very many of them and they don't suffer too greatly. They go to Colgate instead of Cornell. Big deal. The most clearly outstanding whites—the people the meritocracy set up to spot and train for leadership—don't suffer at all. In return, we are able to take some of the edge off of what has been the most explosive issue in our history, the one that set off our bloodiest war and our worst civil disturbances. We create an integrated authority system. We give blacks a stake. It promotes the peace. In addition, case by case, it creates a feeling of doing something to correct our worst historic wrong.

All through the 1970s and 1980s, this quiet but firm establishment support for affirmative action worked to quell incipient revolts against it. Richard Nixon campaigned against quotas and then did not abolish affirmative action. So did Ronald Reagan and so did George Bush.

The closest that affirmative action came to being done away with during the Reagan-Bush years was in 1985, after Reagan was overwhelmingly reelected and the confrontational Donald Regan succeeded James Baker as the White House chief of staff. A group of conservative officials, including Edwin Meese, W. Bradford Reynolds, the Assistant Attorney General for Civil Rights, and William Bennett, had been talking for years about replacing Executive Order 11246 with something similar to the California Civil Rights Initiative. In the second term, they decided to renew the push. Their problem was that in early 1985 Raymond Donovan, the Secretary of Labor and a fellow movement conservative, had resigned and been replaced by Bill Brock, a moderate who wanted to protect the Office of Federal Contract Compliance.

The anti-affirmative-action group made the mistake of over-playing its hand. While Brock was away on a lengthy foreign trip, they presented their idea to Reagan, who seemed interested. But Donald Regan felt that he and Brock were being circumvented and put a stop to it. The attempt on the life of Executive Order 11246 was leaked to the press and the resulting outcry saved the executive order.

"The internal argument was, 'We're expending a lot of political capital on this issue,' " Reynolds recalled not long ago. " 'It's getting in the way of other things that are more important. The less problems for Reagan the better. Let's don't carry this further now. We can always revisit it later.' "

Soon afterward, Reagan nominated Reynolds to be Associate Attorney General and, after a rough hearing, the Senate Judiciary Committee refused to recommend him for the position because of his opposition to affirmative action. In 1990, C. Boyden Gray, an aide to President Bush, tried to get Bush to sign an executive order banning racial preferences in employment; again, there was a leak to the press followed by a backing down. In 1991, an Assistant Secretary of Education named Michael Williams announced that the government would be eliminating scholarships that were reserved for black students only. After another immediate controversy, Bush reversed the policy.

These public disputes aside, the reigning assumption of elected officialdom, including Republican officialdom, was pro-affirmative action. Bob Dole has recently come out against preferences, but for many years he supported it. When she was Secretary of Labor, Elizabeth Dole held a ceremony to celebrate the twenty-fifth anniversary of Executive Order 11246 and presented a plaque to Edward Sylvester, the first head of the contract office. Ten years ago, while working on a magazine profile of Newt Gingrich, I watched him work hard to get gate assignments at the Atlanta airport for a new airline, for the sole reason that its founder was black. Then he called the White House and suggested that Reagan mention this in his inaugural address. Such behavior by a rising leader of the Republican right was completely unremarkable at the time.

The establishment clearly believed that affirmative action had become a permanent part of the American landscape. There was a steady diet of Supreme Court cases; university administrators and corporate officials kept modifying and fine-tuning their programs. What the establishment didn't quite grasp was how bad affirmative action looked from the outside—the way it seemed all-pervasive and undemocratic. A review that Senator Dole recently ordered up from the Library of Congress found that there are 162 separate federal affirmative-action programs, and that leaves out all the state, local, and private ones.

It's arguable that there wasn't a single law passed in Congress that truly endorsed the broad principle of affirmative action until the Civil Rights Act of 1991. Way back in the 1960s, liberals got used to the idea that you could never get Congress to do the right thing on racial matters, so the way to make public policy was through the judicial and executive branches. These were the venues through which affirmative action was pursued. So down through the decades, the muscles that liberals would have used to make a public case for affirmative action atrophied—and the conservatives' were becoming magnificently buffed and toned. What's good about the current crisis for affirmative action is that it means a debate will take place that should have taken place long ago; if it had, affirmative action wouldn't be so vulnerable now.

THE CASE FOR AFFIRMATIVE ACTION

What would the country look like without affirmative action? According to its opponents, a gentle notching downward would take place in black America: black students who now go to Harvard Law School would go to Michigan instead and do very well; black students at Michigan would go to Louisiana State, and so on. The net impact would be small. And maybe then we would get to work on the real issues, like the poor quality of many all-black urban public schools.

The other possibility is that there would be an enormous decrease in black representation everywhere in white-collar (and also blue-collar) America, with a big, noticeable depressive effect on black income, employment, home-ownership, and education levels. The percentage of blacks in managerial and technical jobs doubled during the affirmative action years. During the same period, as Andrew Hacker pointed out in his book *Two Nations*, the number of black police officers rose from 24,000 to 64,000 and the number of black electricians from 14,000 to 43,000. If affirmative action were entirely abolished, does anyone really believe the government would undertake, say, an expensive upgrade of education for blacks as a more meaningful substitute?

Black America is still a substantially separate world. Blacks are by far the most residentially segregated ethnic group and the least likely to intermarry. Without affirmative action the gap would surely become even more pronounced. The lack of faith in the fairness of the system that is so much more a part of the black world than the white would only increase.

The goal of affirmative action is not to reject the spirit of integration in favor of race-consciousness but to bring blacks into the mainstream of national life. The ironic result of affirmative action being abolished could be an increase, not a decrease, in the kind of black demands for reparations and mandated percentages of the action that whites find so annoying: if you're out of the system completely, then you don't seek access to jobs and school places. You just want more resources.

The opponents tend to treat affirmative action as a unitary evil: all the many varieties are equally wrong and disastrous, and the most extreme Frank Washington-type excesses are a fair representation of the totality of the phenomenon. In fact, the country is full of affirmative-action plans that work pretty well and affirmative-action beneficiaries whom people like. Clifford Alexander, who was head of the Equal Employment Opportunity Commission, was Secretary of the Army in the Carter administration; he says that the first time a list of people being promoted to general landed on his desk, he sent it back, demanding that more good black candidates be found. One of these was Colin Powell, who recently departed from his usual sphinx-like silence on public issues to make a speech defending affirmative action. In California, the psychic center of the affirmative-action debate is undergraduate admissions to Berkeley; the initiative literature uses the statistic that "the dropout rate for students admitted under affirmative-action programs often runs as high as 75 percent." According to the university, 60 percent of its black students (there are only about two hundred in each class of three thousand, by the way) graduate within six years, as against 84 percent of white students. Rather than Berkeley cruelly taking its black students up past their level, it has a black graduation rate 50 percent higher than the national average.

It's entirely possible, indeed likely, that the more egregious forms of affirmative action can be jettisoned. This is already happening: the notorious FCC minority tax certificate program was legislatively abolished. . . . As we begin the process of thinking about the remaining bulk of affirmative-action programs, it's important to keep in mind three core principles.

First, the country is so segregated, the natural default position for white people is to have no contact at all with blacks. It's healthy to have some way of pushing people, as they make hiring and contracting and admissions decisions, to go far enough past the bounds of their ordinary realm of contacts to find black candidates. Even the opponents say they want this, but it won't happen if it's not required because the black-white social gulf is so great.

Second, lawsuits and regulations are not the ideal venue for affirmative action. Liberal victories won there tend to be Pyrrhic: they generate enormous public resentment that leads to their eventual demise and gives the whole cause of trying to improve race relations a bad name. A legislation-based affirmative action would perforce be one that was spiritedly debated publicly. Liberals would have to make their case in a way that would convince people, and the result would be compromised-over programs with sustainable public support.

Third, we should recognize that the meritocracy is structured in such a way that one criterion, educational performance, is over-weighted and has become too much the sole path to good jobs and leadership positions. It shows how far we've gone in this direction, how much we accept the present social arrangement as the natural order of things, that affirmative-action plans governing school admissions and entry-level hiring for twenty-two-year-olds are so often criticized as constituting "equality of result." Rationally, a first job or a place in school is an opportunity; it's only because we sort people so firmly so early that it looks like a result. There is a real difference between affirmative-action plans that seek to divide up the spoils and plans that seek to get African Americans into a position where they have a chance to prove themselves through individual performance.

Every child born in America doesn't have access to good schools and doesn't have parents who encourage study. Many blacks go to the worst schools and live in the toughest family circumstances. To argue that by late adolescence black people have run a fair competitive race and that if they're behind whites on the educational standards they deserve to be permanently barred from the professional and managerial classes is absurd. It constitutes not

just a denial of opportunity to individuals but a denial of talent to
the society.

THE CASE OF DR. CHAVIS

Allan Bakke, after graduating from medical school, did his resi-
dency at the Mayo Clinic in Minnesota. Today he is an anesthesi-
ologist in Rochester, Minnesota. Bakke doesn't speak to the press
and he didn't respond to my request for an interview. He does not
appear to have set the world on fire as a doctor. He has no private
practice and works on an interim basis, rather than as a staff physician, at Olmsted Community Hospital.

Patrick Chavis, who took Allan Bakke's place at U.C.-Davis
med school, fits the stereotype of the affirmative-action beneficiary
in one way: as he freely admits, he would not have been admitted
strictly on the basis of his grades and test scores, though they were
good. In other ways, though, he does not fit. He is not a product of
the cushy black upper class: he grew up in South Central Los
Angeles, the eldest of five children of a welfare mother who had
migrated to California from rural Arkansas. Chavis first met his
father three years ago, when he was forty. One day when he was in
high school, one of his teachers used the word "indigents" in class.
That night, upset, he asked his mother if that word meant people
like them. "Who else do you think it means?" she asked him.

Another way in which Patrick Chavis doesn't fit the stereotype
of the affirmative-action beneficiary is that he doesn't give the
impression of being tormented by self-doubt over whether he
really deserves to be where he is. If anything, he seems to assume
a superiority over his white medical-school classmates. He says he
works harder than they do and in tougher conditions. He and his
four black classmates set up a primary-care clinic when they were
at Davis and worked there as volunteers, but they couldn't get any
of the white students to join them. While he was still a resident at
the University of Southern California, he and one of his black
classmates from Davis each put up $500 and opened a small prac-
tice, so that they could "hit the ground running" when they grad-
uated. He ticks off what the black doctors admitted under Davis's
special minorities-only program (which was eliminated after the
Supreme Court's *Bakke* decision, resulting in subsequent classes
having only one or two black members) are doing now: almost all

are in primary care in underserved areas, including his ex-wife, Toni Johnson Chavis, a pediatrician in Compton. If Chavis hadn't gotten into medical school, his patients wouldn't be treated by some better-qualified white obstetrician; they'd have no doctor at all and their babies would be delivered the way Chavis was—by whoever happened to be on duty at the emergency room of the county hospital.

Rather than believing that if it weren't for affirmative action he would be functioning in a color-blind environment, Chavis sees the old-fashioned kind of racial discrimination everywhere. The idea that, as an obstetrician-gynecologist, he could build a practice on the west side of Los Angeles based on middle-class white women is a joke. The Bank of America wouldn't lend him the money to build his house because it is in a rundown black neighborhood. He has staff privileges at St. Francis Hospital in Lynwood, where all the obstetricians are black or Latino, but got into a fiery dispute with Long Beach Memorial Medical Center, where for a while he was the only black OB admitting patients. The hospital put him under professional review, saying he had performed a substandard delivery. Chavis felt the real issue was that the hospital didn't want him admitting Medicaid patients. He sued the hospital for discrimination and won—but the judge overturned the verdict; she mentioned that the jury's award of $1.1 million in damages seemed unwarranted, since he bills Medicaid $800,000 a year. Rather than feeling sheepish about making so much money, Chavis points out that Medical reimburses at the rate of $14 per office visit and $400 per vaginal delivery. His white classmates, with their higher-paying privately insured patients, do fewer deliveries and make more. He has been audited by the state and by the Internal Revenue Service, which he does not attribute to bad luck. "We do it with enthusiasm and with joy, and we fight the system," he says.

So Patrick Chavis fiercely defends affirmative action and holds himself up as an example of the good that it does. "There's no way in hell—if it wasn't for some kind of affirmative action, there wouldn't be any black doctors," he says. "Maybe one or two. Things haven't changed that much."

2

TO FULFILL THESE RIGHTS:
COMMENCEMENT ADDRESS AT HOWARD UNIVERSITY

Lyndon Baines Johnson

I am delighted at the chance to speak at this important and this historic institution. Howard has long been an outstanding center for the education of Negro Americans. Its students are of every race and color and they come from many countries of the world. It is truly a working example of democratic excellence.

Our earth is the home of revolution. In every corner of every continent men charged with hope contend with ancient ways in the pursuit of justice. They reach for the newest of weapons to realize the oldest of dreams, that each may walk in freedom and pride, stretching his talents, enjoying the fruits of the earth.

Our enemies may occasionally seize the day of change, but it is the banner of our revolution they take. And our own future is linked to this process of swift and turbulent change in many lands in the world. But nothing in any country touches us more profoundly, and nothing is more freighted with meaning for our own destiny than the revolution of the Negro American.

In far too many ways American Negroes have been another nation: deprived of freedom, crippled by hatred, the doors of opportunity closed to hope.

In our time change has come to this nation, too. The American Negro, acting with impressive restraint, has peacefully protested

From *Public Papers of the Presidents of the United States,* Lyndon B. Johnson, 1965, Book II (Washington, D.C.: U.S. Government Printing Office, 1966), pp. 635–40.

and marched, entered the courtrooms and the seats of government, demanding a justice that has long been denied. The voice of the Negro was the call to action. But it is a tribute to America that, once aroused, the courts and the Congress, the President and most of the people, have been the allies of progress.

Thus we have seen the high court of the country declare that discrimination based on race was repugnant to the Constitution, and therefore void. We have seen in 1957, and 1960, and again in 1964, the first civil rights legislation in this nation in almost an entire century.

As majority leader of the United States Senate, I helped to guide two of these bills through the Senate. And, as your President, I was proud to sign the third. And now very soon we will have the fourth—a new law guaranteeing every American the right to vote.

No act of my entire administration will give me greater satisfaction than the day when my signature makes this bill, too, the law of this land.*

The voting rights bill will be the latest, and among the most important, in a long series of victories. But this victory—as Winston Churchill said of another triumph for freedom—"is not the end. It is not even the beginning of the end. But it is, perhaps, the end of the beginning."

That beginning is freedom; and the barriers to that freedom are tumbling down. Freedom is the right to share, share fully and equally, in American society—to vote, to hold a job, to enter a public place, to go to school. It is the right to be treated in every part of our national life as a person equal in dignity and promise to all others.

But freedom is not enough. You do not wipe away the scars of centuries by saying: Now you are free to go where you want, and do as you desire, and choose the leaders you please.

You do not take a person who, for years, has been hobbled by chains and liberate him, bring him up to the starting line of a race and then say, "you are free to compete with all the others," and still justly believe that you have been completely fair.

Thus it is not enough just to open the gates of opportunity. All our citizens must have the ability to walk through those gates.

This is the next and the more profound stage of the battle for

---

*The Voting Rights Act of 1965 was approved by President Johnson on August 6, 1965.

civil rights. We seek not just freedom but opportunity. We seek not just legal equity but human ability, not just equality as a right and a theory but equality as a fact and equality as a result.

For the task is to give 20 million Negroes the same chance as every other American to learn and grow, to work and share in society, to develop their abilities—physical, mental and spiritual, and to pursue their individual happiness.

To this end equal opportunity is essential, but not enough, not enough. Men and women of all races are born with the same range of abilities. But ability is not just the product of birth. Ability is stretched or stunted by the family that you live with, and the neighborhood you live in—by the school you go to and the poverty or the richness of your surroundings. It is the product of a hundred unseen forces playing upon the little infant, the child, and finally the man.

This graduating class at Howard University is witness to the indomitable determination of the Negro American to win his way in American life.

The number of Negroes in schools of higher learning has almost doubled in fifteen years. The number of nonwhite professional workers has more than doubled in ten years. The median income of Negro college women tonight exceeds that of white college women. And there are also the enormous accomplishments of distinguished individual Negroes—many of them graduates of this institution, and one of them the first lady ambassador in the history of the United States.*

These are proud and impressive achievements. But they tell only the story of a growing middle-class minority, steadily narrowing the gap between them and their white counterparts.

But for the great majority of Negro Americans—the poor, the unemployed, the uprooted, and the dispossessed—there is a much grimmer story. They still, as we meet here tonight, are another nation. Despite the court orders and the laws, despite the legislative victories and the speeches, for them the walls are rising and the gulf is widening.

Here are some of the facts of this American failure.

Thirty-five years ago the rate of unemployment for Negroes and whites was about the same. Tonight the Negro rate is twice as high.

---

*Mrs. Patricia Harris, U.S. Ambassador to Luxembourg and former associate professor of law at Howard University

In 1948 the 8 percent unemployment rate for Negro teenage boys was actually less than that of whites. By last year that rate had grown to 23 percent, as against 13 percent for whites unemployed.

Between 1949 and 1959, the income of Negro men relative to white men declined in every section of this country. From 1952 to 1963 the median income of Negro families compared to white actually dropped from 57 percent to 53 percent.

In the years 1955 through 1957, 22 percent of experienced Negro workers were out of work at some time during the year. In 1961 through 1963 that proportion had soared to 29 percent.

Since 1947 the number of white families living in poverty has decreased 27 percent while the number of poorer nonwhite families decreased only 3 percent.

The infant mortality of nonwhites in 1940 was 70 percent greater than whites. Twenty-two years later it was 90 percent greater.

Moreover, the isolation of Negro from white communities is increasing, rather than decreasing as Negroes crowd into the central cities and become a city within a city.

Of course Negro Americans as well as white Americans have shared in our rising national abundance. But the harsh fact of the matter is that in the battle for true equality too many—far too many—are losing ground every day.

We are not completely sure why this is. We know the causes are complex and subtle. But we do know the two broad basic reasons. And we do know that we have to act.

First, Negroes are trapped—as many whites are trapped—in inherited, gateless poverty. They lack training and skills. They are shut in, in slums, without decent medical care. Private and public poverty combine to cripple their capacities.

We are trying to attack these evils through our poverty program, through our education program, through our medical care and our other health programs, and a dozen more of the Great Society programs that are aimed at the root causes of this poverty.

We will increase, and we will accelerate, and we will broaden this attack in years to come until this most enduring of foes finally yields to our unyielding will.

But there is a second cause—much more difficult to explain, more deeply grounded, more desperate in its force. It is the devastating heritage of long years of slavery; and a century of oppression, hatred, and injustice.

For Negro poverty is not white poverty. Many of its causes and many of its cures are the same. But there are differences—deep, corrosive, obstinate differences—radiating painful roots into the community, and into the family, and the nature of the individual.

These differences are not racial differences. They are solely and simply the consequence of ancient brutality, past injustice, and present prejudice. They are anguishing to observe. For the Negro they are a constant reminder of oppression. For the white they are a constant reminder of guilt. But they must be faced and they must be dealt with and they must be overcome, if we are ever to reach the time when the only difference between Negroes and whites is the color of their skin.

Nor can we find a complete answer in the experience of other American minorities. They made a valiant and a largely successful effort to emerge from poverty and prejudice.

The Negro, like these others, will have to rely mostly upon his own efforts. But he just cannot do it alone. For they did not have the heritage of centuries to overcome, and they did not have a cultural tradition which had been twisted and battered by endless years of hatred and hopelessness, nor were they excluded—these others—because of race or color—a feeling whose dark intensity is matched by no other prejudice in our society.

Nor can these differences be understood as isolated infirmities. They are a seamless web. They cause each other. They result from each other. They reinforce each other.

Much of the Negro community is buried under a blanket of history and circumstance. It is not a lasting solution to lift just one corner of that blanket. We must stand on all sides and we must raise the entire cover if we are to liberate our fellow citizens.

One of the differences is the increased concentration of Negroes in our cities. More than 73 percent of all Negroes live in urban areas compared with less than 70 percent of the whites. Most of these Negroes live in slums. Most of these Negroes live together—a separated people.

Men are shaped by their world. When it is a world of decay, ringed by an invisible wall, when escape is arduous and uncertain, and the saving pressures of a more hopeful society are unknown, it can cripple the youth and it can desolate the men.

There is also the burden that a dark skin can add to the search for a productive place in our society. Unemployment strikes most swiftly and broadly at the Negro, and this burden erodes hope.

Blighted hope breeds despair. Despair brings indifferences to the learning which offers a way out. And despair, coupled with indifferences, is often the source of destructive rebellion against the fabric of society.

There is also the lacerating hurt of early collision with white hatred or prejudice, distaste or condescension. Other groups have felt similar intolerance. But success and achievement could wipe it away. They do not change the color of a man's skin. I have seen this uncomprehending pain in the eyes of the little, young Mexican-American schoolchildren that I taught many years ago. But it can be overcome. But, for many, the wounds are always open.

Perhaps most important—its influence radiating to every part of life—is the breakdown of the Negro family structure. For this, most of all, white America must accept responsibility. It flows from centuries of oppression and persecution of the Negro man. It flows from the long years of degradation and discrimination, which have attacked his dignity and assaulted his ability to produce for his family.

This, too, is not pleasant to look upon. But it must be faced by those whose serious intent is to improve the life of all Americans.

Only a minority—less than half—of all Negro children reach the age of 18 having lived all their lives with both of their parents. At this moment, tonight, little less than two-thirds are at home with both of their parents. Probably a majority of all Negro children receive federally aided public assistance sometime during their childhood.

The family is the cornerstone of our society. More than any other force it shapes the attitude, the hopes, the ambitions, and the values of the child. And when the family collapses it is the children that are usually damaged. When it happens on a massive scale the community itself is crippled.

So, unless we work to strengthen the family, to create conditions under which most parents will stay together—all the rest: schools, and playgrounds, and public assistance, and private concern, will never be enough to cut completely the circle of despair and deprivation.

There is no single easy answer to all of these problems.

Jobs are part of the answer. They bring the income which permits a man to provide for his family.

Decent homes in decent surroundings and a chance to learn—an equal chance to learn—are part of the answer.

Welfare and social programs better designed to hold families together are part of the answer.

Care for the sick is part of the answer.

An understanding heart by all Americans is another big part of the answer.

And to all of these fronts—and a dozen more—I will dedicate the expanding efforts of the Johnson administration.

But there are other answers that are still to be found. Nor do we fully understand even all of the problems. Therefore, I want to announce tonight that this fall I intend to call a White House conference of scholars, and experts, and outstanding Negro leaders— men of both races—and officials of Government at every level.

This White House conference's theme and title will be "To Fulfill These Rights."

Its object will be to help the American Negro fulfill the rights which, after the long time of injustice, he is finally about to secure.

To move beyond opportunity to achievement.

To shatter forever not only the barriers of law and public practice, but the walls which bound the condition of man by the color of his skin.

To dissolve, as best we can, the antique enmities of the heart which diminish the holder, divide the great democracy, and do wrong—great wrong—to the children of God.

And I pledge you tonight that this will be a chief goal of my administration, and of my program next year, and in the years to come. And I hope, and I pray, and I believe, it will be a part of the program of all America.

For what is justice?

It is to fulfill the fair expectations of man.

Thus, American justice is a very special thing. For, from the first, this has been a land of towering expectations. It was to be a nation where each man could be ruled by the common consent of all—enshrined in law, given life by institutions, guided by men themselves subject to its rule. And all—all of every station and origin—would be touched equally in obligation and in liberty.

Beyond the law lay the land. It was a rich land, glowing with more abundant promise than man had ever seen. Here, unlike any place yet known, all were to share the harvest.

And beyond this was the dignity of man. Each could become whatever his qualities of mind and spirit would permit—to strive, to seek, and, if he could, to find his happiness.

This is American justice. We have pursued it faithfully to the edge of our imperfections, and we have failed to find it for the American Negro.

So, it is the glorious opportunity of this generation to end the one huge wrong of the American Nation and, in so doing, to find America for ourselves, with the same immense thrill of discovery which gripped those who first began to realize that here, at last, was a home for freedom.

All it will take is for all of us to understand what this country is and what this country must become.

The Scripture promises: "I shall light a candle of understanding in thine heart, which shall not be put out."

Together, and with millions more, we can light that candle of understanding in the heart of all America.

And, once lit, it will never again go out.

3

THE SWEET MUSIC OF EQUAL TREATMENT

Ward Connerly

Tonight, my friends, we celebrate. In our hearts and minds, we dance—not in the darkness, but in the warm sunshine to the sweet music of equal treatment for all and special privileges for none.

The thrill of victory is ours. But the victory itself belongs to the American people and to our fellow Californians. It belongs to those who came before us who said, in 1776, "We hold these truths to be self-evident, that all men are created equal, that they are endowed by their Creator with certain unalienable rights, that among these are life, liberty, and the pursuit of happiness."

It belongs to those whose cup is filled with optimism about America and the goodness of its people. It belongs to those who believe in America's passion for fairness. Most importantly, this victory belongs to our children and to our grandchildren, and to their hopes and dreams for a future which will not be impaired by melanin content, by sex, by the country of their birth, or that of their ancestors.

This is not a victory for white men. It is not a victory for white people. It is a victory for all of us.

American democracy is one of the most noble experiments in the history of mankind. People of all colors, with different cultures,

---

Victory speech given by Ward Connerly, chairman of the Yes on Proposition 209 campaign, at the November 5, 1996 election night celebration in Sacramento, California. From Synopsis OnLine.

different ideologies, different religions, coming from different nations, and merging their differences into a common identity to become *one nation, under God, indivisible,* and committed to a system of liberty and justice for all.

The premier laboratory for this experiment is right here in California. And, despite occasional setbacks, the experiment is succeeding. But the seeds of its own destruction are sown when we fail to honor those unalienable rights of some of our citizens.

The opponents of the California Civil Rights Initiative have tried to portray our initiative as a misappropriation of the term "civil rights." But aren't civil rights those "unalienable" rights which attach to each of us as individuals? These are rights which cannot be transferred or surrendered. They are good for the life of the vehicle and should be respected by every government franchise in every village and hamlet of this nation.

We exercised one of those rights today when we voted. We reaffirmed another when we voted for Prop. 209 and proclaimed the sanctity of the principle of equal treatment for all people.

At 8:00 P.M. tonight, when the last vote was cast, we ended an era in American history. We ended the illusion that our government can give some of us a preference based on skin color or gender and have that practice be regarded as something other than discrimination.

We ended our season of denial that different standards were being applied to our citizens based on race, gender, and ethnicity. We rejected the premise that race matters, that America is a racist nation. We rejected the growing view that the goal of becoming a color-blind society is unattainable and unworthy of our pursuit.

There are those who defend racial preferences who often speak in glowing terms about "diversity." Let me be clear: Today's vote was not a rejection of diversity. It was a rejection of using diversity as an excuse to discriminate.

When I went to bed last night, I knew that I would be giving a victory speech tonight and not a "what-might-have-been" speech. The reason lies in an editorial endorsement of one of this state's most important newspapers—UC Berkeley's *Daily Californian.*

Let me read to you language from that editorial:

> Race-based affirmative action is wrong because it discriminates on the basis of race. For three decades, such discriminatory policies have been embraced with the hope that they would reverse

the effects of centuries of racism. To a certain extent, they have. But it is time affirmative action ended. Race and gender preferences now do more harm than good. . . . The goal of affirmative action, to redress centuries of shameful racial discrimination against blacks, Latinos, other minorities and women, is praiseworthy and urgent. But the ends of social policy do not justify the means.

The *Daily Californian* is not alone in reflecting the youth mood about racial and gender preferences. In a mock election held last week, California high school students voted 59 percent to 40 percent in favor of Proposition 209.

There has been a lot of talk this political season about building bridges to the future. The younger generation is the future, and they have already crossed that bridge. They are way ahead of us older folk on building an inclusive society "on the natural." California's youth socialize and date across racial and ethnic lines. They recognize that far too many affirmative action programs divide, rather than unite.

Please indulge me for a moment as I have a personal conversation with my fellow black Americans.

This is an anxious moment for black people. For decades, we have relied on government to secure our rights. Federal troops stood guard so that little children could attend integrated schools. Those same troops had to stand by with bayonets in hand to protect our right to vote.

Make no mistake, America, government had to intervene to protect the civil rights of black Americans.

But somewhere along the lines we became addicted to government and its occupation of our lives. Affirmative action became indispensable instead of transitional. Not only could we not leave home without it, but neither could our children.

I do not often quote President Clinton, but last week, speaking to a predominantly black audience, the president said something which was extremely significant. In reaffirming his support of affirmative action, the president reminded the audience that there comes a time to let go.

For black people and our reliance on affirmative action, the time has, indeed, come to let go. We cannot forever look through the rear view mirror at America's mistakes. We must look through the windshield at its opportunities.

Let the troops go home!

Black Americans have made enormous contributions to American culture. This land is, also, our land . . . from California to the New York islands; from the Redwood forest to the Gulf Stream waters . . . our contributions to America can be evidenced.

But, there is no greater contribution than the price we have paid to America's respect for civil rights. Let us not tarnish that contribution by demanding for ourselves something that we insist should be denied to others. Let us not yield to the temptation of forever looking backward.

To young black Americans: Those who came before you had to climb steep mountains of oppression. Surely, you can travel the freeways of opportunity without special consideration based on the color of your skin.

In my mind's eye, I see this boy of nine or ten sitting at a kitchen table doing his spelling lesson, while a gray-haired woman stands by his side. When he encounters a difficult word, he says, "This is too hard, I can't do it." She says, "Yes, you can." He says, "I can't do it," and he looks longingly outside while his friends play in the field. Finally, the old lady says, "You can do it, and you are not leaving here until you do."

A few moments later, the boy spells the word correctly, and the old lady praises him. She then requires him to spell the word again and again to be certain that it is etched in his memory. After going through several words, the old lady releases him to go outside to play.

As the boy leaves, crying, he says under his breath, "I hate living here." The old lady hears him and responds, "That's OK, but you learned to spell those words, didn't you?"

From those experiences, I learned that if at first you do not succeed, try and try again.

Today, I believe we are saying to young black kids, if at first you don't succeed, redefine success, because your failure must have been the result of culturally biased exams, the lack of role models, and a racist society. Our kids have come to believe that they cannot survive in a world without special consideration. Their competitive spirit has been weakened by this dependency on affirmative action.

We owe it to them to better prepare them for the rigors of a highly competitive world. And we owe it to all that is good about America to not let them sink into the debilitating mentality of believing that our nation is racist at its core.

As we end the era of race and gender preferences, we begin a new chapter in American history. To complete the experiment of American democracy built on principles of equality, there must be a presumptive belief in the goodwill of each other rather than a presumption to the contrary.

There must be respect for our differences, not simply tolerance. In this new era, we must liberate ourselves from the chains of racial labeling and stereotypical thinking. The greatest threat to our system is not racism. It is the lack of respect for those who are different from us. And this problem is not confined to any segment of our society.

A friend of mine is Chicano. He works with his hands every day, when the weather permits, to take care of his family. His English is not so good and his skin is tanned and hardened from the long hours of working in the sun. When he goes to the grocery store or to the mall, he is invisible to us. We see him, but we don't see him. When he pays the cashier, sometimes he gets a "thank you," but often he doesn't. He seeks no preference from us, but he deserves the same respect, as a human being and as a productive member of our village, that we would accord if his skin were white and his English fluent.

We must get involved when a black family is being driven from their home by racists who graffiti their property. We should call them and offer our support. If they know that they have the overwhelming support of their community, they can withstand the idiocy of what they are experiencing, and we help them drive the bigots from their doorstep.

We have to be unafraid to talk about our fears and our expectations. We have to believe in the intrinsic value of our system, that it represents the best hope for mankind, and we must have the courage to try making this system work on the basis of equal treatment for all people.

Jeane Kirkpatrick, a former Ambassador to the United Nations, was in Sacramento about a week ago, and she placed this in perspective, for me. She reminded us that the Soviet empire was not overthrown by outside military force. It collapsed because its people lost faith in their way of life. They lost their conviction in their value system.

When my family came to California in 1947, we were attracted by the lure of equal opportunity. We were seduced by the spirit of California, the promise of that Walt Disney character, Jiminy

Cricket, who said you could wish upon a star, that it made no difference who you are, and all your dreams could come true. That was the attraction of California.

Today, we have restored the spirit of California, the lure that brought my family and so many others to this magical place that we call California.

Like that tree standing by the water, in the old spiritual, we should not be moved from our commitment that California will judge its citizens by their merit and not by their race, gender, or ethnicity.

4

THE DEFUNIS CASE: THE RIGHT TO GO TO LAW SCHOOL

Ronald Dworkin

I

In 1945 a black man named Sweatt applied to the University of Texas Law School, but was refused admission because state law provided that only whites could attend. The Supreme Court declared that this law violated Sweatt's rights under the Fourteenth Amendment to the United States Constitution, which provides that no state shall deny any man the equal protection of its laws.[1] In 1970 a Jew named DeFunis applied to the University of Washington Law School; he was rejected although his test scores and college grades were such that he would have been admitted if he had been a black or a Filipino or a Chicano or an American Indian. DeFunis asked the Supreme Court to declare that the Washington practice, which required less exacting standards of minority groups, violated his rights under the Fourteenth Amendment.[2]

The Washington Law School's admission procedures were complex. Applications were divided into two groups. The majority—not from the designated minority groups—were first screened so as to eliminate all applicants whose predicted average, which is a function of college grades and aptitude lest scores, fell below a certain level. Majority applicants who survived this initial

From *The New York Review of Books* (February 5, 1976): 29–33. Reprinted with permission from *The New York Review of Books*. Copyright © 1976 Nyrev, Inc.

cut were then placed in categories that received progressively more careful consideration. Minority-group applications, on the other hand, were not screened; each received the most careful consideration by a special committee consisting of a black professor of law and a white professor who had taught in programs to aid black law students. Most of the minority applicants who were accepted in the year in which DeFunis was rejected had predicted averages below the cutoff level, and the law school conceded that any minority applicant with his average would certainly have been accepted.

The *DeFunis* case split those political action groups that have traditionally supported liberal causes. The B'nai B'rith Anti-Defamation League and the AFL-CIO, for example, filed briefs as *amici curiae* in support of DeFunis's claim, while the American Hebrew Women's Council, the UAW, and the UMWA filed briefs against it.

These splits among old allies demonstrate both the practical and the philosophical importance of the case. In the past liberals held, within one set of attitudes, three propositions: that racial classification is an evil in itself, that every person has a right to an educational opportunity commensurate with his abilities; and that affirmative state action is proper to remedy the serious inequalities of American society. In the last decade, however, the opinion has grown that these three liberal propositions are in fact not compatible, because the most effective programs of state action are those that give a competitive advantage to minority racial groups.

That opinion has, of course, been challenged. Some educators argue that benign quotas are ineffective, even self-defeating, because preferential treatment will reinforce the sense of inferiority that many blacks already have. Others make a more general objection. They argue that any racial discrimination, even for the purpose of benefiting minorities, will in fact harm those minorities, because prejudice is fostered whenever racial distinctions are tolerated for any purpose whatever. But these are complex and controversial empirical judgments, and it is far too early, as wise critics concede, to decide whether preferential treatment does more harm or good. Nor is it the business of judges, particularly in constitutional cases, to overthrow decisions of other officials because the judges disagree about the efficiency of social policies. This empirical criticism is therefore reinforced by the moral argument that even if reverse discrimination does benefit minorities and does reduce prejudice in the long run, it is nevertheless wrong because distinctions of race are inherently unjust. They are unjust because they violate the rights of individual members of groups not so favored, who may thereby lose a place, as DeFunis did.

DeFunis presented this moral argument, in the form of a constitutional claim, to the courts. The Supreme Court did not, in the end, decide whether the argument was good or bad. DeFunis had been admitted to the law school after one lower court had decided in his favor, and the law school said that he would be allowed to graduate however the case was finally decided. The Court therefore held that the case was moot and dismissed the appeal on that ground. But Justice Douglas disagreed with this neutral disposition of the case; he wrote a dissenting opinion in which he argued that the Court should have upheld DeFunis's claim on the merits.

Many universities and colleges have taken Justice Douglas's opinion as handwriting on the wall, and have changed their practices in anticipation of a later Court decision in which his opinion prevails. In fact, his opinion pointed out that law schools might achieve much the same result by a more sophisticated policy than Washington used. A school might stipulate, for example, that applicants from all races and groups would be considered together, but that the aptitude tests of certain minority applicants would be graded differently, or given less weight in overall predicted average, because experience had shown that standard examinations were for different reasons a poorer test of the actual ability of these applicants. But if this technique is used deliberately to achieve the same result, it is devious, and it remains to ask why the candid program used by the University of Washington was either unjust or unconstitutional.

II

DeFunis plainly has no constitutional right that the state provide him a legal education of a certain quality. His rights would not be violated if his state did not have a law school at all, or if it had a law school with so few places that he could not win one on intellectual merit. Nor does he have a right to insist that intelligence be the exclusive test of admission. Law schools do rely heavily on intellectual tests for admission. That seems proper, however, not because applicants have a right to be judged in that way, but because it is reasonable to think that the community as a whole is better off if its lawyers are intelligent. That is, intellectual standards are justified, not because they reward the clever, but because they seem to serve a useful social policy.

Law schools sometimes serve that policy better, moreover, by supplementing intelligence tests with other sorts of standards: they sometimes prefer industrious applicants, for example, to those who are brighter but lazier. They also serve special policies for which intelligence is not relevant. The Washington Law School, for example, gave special preference not only to minority applicants but also to veterans who had been at the school before entering the military, and neither DeFunis nor any of the briefs submitted in his behalf complained of that preference.

DeFunis does not have an absolute right to a law school place, nor does he have a right that only intelligence be used as a standard for admission. He says he nevertheless has a right that race *not* be used as a standard, no matter how well a racial classification might work to promote the general welfare or to reduce social and economic inequality. He does not claim, however, the he has this right as a distinct and independent political right that is specifically protected by the Constitution, as is his right to freedom of speech and religion. The Constitution does not condemn racial classification directly, as it does condemn censorship or the establishment of a state religion. DeFunis claims that his right that race not be used as a criterion of admission follows from the more abstract right of equality that is protected by the Fourteenth Amendment, which provides that no state shall deny to any person the equal protection of the law.

But the legal arguments made on both sides show that neither the text of the Constitution nor the prior decisions of the Supreme Court decisively settle the question whether, as a matter of law, the Equal Protection Clause makes all racial classifications unconstitutional. The Clause makes the concept of equality a test of legislation, but it does not stipulate any particular conception of that concept.[3] Those who wrote the clause intended to attack certain consequences of slavery and racial prejudice, but it is unlikely that they intended to outlaw all racial classifications, or that they expected such a prohibition to be the result of what they wrote. They outlawed whatever policies would violate equality, but left it to others to decide, from time to time, what it means. There cannot be a good legal argument in favor of DeFunis, therefore, unless there is a good moral argument that all racial classifications, even those that make society as a whole more equal, are inherently offensive to an individual's right to equal protection for himself.

There is nothing paradoxical, of course, in the idea that an individual's right to equal protection may sometimes conflict with an otherwise desirable social policy, including the policy of making the community more equal overall. Suppose a law school were to charge a few middle-class students, selected by lot, double tuition in order to increase the scholarship fund for poor students. It would be serving a desirable policy—equality of opportunity—by means that violated the right of the students selected by lot to be treated equally with other students who could also afford the increased fees. It is, in fact, part of the importance of DeFunis's case that it forces us to acknowledge the distinction between equality as a policy and equality as a right, a distinction that political theory has virtually ignored. He argues that the Washington Law School violated his individual right to equality for the sake of a policy of greater equality overall, in the same way that double tuition for arbitrarily chosen students would violate their rights for the same purpose.

We must therefore concentrate our attention on that claim. We must try to define the central concept on which it turns, which is the concept of an individual right to equality made a constitutional right by the Equal Protection Clause. What rights to equality do citizens have as individuals which might defeat programs aimed at important economic and social policies, including the social policy of improving equality overall?

There are two different sorts of rights they may be said to have. The first is the right to *equal treatment*, which is the right to an equal distribution of some opportunity or resource or burden. Every citizen, for example, has a right to an equal vote in a democracy; that is the nerve of the Supreme Court's decision that one person must have one vote even if a different and more complex arrangement would better secure the collective welfare. The second is the right to *treatment as an equal*, which is the right, not to receive the same distribution of some burden or benefit, but to be treated with the same respect and concern as anyone else. If I have two children, and one is dying from a disease that is making the other uncomfortable, I do not show equal concern if I flip a coin to decide which should have the remaining dose of a drug. This example shows that the right to treatment as an equal is fundamental, and the right to equal treatment, derivative. In some circumstances the right to treatment as an equal will entail a right to equal treatment, but not, by any means, in all circumstances.

DeFunis does not have a right to equal treatment in the assignment of law school places; he does not have a right to a place just because others are given places. Individuals may have a right to equal treatment in elementary education, because someone who is denied elementary education is unlikely to lead a useful life. But legal education is not so vital that everyone has an equal right to it.

DeFunis does have the second sort of right—a right to treatment as an equal in the decision as to which admissions standards should be used. That is, he has a right that his interests be treated as fully and sympathetically as the interests of any others when the law school decides whether to count race as a pertinent criterion for admission. But we must be careful not to overstate what that means.

Suppose an applicant complains that his right to be treated as an equal is violated by tests that place the less intelligent candidates at a disadvantage against the more intelligent. A law school might properly reply in the following way. Any standard will place certain candidates at a disadvantage as against others, but an admission policy may nevertheless be justified if it seems reasonable to expect that the overall gain to the community exceeds the overall loss, and if no other policy that does not provide a comparable disadvantage would produce even roughly the same gain. An individual's right to be treated as an equal means that his potential loss must be treated as a matter of concern, but that loss may nevertheless be outweighed by the gain to the community as a whole. If it is, then the less intelligent applicant cannot claim that he is cheated of his right to be treated as an equal just because he suffers a disadvantage others do not.

Washington may make the same reply to DeFunis. Any admissions policy must put some applicants at a disadvantage, and a policy of preference for majority applicants can reasonably be supposed to benefit the community as a whole, even when the loss to candidates such as Defunis is taken into account. If there are more black lawyers, they will help to provide better legal services to the black community, and so reduce social tensions. It might well improve the quality of legal education for all students, moreover, to have a greater number of blacks as classroom discussants of social problems. Further, if blacks are seen as successful law students, then other blacks who do meet the usual intellectual standards might be encouraged to apply and that, in turn, would raise the intellectual quality of the bar. In any case, preferential admissions of blacks should decrease the difference in wealth and power that now exists between different racial groups, and so make the community more equal overall.

It is, as I said, controversial whether a preferential admissions program will fact promote these various policies, but it cannot be said to be implausible that it will. The disadvantage to applicants such as DeFunis is, on that hypothesis, a cost that must be paid for a greater gain; it is in that way like the disadvantage to less intelligent students that is the cost of ordinary admissions policies.[4]

We now see the difference between DeFunis's case and the case we imagined, in which a law school charged students selected at random higher fees. The special disadvantage to these students was not necessary to achieve the gain in scholarship funds, because the same gain would have been achieved by a more equal distribution of the cost amongst all the students who could afford it. That is not true of DeFunis. He did suffer from the Washington policy more than those majority applicants who were accepted. But that discrimination was not arbitrary; it was a consequence of the meritocratic standards he approves. DeFunis's argument therefore fails. The Equal Protection Clause gives constitutional standing to the right to be treated as an equal, but he cannot find, in that right, any support for his claim that the clause makes all racial classification illegal.

III

If we dismiss DeFunis's claim in this straightforward way, however, we are left with this puzzle. how can so many able lawyers, who supported his claim both in morality and law, have made that mistake? These lawyers all agree that intelligence is a proper criterion for admission to law schools. They do not suppose that anyone's constitutional right to be treated as an equal is compromised by that criterion. Why do they deny that race, in the circumstances of this decade, may also be a proper criterion?

They fear, perhaps, that racial criteria will be misused; that such criteria will serve as an excuse for prejudice against the minorities that are not favored, such as Jews. But that cannot explain their opposition. Any criteria may be misused, and in any case they think that racial criteria are wrong in principle and not simply open to abuse.

Why? The answer lies in their belief that, in theory as well as in practice, *DeFunis* and *Sweatt* must stand of fall together. They believe that it is illogical for liberals to condemn Texas for raising a color barrier against Sweatt, and then applaud Washington for raising a color barrier against DeFunis. The difference between these two cases, they suppose, must be only the subjective preference of liberals for certain minorities now in fashion. If there is something wrong with racial classifications, then it must be something that is wrong with racial classifications as such, not just classifications that work against those groups currently in favor. That is the inarticulate premise behind the slogan, relied on by defendants of DeFunis, that the Constitution is color blind. That slogan means, of course, just the opposite of what it says: it means that the Constitution is so sensitive to color that it makes any institutional racial classification invalid as a matter of law.

It is of the greatest importance, therefore, to test the assumption that Sweatt and DeFunis must stand or fall together. If that assumption is sound, then the straightforward argument against DeFunis must be fallacious after all, for no argument could convince us that segregation of the sort practiced against Sweatt is justifiable or constitutional.[5] Superficially, moreover, the arguments against DeFunis do indeed seem available against Sweatt, because we can construct an argument that Texas might have used to show that segregation benefits the collective welfare, so that the special disadvantage to blacks is a cost that must be paid to achieve an overall gain.

Suppose the Texas admission committee, though composed of men an women who themselves held no prejudice, decided that the Texas economy demanded more white lawyers than they could educate, but could find no use for black lawyers at all. That might have been, after all, a realistic assessment of the commercial market for lawyers in Texas just after World War II. Corporate law firms needed lawyers to serve booming business but could not afford to hire black lawyers, however skillful, because the firms' practices would be destroyed if they did. It was no doubt true that the black community in Texas had great need of skillful lawyers, and would have preferred to use black lawyers if these were available. But the committee might well have thought that the commercial needs of the state as a whole outweighed that special need.

Or suppose the committee judged, no doubt accurately, that alumni gifts to the law school would fall off drastically if it admitted a black student. The committee might deplore that fact, but nevertheless believe that the consequent collective damage would be greater than the damage to black candidates excluded by the racial restriction.

It may be said that these hypothetical arguments are disingenuous, because any policy of excluding blacks would in fact be supported by a prejudice against blacks as such, and arguments of the sort just described would be rationalization only. But if these arguments are, in fact, sound, then they might be accepted by men who do not have the prejudices the objection assumes. It therefore does not follow from the fact that the admissions officers were prejudiced, if they were, they would have rejected these arguments if they had not been.

In any case, arguments such as those I describe were in fact used by officials who might have been free from prejudice against those they excluded. Many decades ago, as the late Professor Bickel reminds us in his brief for the B'nai B'rith, President Lowell of Harvard University argued in favor of a quota limiting the number of Jews who might be accepted by his university. He said that if Jews were accepted in numbers larger than their proportion of the population, as they certainly would have been if intelligence were the only test, then Harvard would no longer be able to provide to the world men of the qualities and temperament it aimed to produce, men, that is, who were more well-rounded and less exclusively intellectual than Jews tended to be, and who, therefore, were better and more likely leaders of other men, both in and out of government. It was no doubt true, when Lowell spoke, that Jews were less likely to occupy important places in government or at the heads of large public companies. If Harvard wished to serve the general welfare by improving the intellectual qualities of the nation's leaders, it was rational not to allow its classes to be filled up with Jews. The men who reached that conclusion might well prefer the company of Jews to that of the Wasps who were more likely to become senators. Lowell suggested he did, though perhaps the responsibilities of his office prevented him from frequently indulging his preference.

It might now be said, however, that discrimination against blacks, even when it does serve some plausible policy, is nevertheless unjustified because it is invidious and insulting. The briefs opposing DeFunis make just the argument to distinguish his claim from Sweatt's. Because blacks were the victims of slavery and legal segregation, they say, any discrimination that excludes blacks will be taken as insulting by them, whatever arguments of general welfare might be made in its support. But it is not true, as a general matter, that any social policy is unjust if those whom it puts at a disadvantage feel insulted. Admission to law school by intelligence is not unjust because those who are less intelligent feel insulted by their exclusion. Everything depends upon whether the feeling of insult is produced by some more objective feature that would disqualify the policy even if the insult were not felt. If segregation does improve the general welfare, even when the disadvantage to blacks is fully taken into account, and if no other reason can be found why segregation is nevertheless unjustified, then the insult blacks feel, while understandable, must be based on misperception.

It would be wrong, in any case, to assume that men in the position of DeFunis will not take *their* exclusion to be insulting. They are very likely to think of themselves, not as members of some large majority group that is privileged overall, but as members of some other minority, such as Jews or Poles or Italians, whom comfortable and successful liberals are willing to sacrifice in order to delay more violent social change. If we wish to distinguish *DeFunis* from *Sweatt* on some argument that uses the concept of an insult, we must show that the treatment of the one, but not the other, is in fact unjust.

IV

So these familiar arguments that might distinguish the two cases are unconvincing. That seems to confirm the view that Sweatt and DeFunis must be treated alike, and therefore that racial classification must be outlawed altogether. But fortunately a more successful ground of distinction can be found to support our initial sense that the cases are in fact very different. This distinction does not rely, as these unconvincing arguments do, on features peculiar to issues of race or segregation, or even on features peculiar to issues of educational opportunity. It relies instead on further analysis of the idea, which was central to my argument against DeFunis, that in certain circumstances a policy which puts many individuals at a disadvantage is nevertheless justified because it makes the community as a whole better off.

Any institution which uses that idea to justify a discriminatory policy faces a series of theoretical and practical difficulties. There are, in the first place, two distinct senses in which a community may be said to be better off as a whole, in spite of the fact that certain of its members are worse off, and any justification must specify which sense is meant. It may be better off in a *utilitarian* sense, that is, because the average or collective level of welfare in the community is improved even though the welfare of some individuals falls. Or it may be better off in an *ideal* sense, that is, because it is more just or in some other way closer to an ideal society, whether or not average welfare is improved. The University of Washington might use either utilitarian or ideal arguments to justify its racial classification. It might argue, for example, that increasing the number of black lawyers reduces racial tension, which improves the welfare of almost everyone in the community. That is a utilitarian argument. Or it might argue that, whatever effect minority preference will have on average welfare, it will make the community more equal and therefore more just. That is an ideal, not a utilitarian argument.

The University of Texas, on the other hand, cannot make an ideal argument for segregation. It cannot claim that segregation makes the community more just whether it improves the average welfare or not. The arguments it makes to defend segregation must therefore all be utilitarian arguments. The arguments I invented, like the argument that white lawyers could do more than black lawyers to improve commercial efficiency in Texas, are utilitarian, since commercial efficiency makes the community better off only if it improves average welfare.

Utilitarian arguments encounter a special difficulty that ideal arguments do not. What is meant by average or collective welfare? How can the welfare of an individual be measured, even in principle, and how can gains in the welfare of different individuals be added and then compared with losses, so as to justify the claim that gains outweigh losses overall? The utilitarian argument that segregation improves average welfare presupposes that such calculations can be made. But how?

Jeremy Bentham, who believed that only utilitarian arguments could justify political decisions, gave the following answer. He said that the effect of a policy on an individual's welfare could be determined by discovering the amount of pleasure or pain the policy brought him, and that effect of the policy on the collective welfare could be calculated by adding together all the pleasure and subtracting all of the pain it brought to everyone. But, as Bentham's critics insisted, it is doubtful whether there exists a simple psychological state of pleasure common to all those who benefit from a policy or of pain common to all those who lose by it; in any case it would be impossible to identify, measure, and add the different pleasures and pains felt by vast numbers of people.

Philosophers and economists who find utilitarian arguments attractive, but who reject Bentham's psychological utilitarianism, propose a different concept of individual and overall welfare. They suppose that whenever an institution or an official must decide upon a policy, the members of the community will each prefer the consequences of one decision to the consequences of others. DeFunis, for example, prefers the consequences of the standard admissions policy to the policy of minority preference Washington used, while the blacks in some urban ghetto might each prefer the consequences of the latter policy to the former. If it can be discovered what each individual prefers, and how intensely, then it might be shown that a particular policy would satisfy on balance more preferences, taking into account their intensity, than alternative policies. On this concept of welfare, a policy makes the community better off in a utilitarian sense if it satisfies the collection of preferences better than alternative policies would, even though it dissatisfies the preferences of some.[6]

Of course, a law school does not have available any means of making accurate judgments about the preferences of all those whom its admissions policies will affect. It may nevertheless make judgments which, though speculative, cannot be dismissed as implausible. It is, for example, plausible to think that in post-war Texas, the preferences of the people were overall in favor of the consequences of segregation in law schools, even if the intensity of the competing preference for integration, and not simply the numbers of those holding that preference, is taken into account. The officials of the Texas law school might have relied upon voting behavior, newspaper editorials, and simply their own sense of their community in reaching that decision. Though they might have been wrong, we cannot now say, even with the benefit of hindsight, that they were.

So even if Bentham's psychological utilitarianism is rejected, law schools may appeal to preference utilitarianism to provide at least a rough and speculative justification for admissions policies that put some classes of applicants at a disadvantage. But once it is made clear that these utilitarian arguments are based on judgments about the actual preferences of members of the community, a fresh and much more serious difficulty emerges.

The utilitarian argument, that a policy is justified if it satisfies more preferences overall, seems at first sight to be an egalitarian argument. It seems to observe strict impartiality. If the community has only enough medicine to treat some of those who are sick, the argument seems to recommend that those who are sickest be treated first. If the community can afford a swimming pool or a new theater, but not both, and more people want the pool, then it recommends that the community build the pool, unless those who want the theater can show that their preferences are so much more intense that they have more weight in spite of the numbers. One sick man is not to be preferred to another because he is worthier of official concern: the tastes of the theater audience are not to be preferred because they are more admirable. In Bentham's phrase, each man is to count as one and no man is to count as more than one.

These simple examples suggest that the utilitarian argument not only respects, but embodies, the right of each citizen to be treated as an equal of any other. The chance that each individual's preferences have to succeed, in the competition for social policy, will depend upon how important his preference is to him, and how many others share it, compared to the intensity and number of competing preferences. His chance will not be affected by the esteem or contempt of either officials or fellow citizens, and he will therefore not be subservient or beholden to them.

But if we examine the range of preferences that individuals in fact have, we shall see that the apparent egalitarian character of a utilitarian argument is often deceptive. Preference utilitarianism asks officials to attempt to satisfy people's preferences so far as this is possible. But the preferences of an individual for the consequences of a particular policy may be seen to reflect, on further analysis, either a *personal* preference for his own enjoyment of some goods or opportunities, or an *external* preference for the assignment of goods and opportunities to others, or both. A white law school candidate might have a personal preference for the consequences of segregation, for example, because the policy improves his own chances of success, or an external preference for those consequences because he has contempt for blacks and disapproves social situations in which the races mix.

The distinction between personal and external preferences is of great importance for this reason. If a utilitarian argument counts external preferences along with personal preferences, then the egalitarian character of that argument is corrupted, because the chance that anyone's preferences have to succeed will then depend, not only on the demands that the personal preferences of others make on scarce resources, but on the respect or affection they have for him or for his way of life. If external preferences tip the balance, then the fact that a policy makes the community better off in a utilitarian sense would not provide a justification compatible with the right of those it disadvantages to be treated as equals.

This corruption of utilitarianism is plain when some people have external preferences because they hold political theories that are themselves contrary to utilitarianism. Suppose many citizens, who are not themselves sick, are racists in political theory, and therefore prefer that scarce medicine be given to a white man who needs it rather than a black man who needs it more. If utilitarianism counts these political preferences at face value, then it will be, from the standpoint of personal preferences, self-defeating, because the distribution of medicine will then not be, from that standpoint, utilitarian at all. In any case, self-defeating or not, the distribution will not be egalitarian in the sense defined. Blacks will suffer, to a degree that depends upon the strength of the racist preference, from the fact that others think them less worthy of respect and concern.

There is a similar corruption when the external preferences that are counted are altruistic or moralistic. Suppose many citizens, who themselves do not swim, prefer the pool to the theater because they approve of sports and admire athletes, or because they think that the theater is immoral and ought to be repressed. If the altruistic preferences are counted, so as to reinforce the personal preferences of swimmers, the result will be a form of double counting: each swimmer will have the benefit not only on his own preference, but also of the preference of someone else who takes pleasure in his success. If the moralistic preferences are counted, the effect will be the same: actors and audiences will suffer because their preferences are held in lower respect by citizens whose personal preferences are not themselves engaged.

In these examples, external preferences are independent of personal preferences. But of course political, altruistic, and moralistic preferences are often not independent, but grafted on to the personal preferences they reinforce. If I am white and sick, I may also hold a racist political theory. If I want a swimming pool for my own enjoyment I may also be altruistic in favor of my fellow athlete, or I may also think that the theater is immoral. The consequences of counting these external preferences will be as grave for equality as if they were independent of personal preference, because those against whom the external preferences run might be unable or unwilling to develop reciprocal external preferences that it would right the balance.

External preferences therefore present a great difficulty for utilitarianism. That theory owes much of its popularity to the assumption that it embodies the right of citizens to be treated as equals. But if external preferences are counted in overall preferences, then this assumption is jeopardized. That is, in itself, an important and neglected point in political theory; it bears, for example, on the liberal thesis, first made prominent by Mill, that the government has no right to enforce popular morality by law. It is often said that this liberal thesis is inconsistent with utilitarianism, because if the preferences of the majority that homosexuality should be repressed, for example, are sufficiently strong, utilitarianism must give way to their wishes. But the preference against homosexuality is an external preference, and the present argument provides a general reason why utilitarians should not count external preferences of any form. If utilitarianism is suitably reconstituted so as to count only personal preferences, then the liberal thesis is a consequence, not an enemy, of that theory.

It is not, however, always possible to reconstitute a utilitarian argument so as to count only personal preferences. Sometimes personal and external preferences are so inextricably tied together, and so mutually dependent, that no practical test for measuring preferences will be able to discriminate the personal and external elements in any individual's overall preference. That is especially true when preferences are affected by prejudice. Consider, for example, the associational preference of a white law student for white classmates. This may be said to be a personal preference for an association with one kind of colleague rather than another. But it is a personal preference that is parasitic upon external preferences: except in very rare cases a white student prefers the company of other whites because he has racist social and political convictions, or because he has contempt for blacks as a group. If these associational preferences are counted in a utilitarian argument used to justify segregation, then the egalitarian character of the argument is destroyed just as if the underlying external preferences were counted directly. Blacks would be denied their right to be treated as equals because the chance that their preferences would prevail in the design of admissions policy would be crippled by the low esteem in which others hold them. In any community in which prejudice against a particular minority is strong, then the personal preferences upon which a utilitarian argument must fix will be saturated with that prejudice; it follows that in such a community no utilitarian argument purporting to justify a disadvantage to the minority can be fair.[7]

This final difficulty is therefore fatal to Texas' utilitarian arguments in favor of segregation. The preferences that might support any such argument are either distinctly external, like the preferences of the community at large for racial separation, or are inextricably combined with and dependent upon external preferences, like the associational preferences of white students for white classmates and white lawyers for white colleagues. These external preferences are so widespread that they must corrupt any such argument. Texas' claim, that segregation makes the community better off in a utilitarian sense, is therefore incompatible with Sweatt's right to treatment as an equal guaranteed by the Equal Protection Clause.

It does not matter to this conclusion whether external preferences figure in the justification of a fundamental policy, or in the justification of derivative policies designed to advance a more fundamental policy. Suppose Texas justifies segregation by pointing to the apparently neutral economic policy of increasing community wealth, which satisfies the personal preferences of everyone for better homes, food, and recreation. If the argument that segregation will improve community wealth depends upon the fact of external preference; if the argument notices, for example, that because of prejudice industry will run more efficiently if factories are segregated; then the argument has the consequence that the black man's personal preferences are defeated by what others think of him.

Utilitarian arguments that justify a disadvantage to members of a race against whom prejudice runs will always be unfair arguments, unless it can be shown that disadvantage would have been justified in the absence of the prejudice. If the prejudice is wide-spread and pervasive, as in fact it is in the case of blacks, that can never be shown. The preferences on which any economic argument justifying segregation must be based will be so intertwined with prejudice that they cannot be disentangled to the degree necessary to make any such contrary-to-fact hypothesis plausible.

We now have an explanation that shows why any form of segregation that disadvantages blacks is, in the United States, an automatic insult to them, and why such segregation offends their right to be treated as equals. The argument confirms our sense that utilitarian arguments purporting to justify segregation are not simply wrong in detail but displaced in principle. This objection to utilitarian arguments is not, however, limited to race or even prejudice. There are other cases in which counting external preferences would offend the rights of citizens to be treated as equals, and it is worth briefly noticing these, if only to protect the argument against the charge that it is constructed ad hoc for the racial case. I might have moralistic preference against professional women, or an altruistic preference for virtuous men. It would be unfair for any law school to count preferences like these in deciding whom to admit to law schools; unfair because these preferences, like racial prejudices, make the success of the personal preferences of an applicant depend on the esteem and approval, rather than on the competing personal preferences, of others.

The same objection does not hold, however, against a utilitarian argument used to justify admission based on intelligence. That policy need not rely, directly or indirectly, on any community sense that intelligent lawyers are intrinsically more worthy of respect. It relies instead upon the law school's own judgment, right or wrong, that intelligent lawyers are more effective in satisfying personal preferences of others, such as the preference for wealth or winning law suits. It is true that law firms and clients prefer the services of intelligent lawyers; that fact might make us suspicious of any utilitarian argument that is said not to depend upon that preference, just as we are suspicious of any argument justifying segregation that is said not to depend upon prejudice. But the widespread preference for intelligent lawyers is, by and large, not parasitic on external preferences: law firms and clients prefer intelligent lawyer because they also hold the opinion that such lawyers will be more effective in serving their personal preferences. Instrumental preferences, of that character, do not themselves figure in utilitarian arguments, though a law school may accept, on its own responsibility, the instrumental hypothesis upon which such preferences depend.

V

We therefore have the distinctions in hand necessary to distinguish *DeFunis* from *Sweatt*. The arguments for an admissions program that discriminates against blacks are all utilitarian arguments, and they are all utilitarian arguments that rely upon external preferences in such a way as to offend the constitutional right of blacks to be treated as equals. The arguments for an admissions program that discriminates in favor of blacks are both utilitarian and ideal. Some of the utilitarian arguments do rely, at least indirectly, on external preferences, such as the preference of certain blacks for lawyers of their own race; but the utilitarian arguments that do not rely on such preferences are strong and may be sufficient. The ideal arguments do not rely upon preferences at all, but on the independent argument that a more equal society is a better society even if its citizens prefer inequality. That argument does not deny anyone's right to be treated as an equal himself.

We are therefore left, in DeFunis, with the simple and straightforward argument with which we began. Racial criteria are not necessarily the right standards for deciding which applicants should be accepted by law schools. But neither are intellectual criteria, nor indeed, any other set of criteria. The fairness—and constitutionality—of any admissions program must be tested in the same way. It is justified if it serves a proper policy that respects the right of all members of the community to be treated as equals, but not otherwise. The criteria used by schools that refused to consider blacks failed that test, but the criteria used by the University of Washington Law School do not.

We are all rightly suspicious of racial classifications. They have been used to deny, rather than to respect, the right of equality, and we are all conscious of the consequent injustice. But if we misunderstand the nature of that injustice because we do not make the simple distinctions that are necessary to understand it, then we are in danger of more injustice still. It may be that preferential admissions programs will not, in fact, make a more equal society, because they may not have the effects their advocates believe they will. That strategic question should be at the center of debate about these programs. But we must not corrupt the debate by supposing that these programs are unfair even if they do work. We must take care not to use the Equal Protection Clause to cheat ourselves of equality.

NOTES

1. *Sweatt v. Painter*, 339 US 629, 70 S.Ct. 848.
2. *DeFunis v. Odegaard*, 94 S.Ct. 1704 (1974).
3. See my "The Jurisprudence of Richard Nixon," *The New York Review of Books*, May 4, 1972.
4. I shall argue later in this essay that there are circumstances in which a policy violates someone's right to be treated as an equal in spite of the fact that the social gains from that policy may be said to outweigh the losses. These circumstances arise when the gains that outweigh the losses include the satisfaction of prejudices and other sorts of preferences that it is improper for officials or institutions to take into account at all. But the hypothetical social gains described in this paragraph do not include gains of that character. Of course, if DeFunis had some other right, beyond the right to be treated as an equal, which the University of Washington's policy violated, then the fact that the policy might achieve an overall social gain would not justify the violation. (See my "Taking Rights Seriously," *The New York Review of Books*, December 17, 1970.) If the Washington admissions procedures included a religious test that violated his right to religious freedom, for example, it would offer no excuse for using such a test that it might make the community more cohesive. But DeFunis does not rely on any distinct right beyond his right to equality protected by the equal protection clause.
5. In the actual *Sweatt* decision, the Supreme Court applied the old rule which held that segregation was constitutionally permitted if facilities were provided for blacks that were "separate but equal." Texas had provided a separate law school for blacks, but the Court held that the school was by no means the equal of the white school. *Sweatt* was decided before the famous *Brown* case in which the Court finally rejected the "separate but equal" rule, and there is no doubt that an all-white law school would be unconstitutional today even if a separate black school provided facilities that were in a material sense the equal of those provided for whites.
6. Many economists and philosophers challenge the intelligibility of preference utilitarianism as well as psychological utilitarianism. They

argue that there is no way, even in principle, to calculate and compare the intensity of individual preferences. Since I wish to establish a different failing in certain utilitarian arguments, I assume for purposes of this essay, that at least rough and speculative calculations about overall community preferences can be made.

7. The argument of this paragraph is powerful but it is not, in itself, sufficient to disqualify all utilitarian arguments that produce substantial disadvantages to minorities who suffer from prejudice. Suppose the government decides, on a utilitarian argument, to allow unemployment to increase because the loss to those who lose their jobs is outweighed by the gain to those who would otherwise suffer from inflation. The burden of this policy will fall disproportionately on blacks, who will be fired first because prejudice runs against them. But though prejudice in this way affects the consequence of the policy, of unemployment, it does not figure, even indirectly, in the utilitarian argument that supports that policy. (It figures, if at all, as a utilitarian argument against it.) We cannot say, therefore, that the special damage blacks suffer from a high unemployment policy is unjust for the reasons described in this essay. It may well be unjust for other reasons: if John Rawls is right, for example, it is unjust because the policy improves the condition of the majority at the expense of those already worse off.

5

CASUALTIES AND MORE CASUALTIES: SURVIVING AFFIRMATIVE ACTION (MORE OR LESS)

Frederick R. Lynch

In the mid-1970s, I became increasingly interested in what I assumed were two sociologically compelling questions: (1) how did white males (and their families, co-workers, and friends) respond to reverse discrimination?; and (2) how were the media portraying affirmative action? I conducted the research and later published the results while teaching in temporary faculty positions on the Los Angeles and San Bernardino campuses of the California State University (CSU) system.

Throughout this period, the nineteen-campus CSU empire became caught up in an intensifying affirmative-action crusade involving blatant race, ethnic, and gender preferences in recruiting faculty, staff, and students. Thus, I was engaging in critical studies of policies championed by my own employer (and most alternative academic employers). This was risky business. Scattered reports from critics of affirmative action made it obvious that academic freedom on the topic was fragile even for tenured scholars, and the tight job market for sociologists rendered the kind of research I was doing doubly dangerous. Nevertheless, curiosity ultimately prevailed over fear and anxiety.

For me this research saga illuminated the powerful taboos which have dominated the American intellectual landscape for more than twenty years, and I learned a great deal from the expe-

Reprinted from *Commentary* (August 1990): 44–47, by permission; all rights reserved.

rience. I would, however, never do such a thing again. My career has been badly damaged. Worse, I have watched a political steam-roller flatten civil liberties and due process as it has moved through institutions designed to be bastions of traditionally liberal values and forums for the free discussion and rational analysis of ideas. The academic and intellectual communities which once embraced Martin Luther King's call to judge an individual by the content of his character, not the color of his skin, now do precisely the opposite. They bow reverentially to the gods of tribalism, while also doing almost everything possible to suppress any challenge to their current orthodoxies.

My interest in affirmative action was whetted in the early 1970s when I began hearing anecdotes about reverse discrimination. Watching for television and newspaper reports on this remarkable policy, I came upon very few. With the exception of some polemical essays, sociologists also paid relatively little attention to the topic. Throughout the 1970s, the anecdotes continued to increase as affirmative-action rhetoric became more strident. Certainly this was the case in the CSU system, where I started teaching as a temporary member of the sociology faculty in 1977.

Like most American colleges and universities, the CSU campuses developed affirmative-action plans, hired affirmative-action officers, and billed themselves as "affirmative-action/equal-opportunity employers." (It was not until the mid-to-late 1980s that the term "equality" was eclipsed by the more hard-line vocabulary of "equity," "diversity," and "access.")

In spite of all this, few of my colleagues in the CSU knew much about affirmative-action programs on their own campuses or in the wider society. One reason was that these programs—in the CSU as elsewhere—had been formulated and implemented quietly. Legal ambiguities wrought by Supreme Court vacillation promoted the use of informal pressures and "discretion" rather than codified or systematic measures.

A second reason for lack of concern among my fellow sociologists with affirmative action was the slowdown in hiring that set in during the mid-1970s. Sociology, the most popular major of the 1960s, was by now becoming one of the least popular. Indeed, the CSU system lost nearly 90 percent of its sociology majors from the mid-1970s to the mid-1980s. In combination with the cuts forced by Proposition 13, the inevitable result was a hiring freeze.

For most of my colleagues, the hiring freeze meant that no white male they personally knew had been denied a job because of his race or gender. If they spoke of affirmative action at all, they did so in vague, simplistic terms. They talked of the policy as the "ideal situation" of an equally qualified white male competing for a position with an equally qualified female or minority candidate—in which case the latter candidate should be given the job. That the realities of affirmative action might involve outright preference of less qualified (or unqualified) women or minorities was dismissed. Nor could these Ph.D.s in sociology grasp the elementary economic fact that, in a tight labor market, affirmative action must necessarily operate in a zero-sum context: when one person was hired because of race, ethnicity, or gender, others were thereby excluded on the same discriminatory grounds.

Yet to recognize that affirmative action could not help without hurting ran up against an absolute dictum of the Marxist/feminist orthodoxy which had crept into the everyday academic world view of the 1970s and 1980s: the idea that only certified minorities—especially blacks and women—could be victims. To suggest that white males were being injured by affirmative action invited righteous scorn and contempt—even among white males themselves.

The question that intrigued me was how these same (or similar) white males would respond when and if they themselves encountered reverse discrimination. Would they protest? Would they accord one another support and understanding?

In 1984, I obtained a small grant from the Institute for Educational Affairs which enabled me to hire two research assistants. In the ensuing months we found our way to 34 white males in a variety of occupations who had good reason to believe that they had been the victims of reverse discrimination in seeking jobs or promotions. After dropping two of the 34 because it was not clear that affirmative action had been a decisive factor in their cases, we wound up with 32 subjects. The data we got from them were supplemented by background interviews with a dozen personnel or affirmative-action officers, employment counselors, and corporate executives. Many informal interviews with others who learned of the research and wanted to talk added to our sense of what was happening.

By coincidence, our 32 formal interviews equaled the number of college-student participants in a laboratory experiment which had been conducted in 1980 by a sociologist named Stephen

Johnson. Johnson discovered that white male students who had lost a puzzle-solving exercise to a fictitious competitor expressed more hostility toward the victor when told that he was black and had been given a bonus score by the experimenter to compensate for his cultural disadvantages. The student subjects, however, expressed less hostility toward black victors than toward white ones when told that they had lost because of the competitor's superior performance.

Suggestive though they were, Johnson's laboratory results were simply too limited to predict the real-world effects of reverse discrimination. Practically no one could truly guess at the responses we would find "out there." Using a semi-structured interview format—which let the subjects discuss their experiences in their own words—we discovered a wide and deep spectrum of responses ranging from acquiescence to anger to protest.

The vast majority—20 out of 32—simply endured reverse discrimination without protest, though many were quietly angry. Among the other twelve, six quit the jobs in which they had encountered discrimination; four protested, including three who took legal action—to no avail; and two circumvented barriers through other organizational means.

Our subjects were not angry white racists eager to take to the streets. On the contrary, the mostly middle-class males we interviewed felt bewildered and isolated by what had happened to them. Hardly a one of them was willing to voice any open antagonism toward affirmative action. Why?

First, they feared being labeled "racist" if they complained about programs that purportedly redressed past discrimination. In fact, almost to a man they took pains to explain to the interviewers that they understood and deplored the history of racism in America. Yet many had sustained real career injuries and felt betrayed by the system. Said a middle-management state worker: "A lot of us were sold a bill of goods. We were told if you went to college, you could write your own ticket. But . . . affirmative action has lowered standards to the point where education almost counts against you. . . ."

Unlike minority or female victims of discrimination, white males could not necessarily count on in-group support. Wives aside ("My wife is mad as hell; she's angrier than, I am"), only half reported any such support from friends and co-workers.

This seems to be why teachers selected by computer for

transfer in a massive racial-balancing plan by the Los Angeles Unified School district were especially bitter. Commented one: "You found out who your friends were. I found I didn't have as many as I thought." Said another: "My friends and co-workers didn't know how to handle this. They wanted to empathize but [as political liberals] felt cognitive dissonance." A third stated dryly, "People don't like victims."

Deeply ingrained norms regarding silent, "manly" behavior and individual responsibility have crushed any sort of collective awareness and class action by white males. "When it hits you," a community-college instructor stated, "You don't want to admit it at first. Instead, you think it must be something in you. You doubt yourself. You repress it, try to forget it." No one wanted to be accused of "alibiing."

A Ph.D. in political science and a once aspiring university professor (now a government worker) articulated a common concern: "Why didn't I say anything about it? Pride, I guess. I didn't want to make excuses." Many others feared for the future of their careers if they vented their objections. They felt that if they did not "rock the boat," things would work out later.

Another key factor in keeping silent was the fear of not being believed. Reverse discrimination simply sounded too outlandish and incredible without external validation by the mass media—and the mass media were not providing such validation.

This neglect by the news and entertainment industry—especially in the 1970s—was quickly confirmed even before we began interviewing. I simply counted the number of articles on affirmative action indexed in the *Reader's Guide to Periodical Literature* from 1968 to 1980, and the number of minutes on the network newscasts as tabulated in the *Vanderbilt Television News Index and Abstracts* (from its inception in 1972 through 1980). What I discovered was that, until the *Bakke* case moved to the U.S. Supreme Court in 1977, there was about one article per year in each of the major newsweeklies and about twelve to fifteen minutes per year (and sometimes much less) on the networks on topics related to affirmative action. There was a slight fall-off after *Bakke.*

Qualitative evidence reinforced quantitative data. In comparison with other race-related issues, especially the school-busing battles, affirmative action was not box-office. It was treated as a non-issue and rarely, if ever, mentioned in press coverage of the 1980, 1984, and 1988 presidential campaigns, not even in cover stories by major news magazines about Jesse Jackson. As for commercial television, on those few occasions when affirmative action was dealt with—such as a 1975 episode of "All in the Family"—it was portrayed in its "ideal" form and in highly sympathetic terms.

There were also several issues to which affirmative action seemed "naturally" related, but where it remained the other shoe that never dropped. For example, very few reporters or commentators noted the clash between the egalitarian thrust of affirmative action and the drive for higher standards in education and business. And, until the late 1980s, few journalists ever pointed to the role of affirmative action in promoting discord in the Democratic party.

Yet by the mid-1980s, the emergence of blue-collar, white, male "Reagan Democrats" compelled the guarded attention of political analysts and pollsters. Thus, after the 1984 Reagan landslide, Michigan Democrats commissioned Stanley Greenberg to study "Democratic defection" in their state. Greenberg and his associates gathered discussion groups of white, working-class Democrats and posed a series of questions designed to assess their political mood. Asked, "Who do you think gets the raw deal?" they responded:

> "We do."
> "The middle-class white guy."
> "The working middle class."
> "Cause women get advantages, the Hispanics get advantages, Orientals get advantages. Everybody but the white male race gets advantages now."

and:

> "I have been here all my life working, paying taxes and the whole shot, and I can't start my own business unless I have 30 percent down on whatever I want to buy. I have the experience on the job, I have put in for openings, and they have come right out and told me in personnel that the government has come down and said that I can't have the job because they have to give it to the minorities."

Greenberg and his sponsors were stunned and chagrined by this fury over affirmative action among working-class whites. Clearly preferential treatment had poisoned traditional Democratic appeals to "fairness" and "justice," and it also seemed that racial preferences were turning white working-class males against government programs in general. Similar data were obtained in a 1985 "Democrats Listening to America" poll of 5,500 voters, as well as in a replication of the Michigan study in 1987.

The response of the Democratic party to findings such as Greenberg's was instructive: it tried to suppress the reports. As the social critic Charles Murray observed of the ill effects of affirmative action: "Hardly a policy-maker or academic anywhere wants to examine these results and fewer still want to speak of them."

In discussing the hostile reception accorded in the 1970s to his work on school busing (which demonstrated that it was causing white flight and other problems), the eminent sociologist James Coleman suggested that when senior scholars act as a lightning rod for controversial research, it makes the world safer for their less secure juniors laboring in the same field. As I have good reason to know, Coleman was right. For it took a number of books and articles by well-known scholars to pave the way for my own work.

Nathan Glazer was the first sociologist to break the ice, with *Affirmative Discrimination* in 1975. Nearly a decade later came Charles Murray's *Losing Ground,* which appeared just as I was launching my interviews. During these same years, articles criticizing affirmative action also began to appear here and there, making it easier for me to publish two of my own articles and to edit a special issue of *The American Behavioral Scientist* on the subject.

But then, in a deeply ironic twist, I began discovering that I myself had joined the subjects of my own study as a victim of reverse discrimination. Which is to say that while my résumé continued to grow with more publications and references, I was unable to move beyond temporary faculty status to a tenure-track position.

No doubt my career struggles were in part linked to the huge surplus of baby-boomer Ph.D.s. Furthermore, I had a Ph.D. from the University of California at Riverside, not the more prestigious UC-Berkeley. And I was growing older. But there could be little doubt that reverse discrimination was a major cause of my stalled career.

Once, for example, I was informed by a plainly discomfited chairman that I had lost a position at Sweet Briar College strictly because I was male. On another occasion the department chairman at Pomona College told me that the only sociologist he could hire was a black. On yet a third occasion, Occidental College abruptly canceled an interview, later notifying me (and several other candidates) that it had hired a female "native of Jamaica."

Making matters even worse, there was my research on affirmative action. Job nibbles usually ceased the moment I mentioned it. When I was interviewed at a seven-sisters college in the early 1980s, the chairman pleaded with me: "Please, I want you to get this job. Don't talk about your affirmative-action research." A scheduled interview at a Southwestern university was suddenly canceled in 1987 after the dean learned of the topic of my research. In 1990, the political implications of my research sabotaged an otherwise successful interview at a large Midwestern state university.

To keep my research afloat, I needed financial support, but initial queries to such major foundations as Ford, Rockefeller, and Carnegie met with bewilderment or contempt. Fortunately, smaller, less ideologically orthodox foundations like Earhart and Sarah Scaife were more responsive. Help from Earhart made it possible for me to complete the project and analyze its results in a book, *Invisible Victims: White Males and the Crisis of Affirmative Action.* The editors at Greenwood Press were more willing to take a risk with such a manuscript than several larger publishers who hinted or admitted outright that their firms subscribed to a "party line" on this issue.

At first, my colleagues treated my complaints about reverse discrimination exactly as the few complaints made by the subjects of my research project were treated by the people around them: as a form of "alibiing." But by the late 1980s, acknowledgment of race-and-gender pressures became more explicit. Universities openly began to advertise "targets of diversity" and other set-aside positions for minorities and women.

Then, in the late 1980s, limited hiring began again in sociology and related fields at both CSU Los Angeles and San Bernardino. Suddenly, colleagues who had once dismissed complaints about reverse discrimination were now instructed to implement such practices.

In 1986, 19.2 percent of newly hired, tenure-track CSU faculty were minorities and 34.8 percent were women. By 1988, 23.4 percent of new hires were minorities and 38.4 percent were women. Since there have been few female, black, or Hispanic Ph.D.s in the high-demand fields of physical science, business, engineering, and math, most female, non-Asian minority faculty were likely to be hired in education and in the glutted, low-demand humanities and social sciences. It is reasonable to assume that administrative prompting to hire females and minorities created pressures—however subtle—against hiring white males.

Less subtle were pools of set-aside faculty positions reserved for minorities and females established at San Bernardino and some other CSU campuses. In 1989, a black female (*sans* Ph.D.) was hired by the sociology department to fill such a set-aside position, with a high salary and reduced teaching load which included classes I had taught for several years. Since I was directly affected, I was able to check out the futility of legal redress as reported by some of my interview subjects. Their accounts were grimly confirmed. The representative of the State Fair Housing and Employment Commission rationalized the CSU set-asides as a legally acceptable attempt to bring its work force into "balance" and I was informed by the Equal Employment Opportunity Commission that Cal State's use of set-asides was "voluntary affirmative action." Unless I had direct, "smoking-gun" evidence that I had been denied employment because I was a white male, nothing could be done.

Interestingly, both of these defenses of CSU's set-asides were offered *after* the Supreme Court, in *Richmond* v. *Croson,* specifically limited the use of voluntary set-asides by state or local government agencies. No wonder, then, that Cal State Northridge saw no risk in running a large ad in the *Chronicle of Higher Education* announcing that it was "setting aside a pool of faculty positions to allocate to those departments that identify well-qualified minority candidates for either full-time tenure Crack or lecturer appointments." The CSU system has also provided 200 minority and female Ph.D. aspirants with up to $30,000 each through a set-aside forgivable loan program.

My subjects' accounts of union paralysis on reverse discrimination were also confirmed by my own experience. Our fledgling faculty union was even more strident than the CSU in its calls for "diversity, equity, and affirmative action,." The union was content that the CSU's programs be merely "legally defensible." Publicly, it would take no stand on reverse discrimination; privately, there was recognition of the problem, a little anguish, and no action. "People still can't deal with this issue," a UCLA sociologist recently told me, "they don't want to be critical." Indeed they don't, as I and so many others have learned from bitter personal experience.

6

FROM EQUAL OPPORTUNITY TO "AFFIRMATIVE ACTION"

Thomas Sowell

The very meaning of the phrase "civil rights" has changed greatly since the *Brown* decision in 1954, or since the Civil Rights Act of 1964. Initially, civil rights meant, quite simply, that all individuals should be treated the same under the law, regardless of their race, religion, sex, or other such social categories. For blacks, especially, this would have represented a dramatic improvement in those states where law and public policy mandated racially separate institutions and highly discriminatory treatment.

Many Americans who supported the initial thrust of civil rights, as represented by the *Brown* v. *Board of Education* decision and the Civil Rights Act of 1964, later felt betrayed as the original concept of equal individual *opportunity* evolved toward the concept of equal group *results.* The idea that statistical differences in results were weighty presumptive evidence of discriminatory processes was not initially an explicit part of civil rights law. But neither was it merely an inexplicable perversion, as many critics seem to think, for it followed logically from the civil rights *vision.*

If the causes of intergroup differences can be dichotomized into discrimination and innate ability, then nonracists and nonsexists must expect equal results from nondiscrimination. Conversely, the persistence of highly disparate results must indicate that discrimination continues to be pervasive among recalcitrant employers, culturally biased tests, hypocritical educational institutions, etc. The early leaders and supporters of the civil rights movement did not advocate such corollaries, and many explicitly repudiated them, especially during the congressional debates that preceded passage of the Civil Rights Act of 1964.[1] But the corollaries were implicit in the vision—and in the long run that proved to be more decisive than the positions taken by the original leaders in the cause of civil rights. In the face of crying injustices, many Americans accepted a vision that promised to further a noble cause, without quibbling over its assumptions or verbal formulations. But visions have a momentum of their own, and those who accept their assumptions have entailed their corollaries, however surprised they may be when these corollaries emerge historically.

FROM RIGHTS TO QUOTAS

"Equal opportunity" laws and policies require that individuals be judged on their qualifications as individuals, *without regard* to race, sex, age, etc. "Affirmative action" requires that they be judged *with regard* to such group membership, receiving preferential or compensatory treatment in some cases to achieve a more proportional "representation" in various institutions and occupations.

The conflict between equal opportunity and affirmative action developed almost imperceptibly at first, though it later became a heated issue, repeatedly debated by the time the Civil Rights Act of 1964 was being considered by Congress. The term "affirmative action" was first used in a racial discrimination context in President John F. Kennedy's Executive Order No. 10,925 in 1961. But, as initially presented, affirmative action referred to various activities, such as monitoring subordinate decision makers to ensure the fairness of their hiring and promotion decisions, and spreading information about employment or other opportunities so as to encourage previously excluded groups to apply—after which the actual selection could be made *without regard* to group membership. Thus, it was both meaningful and consistent for President Kennedy's Executive Order to say that federal contractors should "take affirmative action to ensure that the applicants are employed, and that employees are treated during employment, without regard to their race, creed, color, or national origin."

Tendencies toward shifting the emphasis from equality of prospective opportunity toward statistical parity of retrospective results were already observed, at both state and federal levels, by the time that the Civil Rights Act of 1964 was under consideration in Congress. Senator Hubert Humphrey, while guiding this bill through the Senate, assured his colleagues that it "does not require an employer to achieve any kind of racial balance in his work force by giving preferential treatment to any individual or group."[2] He pointed out that subsection 703(j) under Title VII of the Civil Rights Act "is added to state this point expressly."[3] That subsection declared that nothing in Title VII required an employer "to grant preferential treatment to any individual or group on account of any imbalance which may exist" with respect to the numbers of employees in such groups "in comparison with the total number or percentage of persons of such race, color, religion, sex, or national origin in any community, State, section or other area."

Virtually all the issues involved in the later controversies over affirmative action, in the specifically numerical sense, were raised in the legislative debates preceding passage of the Civil Rights Act. Under subsection 706(g) of that Act, an employer was held liable only for his own "intentional" discrimination,[4] not for societal patterns reflected in his work force. According to Senator Humphrey, the "express requirement of intent is designed to make it wholly clear that inadvertent or accidental discriminations will not violate the Title or result in the entry of court orders."[5] Vague claims of differential institutional policy impact—"institutional racism"—were not to be countenanced. For example, tests with differential impact on different groups were considered by Humphrey to be "legal unless used for the purpose of discrimination."[6] There was no burden of proof placed upon employers to "validate" such tests.

In general there was to be no burden of proof on employers; rather the Equal Employment Opportunity Commission (EEOC) created by the Act "must prove by a preponderance" that an adverse decision was based on race (or, presumably, other forbidden categories), according to Senator Joseph Clark, another leading advocate of the Civil Rights Act.[7] Senator Clark also declared that the Civil Rights Act "will not require an employer to change existing seniority lists," even though such lists might have differential impact on blacks as the last hired and first fired.[8] Still another supporter, Senator Harrison Williams, declared that an employer with an all-white work force could continue to hire "only the best qualified persons even if they were all white."[9]

In short, Congress declared itself in favor of equal opportunity and opposed to affirmative action. So has the American public. Opinion polls show a majority of blacks opposed to preferential treatment, as is an even larger majority of women.[10] Federal administrative agencies and the courts led the change from the prospective concept of individual equal opportunity to the retrospective concept of parity of group "representation" (or "correction" of "imbalances").

The key development in this process was the creation of the Office of Federal Contract Compliance in the U.S. Department of Labor by President Lyndon Johnson's Executive Order No. 11,246 in 1965. In May 1968, this office issued guidelines containing the fateful expression "goals and timetables" and "representation." But as yet these were still not quotas, for 1968 guidelines spoke of "goals and timetables for the prompt achievement of full and equal employment opportunity." By 1970, however, new guidelines referred to "results-oriented procedures," which hinted more strongly at what was to come. In December 1971, the decisive guidelines were issued, which made it clear that "goals and timetables" were meant to "increase materially the utilization of minorities and women," with "under-utilization" being spelled out as "having fewer minorities or women in a particular job classification than would reasonably be expected by their availability . . ."[11] Employers were required to confess to "deficiencies in the utilization" of minorities and women whenever this statistical parity could not be found in all job classifications, as a first step toward correcting this situation. The burden of proof—and remedy—was on the employer. "Affirmative action" was now decisively transformed into a numerical concept, whether called "goals" or "quotas."[12]

Though lacking in either legislative authorization or public support for numerical group preferences, administrative agencies of government were able to enforce such policies with the support of the federal courts in general and the U.S. Supreme Court in particular. In the landmark *Weber* case the Supreme Court simply rejected "a literal interpretation" of the words of the Civil Rights Act. Instead, it sought the "spirit" of the Act, its "primary concern" with the economic problems of blacks. According to Justice William Brennan, writing the majority opinion, these words do not bar "temporary, voluntary, affirmative action measures undertaken to eliminate manifest racial imbalance in traditionally segregated job categories."[13] This performance received the sarcastic tribute of Justice Rehnquist that it was "a *tour de force* reminiscent not of jurists such as Hale, Holmes, and Hughes but of escape artists such as Houdini."[14] Rehnquist's dissent inundated the Supreme Court with the legislative history of the Act, and Congress' repeated and emphatic rejection of the whole approach of correcting imbalances or compensating for the past.[15] The spirit of the Act was as contrary to the decision as was the letter.

EQUALITY OF RIGHTS AND RESULTS

Those who carry the civil rights vision to its ultimate conclusion see no great difference between promoting equality of opportunity and equality of results. If there are not equal results among groups presumed to have equal genetic potential, then some inequality of opportunity must have intervened somewhere, and the question of precisely where is less important than the remedy of restoring the less fortunate to their just position. The fatal flaw in this kind of thinking is that there are many reasons, besides genes and discrimination, why groups differ in their economic performances and rewards. Groups differ by large amounts demographically, culturally, and geographically—and all of these differences have profound effects on incomes and occupations.

Age differences are quite large. Blacks are a decade younger than the Japanese. Jews are a quarter of a century older than Puerto Ricans. Polish Americans are twice as old as American Indians.[16] These represent major differences in the quantity of work experience, in an economy where income differences between age brackets are even greater than black-white income differences.[17] Even if the various racial and ethnic groups were identical in every other respect, their age differences alone would prevent their being equally represented in occupations requiring experience or higher education. Their very different age distributions likewise prevent their being equally represented in colleges, jails, homes for the elderly, the armed forces, sports, and numerous other institutions and activities that tend to have more people from one age bracket than from another.

Cultural differences add to the age differences. . . . [Half] of all Mexican American wives were married in their teens, while only

10 percent of Japanese American wives married that young.[18] Such very different patterns imply not only different values but also very different future opportunities. Those who marry and begin having children earlier face more restricted options for future education and less geographic mobility for seeking their best career opportunities. Even among those young people who go on to colleges and universities, their opportunities to prepare themselves for the better paid professions are severely limited by their previous educational choices and performances, as well as by their selections of fields of study in the colleges and universities. All of these things vary enormously from one group to another.

For example, mathematics preparation and performance differ greatly from one ethnic group to another and between men and women. A study of high school students in northern California showed that four-fifths of Asian youngsters were enrolled in the sequence of mathematics courses that culminate in calculus, while only one-fifth of black youngsters were enrolled in such courses. Moreover, even among those who began this sequence in geometry, the percentage that persisted all the way through to calculus was several times higher among the Asian students.[19] Sex differences in mathematics preparation are comparably large. Among both black and white freshmen at the University of Maryland, the men had had four years of mathematics in high school more than twice as often as the women.[20]

Mathematics is of decisive importance for many more professions than that of mathematician. Whole ranges of fields of study and work are off-limits to those without the necessary mathematical foundation. Physicists, chemists, statisticians, and engineers are only some of the more obvious occupations. In some colleges, one cannot even be an undergraduate economics major without having had calculus, and to go on to graduate school and become a professional economist requires much more mathematics, as well as statistical analysis. Even in fields where mathematics is not an absolute prerequisite, its presence or absence makes a major difference in one's ability to rise in the profession. Mathematics is becoming an important factor in the social sciences and is even beginning to invade some of the humanities. To be mathematically illiterate is to carry an increasing burden into an increasing number of occupations. Even the ability to pass a civil service examination for modest clerical jobs is helped or hindered by one's facility in mathematics.

It is hardly surprising that test scores reflect these group differences in mathematics preparation. Nationwide results on the Scholastic Aptitude Test (SAT) for college applicants show Asians and whites consistently scoring higher on the quantitative test than Hispanics or blacks, and men scoring higher than women.[21] Nor are these differences merely the result of socioeconomic "disadvantage" caused by "society. " Black, Mexican American, and American Indian youngsters from families with incomes of $50,000 and up score lower than Asians from families whose incomes are just $6,000 and under.[22] Moreover, Asians as a group score higher than whites as a group on the quantitative portion of the SAT and the Japanese in Japan specialize in mathematics, science, and engineering to a far greater extent than do American students in the United States.[23] Cultural differences are real, and cannot be talked away by using pejorative terms such as "stereotypes" or "racism."

The racial, ethnic, and sex differences in mathematics that begin in high school (or earlier) continue on through to the Ph.D. level, affecting career choices and economic rewards. Hispanic Ph.D.s outnumber Asian Ph.D.s in the United States by three-to-one in history, but the Asians outnumber the Hispanics by ten-to-one in chemistry.[24] More than half of all Asian Ph.D.s are in mathematics, science, or engineering, and more than half the Asians who teach college teach in those fields. By contrast, more than half of all black doctorates are in the field of education, a notoriously undemanding and less remunerative field. So are half the doctorates received by American Indians, not one of whom received a Ph.D. in either mathematics or physics in 1980.[25] Female Ph.D.s are in quantitatively based fields only half as frequently as male Ph.D.s.[26]

Important as mathematics is in itself, it is also a symptom of broader and deeper disparities in educational choices and performances in general. Those groups with smaller quantities of education tend also to have lower qualities of education, and these disparities follow them all the way through their educational careers and into the job market. The children of lower income racial and ethnic groups typically score lower on tests all through school and attend lower quality colleges when they go to college at all, as well as majoring in the easier courses in fields with the least economic promise. How much of this is due to the home environment and how much to the deficiencies of the public schools in their neighborhoods is a large question that cannot be answered here. But what is clear is that what is called the "same" education, measured in years of schooling, is not even remotely the same in reality.

The civil rights vision relies heavily on statistical "disparities" in income and employment between members of different groups to support its sweeping claims of rampant discrimination. The U.S. Civil Rights Commission, for example, considers itself to be "controlling for those factors"[27] when it examines people of the same age with the same number of years of schooling—resolutely ignoring the substance of that schooling.

Age and education do not begin to exhaust the differences between groups. They are simply more readily quantitative than some other differences. The geographic distributions of groups also vary greatly, with Mexican Americans being concentrated in the southwest, Puerto Ricans in the northeast, half of blacks in the South, and most Asians in California and Hawaii. Differences in income between the states are also larger than black-white income differences, so that these distributional differences affect national income differences. A number of past studies, for example, have shown black and Puerto Rican incomes to be very similar nationally, but blacks generally earn higher incomes than Puerto Ricans in New York and other places where Puerto Ricans are concentrated.[28] Their incomes nationally have shown up in the studies as similar, because there are very few Puerto Ricans living in low-income southern states.

One of the most important causes of differences in income and employment is the way people work—some diligently, carefully, persistently, cooperatively, and without requiring much supervision or warnings about absenteeism, tardiness, or drinking, and others requiring much such concern over such matters. Not only are such things inherently difficult to quantify; any suggestion that such differences even exist is sure to bring forth a storm of condemnation. In short, the civil rights vision has been hermetically sealed off from any such evidence. Both historical and contemporary observations on intergroup differences in work habits, discipline, reliability, sobriety, cleanliness, or cooperative attitude—anywhere in the world—are automatically dismissed as evidence only of the bias or bigotry of the observers. "Stereotypes" is the magic word that makes thinking about such things unnecessary. Yet despite this closed circle of reasoning that surrounds the civil rights vision, there is some evidence that cannot be disposed of in that way.

Self-employed farmers, for example, do not depend for their

rewards on the biases of employers or the stereotypes of observers. Yet self-employed farmers of different ethnicity have fared very differently on the same land, even in earlier pre-mechanization times, when the principal input was the farmer's own labor. German farmers, for example, had more prosperous farms than other farmers in colonial America[29]—and were more prosperous than Irish farmers in eighteenth-century Ireland,[30] as well as more prosperous than Brazilian farmers in Brazil,[31] Mexican farmers in Mexico,[32] Russian farmers in Russia,[33] and Chilean farmers in Chile.[34] We may ignore the forbidden testimony from all these countries as to how hard the German farmers worked, how frugally they lived, or how sober they were. Still, the results speak for themselves.

That Jews earn far higher incomes than Hispanics in the United States might be taken as evidence that anti-Hispanic bias is stronger than anti-Semitism—if one followed the logic of the civil rights vision. But this explanation is considerably weakened by the greater prosperity of Jews than Hispanics in *Hispanic countries* throughout Latin America.[35] Again, even if one dismisses out of hand all the observers who see great differences in the way these two groups work, study, or save, major tangible differences in economic performance remain that cannot be explained in terms of the civil rights vision.

One of the commonly used indices of intergroup economic differences is family income. Yet families are of different sizes from group to group, reflecting differences in the incidence of broken homes. Female-headed households are several times more common among blacks than among whites, and in both groups these are the lowest income families. Moreover, the proportion of people working differs greatly from group to group. More than three-fifths of all Japanese American families have multiple income earners while only about a third of Puerto Rican families do. Nor is this a purely socioeconomic phenomenon. Blacks have similar incomes to Puerto Ricans, but the proportion of black families with a woman working is nearly three times that among Puerto Ricans.[36]

None of this disproves the existence of discrimination, nor is that its purpose. What is at issue is whether statistical differences mean discrimination, or whether there are innumerable demographic, cultural, and geographic differences that make this crucial automatic inference highly questionable.

EFFECTS VERSUS HOPES

Thus far, we have not even considered the actual effects of the incentives and constraints created by affirmative action policies—as distinguished from the rationales, hopes, or claims made for these policies. Because these policies are invoked on behalf of the most disadvantaged groups, and the most disadvantaged classes within these groups, it is especially important to scrutinize the factual record of what has happened to the economic position of such people under both equal opportunity and affirmative policies.

Before crediting either political policy with economic gains, it is worth considering what trends were already under way before they were instituted. Much has been made of the number of blacks in high-level occupations before and after the Civil Rights Act of 1964. What has been almost totally ignored is the historical *trend* of black representation in such occupations before the Act was passed. In the period from 1954 to 1964, for example, the number of blacks in professional, technical, and similar high-level positions more than doubled.[37] In other kinds of occupations, the advance of blacks was even greater during the 1940s—when there was little or no civil rights policy—than during the 1950s when the civil rights revolution was in its heyday.[38]

The rise in the number of blacks in professional and technical occupations in the two years from 1964 to 1966 (after the Civil Rights Act) was in fact less than in the one year from 1961 to 1962 (before the Civil Rights Act).[39] If one takes into account the growing black population by looking at percentages instead of absolute numbers, it becomes even clearer that the Civil Rights Act of 1964 represented no acceleration in trends that had been going on for many years. The percentage of employed blacks who were professional and technical workers rose less in the five years following the Civil Rights Act of 1964 than in the five years preceding it. The percentage of employed blacks who were managers and administrators was the same in 1967 as in 1964—and in 1960. Nor did the institution of "goals and timetables" at the end of 1971 mark any acceleration in the long trend of rising black representation in these occupations. True, there was an appreciable increase in the percentage of blacks in professional and technical fields from 1971 to 1972, but almost entirely offset by a reduction in the percentage of blacks who were managers and administrators.[40]

The history of Asians and Hispanics likewise shows long-term upward trends that began years before the Civil Rights Act of 1964 and were not noticeably accelerated by the Act or by later "affirmative action" policies. The income of Mexican Americans rose relative to that of non-Hispanic whites between 1959 and 1969 (after the Civil Rights Act), but no more so than from 1949 to 1959 (before the Act).[41] Chinese and Japanese Americans overtook other Americans in income by 1959—five years before the Civil Rights Act.

Ignoring trends already in progress for years makes before-and-after comparisons completely misleading. Yet that is precisely the approach of supporters of the civil rights vision, who proceed as if "before" was a static situation. Yet the notion that the Civil Rights Act and "affirmative action" have had a dramatic impact on the economic progress of minorities has become part of the folklore of the land, established primarily through repetition and vehemence, rather than evidence.

The evidence of the *political* impact of civil rights changes in the 1960s is far more clear-cut. The number of black elected officials, especially in the South, increased manyfold in a relatively few years, including blacks elected to public office in some places for the first time since the Reconstruction era after the Civil War. Perhaps even more important, white elected officials in the South had to change both their policies and their rhetoric to accommodate the new political reality that blacks could vote.

What is truly surprising—and relatively ignored—is the economic impact of affirmative action on the disadvantaged, for whom it is most insistently invoked. The relative position of disadvantaged individuals within the groups singled out for preferential treatment has generally *declined* under affirmative action. This is particularly clear in data for individuals, as distinguished from families.

Family income data have too many pitfalls to be taken at face value. There are, for example, significant variations in what constitutes a family, both from time to time and from group to group. But since many people insist on using such data, these statistics cannot be passed over in silence. In 1969, *before* the federal imposition of numerical "goals and time-tables," Puerto Rican family income was 63 percent of the national average. By 1977, it was down to 50 percent. In 1969, Mexican American family income was 76 percent of the national average. By 1977 it was down to 73 percent. Black family income fell from 62 percent of the national average to 60 percent over the same span.[42]

There are many complex factors behind these numbers. The point here is simply that they do not support the civil rights vision. A finer breakdown of the data for blacks shows the most disadvantaged families—the female-headed, with no husband present—to be not only the poorest and with the slowest increase in money income during the 1970s (a decline in *real* income) but also with money incomes increasing even more slowly than among white, female-headed families. By contrast, black husband-wife families had money incomes that were rising faster than that of their white counterparts.[43] It is part of a more general pattern of the most disadvantaged falling farther behind during the affirmative action era, while the already advantaged forged ahead.

Individual data tell the same story, even more clearly. Those blacks with less education and less job experience—the truly disadvantaged—have been falling farther and farther behind their white counterparts under affirmative action, during the very same years when blacks with more education and more job experience have been advancing economically, both absolutely and relative to their white counterparts. First, the disadvantaged: Black male high school dropouts with less than six years of work experience earned 79 percent of the income of white male high school dropouts with less than six years of work experience in 1967 (before affirmative action quotas) and this *fell* to 69 percent by 1978 (after affirmative action quotas). Over these very same years, the income of black males who had completed college and had more than six years of work experience *rose* from 75 percent of the income of their white counterparts to 98 percent.[44] Some economic trends can be explained in terms of general conditions in the economy, but such diametrically opposite trends during the very same span of years obviously cannot.

There is additional evidence that the advantaged have benefited under affirmative action while the disadvantaged have fallen behind. Black faculty members with numerous publications and Ph.D.s from top-rated institutions earned more than white faculty members with the same high qualifications, but black faculty members who lacked a doctorate or publications earned less than whites with the same low qualifications.[45] The pattern of diametrically opposite trends in economic well-being among advantaged and disadvantaged blacks is also shown by the general internal distribution of income among blacks. The top fifth of blacks have absorbed a growing proportion of all income received by blacks, while each of the bottom three-fifths has received declining shares.[46] Black college-educated couples with husband and wife working had by 1980 achieved incomes higher than white couples of the same description.[47] Meanwhile, at the other end of the spectrum, the black female-headed household was receiving only 62 percent of the income of white, female-headed households—down from 70 percent in 1970.[48]

None of this is easily reconcilable with the civil rights vision's all-purpose explanation, racism and discrimination. To explain such diametrically opposite trends within the black community on the basis of whites' behavior would require us to believe that racism and discrimination were growing and declining at the same time. It is much more reconcilable with ordinary economic analysis.

Affirmative action hiring pressures make it costly to have no minority employees, but continuing affirmative action pressures at the promotion and discharge phases also make it costly to have minority employees who do not work out well. The net effect is to increase the demand for highly qualified minority employees while decreasing the demand for less qualified minority employees or for those without a sufficient track record to reassure employers.

Those who are most vocal about the need for affirmative action are of course the more articulate minority members—the advantaged who speak in the name of the disadvantaged. Their position on the issue may accord with their own personal experience, as well as their own self-interest. But that cannot dismiss the growing evidence that it is precisely the disadvantaged who suffer from affirmative action.

By the Numbers

Averages versus Variance

One of the remarkable aspects of affirmative action is that, while numbers—and *assumptions* about numbers—abound, proponents of the program are almost never challenged to produce positive numerical evidence for its effectiveness or to support their statistical presuppositions. The mere fact that some group is x percent of the population but only y percent of the employees is taken as weighty presumption of employer discrimination. There are serious statistical problems with this approach, quite aside from substantial group differences in age, education, and cultural values.

Even in a random world of identical things, to say that something happens a certain way *on the average* is not to say that it happens that way *every time*. But affirmative action deals with averages almost as if there were no variance. If Hispanics are 8 percent of the carpenters in a given town, it does not follow that every employer of carpenters in that town would have 8 percent Hispanics if there were no discrimination. Even if carpenters were assigned to employers by drawing lots (or by some other random process), there would be *variance* in the proportion of Hispanic carpenters from one employer to another. To convict those employers with fewer Hispanics of discrimination in hiring would be to make statistical variance a federal offense.

To illustrate the point, we can consider some process where racial, sexual, or ideological factors do not enter, such as the flipping of a coin. There is no reason to expect a persistent preponderance of heads over tails (or vice versa) on the average, but there is also no reason to expect exactly half heads and half tails every time we flip a coin a few times. That is, *variance* will exist.

To illustrate the effect of statistical variance, a coin was flipped ten times and then this experiment was repeated ten times. Here are the results:

Heads	3	4	3	4	6	7	2	4	5	3
Tails	7	6	7	6	4	3	8	6	5	7

At one extreme, there were seven heads and three tails, and at the other extreme eight tails and two heads. Statistics not only have averages, they have variance.

Translate this into employment decisions. Imagine that you are the employer who ends up with eight employees from one group and two from another, even though both groups are the same size and no different in qualifications, and even though you have been unbiased in selecting. Try explaining to EEOC and the courts that you ended up with four times as many employees from one group by random chance! You may be convicted of discrimination, even if you have only been guilty of statistical variance.

Of course some employers are biased, just as some coins are biased because of the way their weight is distributed on the design. This particular coin might have been biased; over all, it came up heads 41 percent of the time and tails 59 percent. But even if the coin was biased toward tails, it still came up heads seven times out of ten in one set of flips. If an employer were similarly biased in *favor* of a particular group, he could still be convicted of discrimination *against* that very group, if they ended up with less than half the "representation" of some other group.

No one needs to assume that this particular coin was unbiased or even that the results were accurately reported. Anyone can collect ten people and have them flip a coin ten times, to see the statistical variance for himself. Frivolous as this might seem, the results have deadly serious implications for the way people are convicted of violating federal laws, regulations, and guidelines. It might be especially instructive if this little experiment were performed by editorial writers for publications that fervently support affirmative action, or by clerks of the Supreme Court.

Even when conclusions are based only on differences that statisticians call "statistically significant," this by no means eliminates the basic problem. What is statistically significant depends upon the probability that such a result would have happened by random chance. A common litmus test used by statisticians is whether the event would occur more than 5 times out of a hundred by random chance. Applying this common test of statistical significance to affirmative action means that even in the most extreme case imaginable—zero discrimination and zero difference among racial, ethnic, and other groups—the EEOC could still run 10,000 employers' records through a computer and come up with about 500 "discriminators."

The illustration chosen is in fact too favorable to the proponents of affirmative action, because it shows the probability of incorrectly calling an employer a discriminator when there is only *one* group in question that might be discriminated against. Affirmative action has a number of groups whose statistical employment patterns can lead to charges of discrimination. To escape a false charge of discrimination, an employer must avoid being in the fatal 5 percent for *all* the groups in question simultaneously. That becomes progressively harder when there are more groups.

While there is a 95 percent chance for a nondiscriminatory employer to escape when there is only one group, this falls to 86 percent when there are three separate groups and to 73 percent when there are six.[49] That is, even in a world of zero discrimination and zero differences among groups, more than one-fourth of all employers would be called "discriminators" by this common test of statistical significance, when there are six separate groups in question.

What this means is that the courts have sanctioned a procedure which insures that large-scale statistical "discrimination" will exist forever, regardless of what the actual facts may be. They have made statistical variance a federal offense.[50]

SHOPPING FOR DISCRIMINATION

Often the very same raw data point to different conclusions at different levels of aggregation. For example, statistics have shown that black faculty members earn less than white faculty members, but as these data are broken down by field of specialization, by number of publications, by possession (or nonpossession) of a Ph.D. and by the ranking of the institution that issued it, then the black-white income difference not only shrinks but disappears, and in some fields reverses—with black faculty earning more than white faculty with the same characteristics.[51] For those who accept statistics as proof of discrimination, how much discrimination there is, and in what direction, depends upon how finely these data are broken down.

There is no "objective" or "scientific" way to decide at what level of aggregation to stop breaking the data down into finer categories. Nor have the laws or the courts specified in advance what will and will not be the accepted way to break down the statistics. Any individual or organization contemplating a lawsuit against an employer can arrange that employer's statistics in any number of possible ways and then go shopping among the possibilities for the one that will present the employment pattern in the worst light. This is a very effective strategy in a society in which groups differ enormously in their characteristics and choices, while the prevailing vision makes deviations from a random distribution evidence against the employer.

A discrimination case can depend entirely on what level of statistical breakdown the judge accepts, for different groups will be represented—or "underrepresented"—differently according to how precisely occupations and qualifications are defined. While there were more black than Asian American "social scientists" receiving a Ph.D. in 1980, when social scientists were broken down further, there were nearly three times as many Asian as black *economists.*[52] While male recipients of Ph.D.s in the social sciences outnumbered female recipients of Ph.D.s by slightly less than two-to-one in 1980, men outnumbered women by more than four-to-one among doctorates in economics and by ten-to-one among doctorates in econometrics.[53] What is the employer hiring: social scientists, economists, or econometricians? He may in fact be looking for an econometrician specializing in international trade—and there may be no statistics available on that. Nor can anyone infer the proportion of women or minority members available in that specialty from their distribution in broader categories, for the distribution changes at every level of aggregation.

The same principle applies in other fields as well. A computer manufacturer who is looking for an engineer is not looking for the same kind of engineer as a company that builds bridges. Nor is there the slightest reason to expect all groups to be distributed the same in these subspecialties as they are among engineers in general. Even within a narrow occupational range such as mathematical specialists, blacks outnumber Asian Americans in gross numbers but Asian Americans outnumber blacks more than two-to-one among statisticians.[54]

When comparing any employer's work force with the available labor pool to determine "underrepresentation," everything depends on how that labor pool is defined—at what level of aggregation. Those who wish to argue for discrimination generally prefer broad, loose, heterogeneous categories. The concept of a "qualified" worker aids that approach. When the barely qualified is treated as being the same as the most highly skilled and experienced, it is the same as staying at a very general level of aggregation. Anything that creates or widens the disparity between what the job requires and how the categories are defined increases the potential for statistical "discrimination."

An employer may be guilty or innocent according to what level of statistical aggregation a judge accepts, after the plaintiffs have shopped around among the many possibilities. But that is only part of the problem. A more fundamental problem is that *the burden of proof is on the accused* to prove his innocence, once suspicious numbers have been found. Shopping around for suspicious numbers is by no means difficult, especially for a federal agency, given statistical variance, multiple groups, multiple occupations, and wide-ranging differences in the characteristics and choices of the groups themselves.

Statistical aggregation is a major factor not only in courts of law but also in the court of public opinion. Many statistics from a very general level of aggregation are repeatedly presented in the media as demonstrating pervasive discrimination. The finer breakdowns are more likely to appear in specialized scholarly journals, read by a relative handful of people. Yet these finer breakdowns of statistics often tell a drastically different story, not only for black-white differences and male-female differences but for other groups as well.

For example, American Indian males earn significantly less than white males, and Asian males earn significantly more. Yet, as one holds a wide range of variables constant, these income differences shrink to the vanishing point. Asian Americans, for example, are distributed geographically in a very different pattern from whites. Asians are concentrated in higher income states, in more urban areas, and have more education. When all of this is held constant, their income advantage vanishes.[55] By the same token, when various demographic and cultural variables—notably proficiency in the English language—are held constant, the income disadvantages of Hispanic and American Indian males also disappear.[56]

It can hardly be expected that discrimination lawsuits and discrimination as a political issue will be correspondingly reduced any time soon. The methods by which it is measured in the courts and in politics insures that it will be a continuing source of controversy.

Poverty and huge intergroup differences in income are serious matters, whether or not discrimination is the cause—and whether or not affirmative action is the cure. Yet any attempt to deal with these very real disadvantages must first cut through the fog generated by a vision more powerful than its evidence—and, in fact, a vision shaping what courts will accept as evidence.

NOTES

1. U.S. Equal Employment Opportunity Commission, *Legislative History of Titles VII and XI of Civil Rights Act of 1964* (Washington, D.C.: U.S. Government Printing Office, no date) pp. 1007–1008, 1014, 3005, 3006, 3013, 3160, and *passim.*

2. Ibid., p. 3005.

3. Ibid.

4. Ibid., p. 1014.

5. Ibid., p. 3006.

6. Ibid., p. 3160.

7. Ibid., p. 3015.

8. Ibid., p. 3013.

9. Quoted in Nathan Glazer, *Affirmative Discrimination* (New York: Basic Books, 1975), p. 45.

10. For example, *Gallup Opinion Index*, Report 143 (June 1977), p. 23.

11. Nathan Glazer, *Affirmative Discrimination*, p. 49.

12. Much semantic effort has gone into claiming that quotas are rigid requirements while "goals" under "affirmative action" are flexible. Historically, however, quotas have existed in sales, immigration, production, and many other areas, sometimes referring to minima, sometimes to maxima, and with varying degrees of flexibility. The idea that "quota" implies rigidity is a recent redefinition. The objection to quotas is that they are quantitative rather than qualitative criteria, not that they are rigidly rather than flexibly quantitative.

13. *United Steelworkers of America* v. *Weber*, 443 US 193 (1979), p. 207, note 7.

14. Ibid., p. 222.

15. Ibid., pp. 226–52.

16. Thomas Sowell, *Markets and Minorities* (New York: Basic Books, 1981), p. 11.

17. U.S. Bureau of the Census, *Social Indicators, 1976* (Washington, D.C.: U.S. Government Printing Office, 1977), pp. 454–56.

18. Peter Uhlenberg, "Demographic Correlates of Group Achievement: Contrasting Patterns of Mexican-Americans and Japanese-Americans," *Race, Creed, Color, or National Origin*, ed. Robert K. Yin (Itasca, Ill.: F. E. Peacock Publishers, 1973), p. 91.

19. Lucy W. Sells, "Leverage for Equal Opportunity Through Mastery of Mathematics," *Women and Minorities in Science*, ed. Sheila M. Humphreys (Boulder, Colo.: Westview Press, 1982), pp. 12, 16.

20. Ibid., p. 11.

21. College Entrance Examination Board, *Profiles, College-Bound Seniors, 1981* (New York: College Entrance Examination Board, 1982), pp. 12, 22, 41, 51, 60, 65.

22. Ibid., pp. 27, 36, 46, 55.

23. Ibid., pp. 60, 79; Alexander Randall, "East Meets West," *Science*, November 1981, p. 72.

24. National Research Council, *Science, Engineering, and Humanities Doctorates in the United States* (Washington, D.C.: National Academy of Sciences, 1980), pp. 13, 39.

25. National Research Council, *Summary Report: 1980 Doctorate Recipients from United States Universities* (Washington, D.C.: National Academy Press, 1981), pp. 26, 29.

26. Sue E. Berryman,"Trends in and Causes of Minority and Female Representation Among Science and Mathematics Doctorates," mimeographed, The Rand Corporation, 1983, p. 13.

27. U.S. Commission on Civil Rights, *Unemployment and Underemployment Among Blacks, Hispanics, and Women* (Washington, D.C.: U.S. Commission on Civil Rights, 1982), p. 58.

28. Thomas Sowell, *Ethnic America* (New York: Basic Books, 1981), p. 222.

29. J. C. Furnas, *The Americans* (New York: G. P. Putnam's Sons, 1969), p. 86; Daniel Boorstin, *The Americans* (New York: Random House, 1958), Vol. 1, p. 225.

30. Arthur Young, *A Tour in Ireland* (Shannon, Ireland: Irish University Press, 1970), Vol. 1, pp. 377–79.

31. Thomas H. Holloway, *Immigrants on the Land* (Chapel Hill, N.C.: University of North Carolina Press, 1980), p. 151.

32. Harry Leonard Sawatzky, *They Sought a Country* (Berkeley: University of California Press, 1971), pp. 129, 244. Apparently Germans prospered in Honduras as well. Ibid., pp. 361, 365.

33. Hattie Plum Williams, *The Czar's Germans* (Lincoln, Neb.: American Historical Society of Germans from Russia, 1975), pp. 135, 159.

34. Carl Solberg, *Immigration and Nationalism* (Austin: University of Texas Press, 1970), pp. 27, 40.

35. Judith Laikin Elkin, *Jews of the Latin American Republics* (Chapel Hill, N.C.: University of North Carolina Press, 1980), pp. 214–37. See also Robert Weisbrot, *The Jews of Argentina* (Philadelphia: The Jewish Publication Society of America, 1979), pp. 175–84.

36. Thomas Sowell, *Ethnic America*, p. 238.

37. Daniel P. Moynihan, "Employment, Income, and the Ordeal of the Negro Family," *Daedalus*, Fall 1965, p. 752.

38. Daniel O. Price, *Changing Characteristics of the Negro Population* (Washington, D.C.: U.S. Government Printing Office, 1969), pp. 117, 118.

39. *Employment and Training Report of the President, 1981* (Washington, D.C.: U.S. Government Printing Office, 1981), P. 150.

40. Ibid., p. 151.

41. Thomas Sowell, *Ethnic America*, p. 260.

42. Thomas Sowell, *The Economics and Politics of Race* (New York: William Morrow, 1983), p. 187.

43. *U.S. Bureau of the Census, Social Indicators III* (Washington, D.C.: U.S. Government Printing Office, 1980), p. 485.

44. Finis Welch, "Affirmative Action and Its Enforcement," *American Economic Review,* May 1981, p. 132.

45. Thomas Sowell, *Affirmative Action Reconsidered* (Washington, D.C.: American Enterprise Institute, 1975), pp. 16–22.

46. Martin Kilson, "Black Social Classes and Intergenerational Policy," *The Public Interest,* Summer 1981, p. 63.

47. U.S. Bureau of the Census, *Current Population Reports,* Series P-20, No. 366 (Washington, D.C.: U.S. Government Printing Office, 1981), pp. 182, 184.

48. U.S. Bureau of the Census, *Current Population Reports,* Series P-60, No. 80, p. 37; ibid., Series P-60, No. 132, pp. 41–42.

49. The probability that a nondiscriminatory employer will escape a false charge of discrimination is 95 percent, when the standard of "statistical significance" is that his employment pattern would not occur more than 5 times out of 100 by random chance. But the probability of escaping the same false charge for three separate groups simultaneously is $(.95)^3$ or about 86 percent. When there are six separate groups, the probability is $(.95)^6$ or about 73 percent. Not all groups are separate; women and the aged, for example, overlap racial and ethnic groups. This complicates the calculation without changing the basic principle.

50. The greater ease of "proving" discrimination statistically, when there are multiple groups, multiple jobs, and substantial demographic, cultural, and other differences between groups, may either take the form of finding more "discriminators" at a given level of statistical significance (5 percent, for example) or using a more stringent standard of statistical significance (1 percent, for example) to produce a more impressive-looking case against a smaller number of "discriminators."

51. Thomas Sowell, *Affirmative Action Reconsidered* (Washington, D.C.: American Enterprise Institute, 1975), pp. 16–22.

52. Commission on Human Resources, National Research Council, *Summary Report: 1980 Doctorate Recipients from United States Universities* (National Academy Press, 1981), p. 27.

53. Ibid., p. 25.

54. U.S. Bureau of the Census, *Current Population Reports,* Series P-23, No. 120 (Washington, D.C.: U.S. Government Printing Office, 1982), p. 5.

55. Barry R. Chiswick, "An Analysis of the Earnings and Employment of Asian-American Men," *Journal of Labor Economics,* April 1983, pp. 197–214.

56. Walter McManus,William Gould, and Finis Welch, "Earnings of Hispanic Men: The Role of English Language Performance," ibid., pp. 101–30; Gary D. Sandefur, "Minority Group Status and the Wages of White, Black, and Indian Males," *Social Science Research,* March 1983, pp. 44–68.

7

NIHILISM IN BLACK AMERICA

Cornel West

Recent discussions about the plight of African Americans—especially those at the bottom of the social ladder—tend to divide into two camps. On the one hand, there are those who highlight the *structural* constraints on the life chances of black people. Their viewpoint involves a subtle historical and sociological analysis of slavery, Jim Crowism, job and residential discrimination, skewed unemployment rates, inadequate health care, and poor education. On the other hand, there are those who stress the *behavioral* impediments on black upward mobility. They focus on the waning of the Protestant ethic—hard work, deferred gratification, frugality, and responsibility—in much of black America.

Those in the first camp—the liberal structuralists—call for full employment, health, education, and child-care programs, and broad affirmative action practices. In short, a new, more sober version of the best of the New Deal and the Great Society: more government money, better bureaucrats, and an active citizenry. Those in the second camp—the conservative behaviorists—promote self-help programs, black business expansion, and nonpreferential job practices. They support vigorous "free market" strategies that depend on fundamental changes in how black people act and live. To put it bluntly, their projects rest largely upon a cultural revival of the Protestant ethic in black America.

Unfortunately, these two camps have nearly suffocated the crucial debate that should be taking place about the prospects for black America. This debate must go far beyond the liberal and conservative positions in three fundamental ways. First, we must acknowledge that structures and behavior are inseparable, that institutions and values go hand in hand. How people act and live are shaped—though in no way dictated or determined—by the larger circumstances in which they find themselves. These circumstances can be changed, their limits attenuated, by positive actions to elevate living conditions.

Second, we should reject the idea that structures are primarily economic and political creatures—an idea that sees culture as an ephemeral set of behavioral attitudes and values. Culture is as much a structure as the economy or politics; it is rooted in institutions such as families, schools, churches, synagogues, mosques, and communication industries (television, radio, video, music). Similarly, the economy and politics are not only influenced by values but also promote particular cultural ideals of the good life and good society.

Third, and most important, we must delve into the depths where neither liberals nor conservatives dare to tread, namely, into the murky waters of despair and dread that now flood the streets of black America. To talk about the depressing statistics of unemployment, infant mortality, incarceration, teenage pregnancy, and violent crime is one thing. But to face up to the monumental eclipse of hope, the unprecedented collapse of meaning, the incredible disregard for human (especially black) life and property in much of black America is something else.

The liberal/conservative discussion conceals the most basic issue now facing black America: *the nihilistic threat to its very existence.* This threat is not simply a matter of relative economic deprivation and political powerlessness—though economic well-being and political clout are requisites for meaningful black progress. It is primarily a question of speaking to the profound sense of psychological depression, personal worthlessness, and social despair so widespread in black America.

The liberal structuralists fail to grapple with this threat for two reasons. First, their focus on structural constraints relates almost exclusively to the economy and politics. They show no understanding of the structural character of culture. Why? Because they tend to view people in egoistic and rationalist terms according to which they are motivated primarily by self-interest and self-preservation. Needless to say, this is partly true about most of us. Yet, people, especially degraded and oppressed people, are also hungry for identity, meaning, and self-worth.

The second reason liberal structuralists overlook the nihilistic threat is a sheer failure of nerve. They hesitate to talk honestly about culture, the realm of meanings and values, because doing so seems to lend itself too readily to conservative conclusions in the narrow way Americans discuss race. If there is a hidden taboo among liberals, it is to resist talking *too much* about values because such discussions remove the focus from structures and especially because they obscure the positive role of government. But this failure by liberals leaves the existential and psychological realities of black people in the lurch. In this way, liberal structuralists neglect the battered identities rampant in black America.

As for the conservative behaviorists, they not only misconstrue the nihilistic threat but inadvertently contribute to it. This is a serious charge, and it rests upon several claims. Conservative behaviorists talk about values and attitudes as if political and economic structures hardly exist. They rarely, if ever, examine the innumerable cases in which black people do act on the Protestant ethic and still remain at the bottom of the social ladder. Instead, they highlight the few instances in which blacks ascend to the top, as if such success is available to all blacks, regardless of circumstances. Such a vulgar rendition of Horatio Alger in blackface may serve as a source of inspiration to some—a kind of model for those already on the right track. But it cannot serve as a substitute for serious historical and social analysis of the predicaments of and prospects for all black people, especially the grossly disadvantaged ones.

Conservative behaviorists also discuss black culture as if acknowledging one's obvious victimization by white supremacist practices (compounded by sexism and class condition) is taboo. They tell black people to see themselves as agents, not victims. And on the surface, this is comforting advice, a nice cliché for downtrodden people. But inspirational slogans cannot substitute for substantive historical and social analysis. While black people have never been simply victims, wallowing in self-pity and begging for white giveaways, they have been—and are—*victimized*. Therefore, to call on black people to be agents makes sense only if we also examine the dynamics of this victimization against which their agency will, in part, be exercised. What is particularly naive and peculiarly vicious about the conservative behavioral outlook is that it tends to deny the lingering effect of black history—a history inseparable from though not reducible to victimization. In this way, crucial and indispensable themes of self-help and personal responsibility are wrenched out of historical context and contemporary circumstances—as if it is all a matter of personal will.

This ahistorical perspective contributes to the nihilistic threat within black America in that it can be used to justify right-wing cutbacks for poor people struggling for decent housing, child care, health care, and education. As I pointed out above, the liberal perspective is deficient in important ways, but even so liberals are right on target in their critique of conservative government cutbacks for services to the poor. These ghastly cutbacks are one cause of the nihilist threat to black America.

The proper starting point for the crucial debate about the prospects for black America is an examination of the nihilism that increasingly pervades black communities. *Nihilism is to be understood here not as a philosophic doctrine that there are no rational grounds for legitimate standards or authority; it is, far more, the lived experience of coping with a life of horrifying meaninglessness, hopelessness, and (most important) lovelessness.* The frightening result is a numbing detachment from others and a self-destructive disposition toward the world. Life without meaning, hope, and love breeds a coldhearted, mean-spirited outlook that destroys both the individual and others.

Nihilism is not new in black America. The first African encounter with the New World was an encounter with a distinctive form of the Absurd. The initial black struggle against degradation and devaluation in the enslaved circumstances of the New World was, in part, a struggle against nihilism. In fact, the major enemy of black survival in America has been and is neither oppression nor exploitation but rather the nihilistic threat—that is, loss of hope and absence of meaning. For as long as hope remains and meaning is preserved, the possibility of overcoming oppression stays alive. The self-fulfilling prophecy of the nihilistic threat is that without hope there can be no future, that without meaning there can be no struggle.

The genius of our black foremothers and forefathers was to create powerful buffers to ward off the nihilistic threat, to equip black folk with cultural armor to beat back the demons of hope-lessness, meaninglessness, and lovelessness. These buffers con-sisted of cultural structures of meaning and feeling that created and sustained communities; this armor constituted ways of life and struggle that embodied values of service and sacrifice, love and care, discipline and excellence. In other words, traditions for black surviving and thriving under usually adverse New World conditions were major barriers against the nihilistic threat. These traditions consist primarily of black religious and civic institutions that sustained familial and communal networks of support. If cul-tures are, in part, what human beings create (out of antecedent fragments of other cultures) in order to convince themselves not to commit suicide, then black foremothers and forefathers are to be applauded. In fact, until the early seventies black Americans had the lowest suicide rate in the United States. But now young black people lead the nation in suicides.

What has changed? What went wrong? The bitter irony of inte-gration? The cumulative effects of a genocidal conspiracy? The vir-tual collapse of rising expectations after the optimistic sixties? None of us fully understands why the cultural structures that once sus-tained black life in America are no longer able to fend off the nihilistic threat. I believe that two significant reasons why the threat is more powerful now than ever before are the saturation of market forces and market moralities in black life and the present crisis in black leadership. The recent market-driven shattering of black civil society—black families, neighborhoods, schools, churches, mosques—leaves more and more black people vulnerable to daily lives endured with little sense of self and fragile existential moorings.

Black people have always been in America's wilderness in search of a promised land. Yet many black folk now reside in a jungle ruled by a cutthroat market morality devoid of any faith in deliverance or hope for freedom. Contrary to the superficial claims of conservative behaviorists, these jungles are not primarily the result of pathological behavior. Rather, this behavior is the tragic response of a people bereft of resources in confronting the workings of U.S. capitalist society. Saying this is not the same as asserting that individual black people are not responsible for their actions—black murderers and rapists should go to jail. But it must be recognized that the nihilistic threat contributes to criminal behavior. It is a threat that feeds on poverty and shattered cultural institutions and grows more powerful as the armors to ward against it are weakened.

*   *   *

But why is this shattering of black civil society occurring? What has led to the weakening of black cultural institutions in asphalt jungles? Corporate market institutions have contributed greatly to their collapse. By corporate market institutions I mean that complex set of interlocking enterprises that have a disproportionate amount of capital, power, and exercise a disproportionate influence on how our society is run and how our culture is shaped. Needless to say, the primary motivation of these institutions is to make profits, and their basic strategy is to convince the public to consume. These institutions have helped create a seductive way of life, a culture of consumption that capitalizes on every opportunity to make money. Market calculations and cost-benefit analyses hold sway in almost every sphere of U.S. society.

The common denominator of these calculations and analyses is usually the provision, expansion, and intensification of *pleasure.* Pleasure is a multivalent term; it means different things to many people. In the American way of life pleasure involves comfort, convenience, and sexual stimulation. Pleasure, so defined, has little to do with the past and views the future as no more than a repetition of a hedonistically driven present. This market morality stigmatizes others as objects for personal pleasure or bodily stimulation. Conservative behaviorists have alleged that traditional morality has been undermined by radical feminists and the cultural radicals of the sixties. But it is clear that corporate market institutions have greatly contributed to undermining traditional morality in order to stay in business and make a profit. The reduction of individuals to objects of pleasure is especially evident in the culture industries—television, radio, video, music—in which gestures of sexual foreplay and orgiastic pleasure flood the marketplace.

Like all Americans, African Americans are influenced greatly by the images of comfort, convenience, machismo, femininity, violence, and sexual stimulation that bombard consumers. These seductive images contribute to the predominance of the market-inspired way of life over all others and thereby edge out non-market values—love, care, service to others—handed down by preceding generations. The predominance of this way of life among those living in poverty-ridden conditions, with a limited capacity to ward off self-contempt and self-hatred, results in the possible triumph of the nihilistic threat in black America.

*   *   *

A major contemporary strategy for holding the nihilistic threat at bay is a direct attack on the sense of worthlessness and self-loathing in black America. This *angst* resembles a kind of collective clinical depression in significant pockets of black America. The eclipse of hope and collapse of meaning in much of black America is linked to the structural dynamics of corporate market institutions that affect all Americans. Under these circumstances black existential *angst* derives from the lived experience of ontological wounds and emotional scars inflicted by white supremacist beliefs and images permeating U.S. society and culture. These beliefs and images attack black intelligence, black ability, black beauty, and black character daily in subtle and not-so-subtle ways. Toni Morrison's novel *The Bluest Eye*, for example, reveals the devastating effect of pervasive European ideals of beauty on the self-image of young black women. Morrison's exposure of the harmful extent to which these white ideals affect the black self-image is a first step toward rejecting these ideals and overcoming the nihilistic self-loathing they engender in blacks.

The accumulated effect of the black wounds and scars suffered in a white-dominated society is a deep-seated anger, a boiling sense of rage, and a passionate pessimism regarding America's will to justice. Under conditions of slavery and Jim Crow segregation, this anger, rage, and pessimism remained relatively muted because of a well-justified fear of brutal white retaliation. The major breakthroughs of the sixties—more psychically than politically—swept this fear away. Sadly, the combination of the market way of life, poverty-ridden conditions, black existential *angst*, and the lessening of fear of white authorities has directed most of the anger, rage, and despair toward fellow black citizens, especially toward black women who are the most vulnerable in our society and in black communities. Only recently has this nihilistic threat—and its ugly inhumane outlook and actions—surfaced in the larger American society. And its appearance surely reveals one of the many instances of cultural decay in a declining empire.

What is to be done about this nihilistic threat? Is there really any hope, given our shattered civil society, market-driven corporate enterprises, and white supremacism? If one begins with the threat of concrete nihilism, then one must talk about some kind of *politics of conversion.* New models of collective black leadership must promote a version of this politics. Like alcoholism and drug addiction, nihilism is a disease of the soul. It can never be completely cured, and there is always the possibility of relapse. But there is always a chance for conversion—a chance for people to believe that there is hope for the future and a meaning to struggle. This chance rests neither on an agreement about what justice consists of nor on an analysis of how racism, sexism, or class subordination operate. Such arguments and analyses are indispensable. But a politics of conversion requires more. Nihilism is not overcome by arguments or analyses; it is tamed by love and care. Any disease of the soul must be conquered by a turning of one's soul. This turning is done through one's own affirmation of one's worth—an affirmation fueled by the concern of others. A love ethic must be at the center of a politics of conversion.

A love ethic has nothing to do with sentimental feelings or tribal connections. Rather it is a last attempt at generating a sense of agency among a downtrodden people. The best exemplar of this love ethic is depicted on a number of levels in Toni Morrison's great novel *Beloved*. Self-love and love of others are both modes toward increasing self-valuation and encouraging political resistance in one's community. These modes of valuation and resistance are rooted in a subversive memory—the best of one's past without romantic nostalgia—and guided by a universal love ethic. For my purposes here, *Beloved* can be construed as bringing together the loving yet critical affirmation of black humanity found in the best of black nationalist movements, the perennial hope against hope for trans-racial coalition in progressive movements, and the painful struggle for self-affirming sanity in a history in which the nihilistic threat *seems* insurmountable.

The politics of conversion proceeds principally on the local level—in those institutions in civil society still vital enough to promote self-worth and self-affirmation. It surfaces on the state and national levels only when grassroots democratic organizations put forward a collective leadership that has earned the love and respect of and, most important, has proved itself *accountable* to these organizations. This collective leadership must exemplify moral integrity, character, and democratic statesmanship within itself and within its organizations.

Like liberal structuralists, the advocates of a politics of conversion never lose sight of the structural conditions that shape the sufferings and lives of people. Yet, unlike liberal structuralism, the politics of conversion meets the nihilistic threat head-on. Like conservative behaviorism, the politics of conversion openly confronts the self-destructive and inhumane actions of black people. Unlike conservative behaviorists, the politics of conversion situates these actions within inhumane circumstances (but does not thereby exonerate them). The politics of conversion shuns the limelight—a limelight that solicits status seekers and ingratiates egomaniacs. Instead, it stays on the ground among the toiling everyday people, ushering forth humble freedom fighters—both followers and leaders—who have the audacity to take the nihilistic threat by the neck and turn back its deadly assaults. . . .

The fundamental crisis in black America is twofold: too much poverty and too little self-love. The urgent problem of black poverty is primarily due to the distribution of wealth, power, and income—a distribution influenced by the racial caste system that denied opportunities to most "qualified" black people until two decades ago.

The historic role of American progressives is to promote redistributive measures that enhance the standard of living and quality of life for the have-nots and have-too-littles. Affirmative action was one such redistributive measure that surfaced in the heat of battle in the 1960s among those fighting for racial equality. Like earlier *de facto* affirmative action measures in the American past—contracts, jobs, and loans to select immigrants granted by political machines; subsidies to certain farmers; FHA mortgage loans to specific home buyers; or GI Bill benefits to particular courageous Americans—recent efforts to broaden access to America's prosperity have been based upon preferential policies. Unfortunately, these policies always benefit middle-class Americans disproportionately. The political power of big business in a big government circumscribes redistributive measures and thereby tilts these measures away from the have-nots and have-too-littles.

Every redistributive measure is a compromise with and concession from the caretakers of American prosperity—that is, big business and big government. Affirmative action was one such compromise and concession achieved after the protracted struggle of American progressives and liberals in the courts and in the streets. Visionary progressives always push for substantive redistributive measures that make opportunities available to the have-

nots and have-too-littles, such as more federal support to small
farmers, or more FHA mortgage loans to urban dwellers as well as
suburban home buyers. Yet in the American political system,
where the powers that be turn a skeptical eye toward any program
aimed at economic redistribution, progressives must secure whatever redistributive measures they can, ensure their enforcement,
then extend their benefits if possible.

If I had been old enough to join the fight for racial equality in
the courts, the legislatures, and the board rooms in the 1960s (I *was*
old enough to be in the streets), I would have favored—as I do
now—a class-based affirmative action in principle. Yet in the heat
of battle in American politics, a redistributive measure in principle
with no power and pressure behind it means no redistributive
measure at all. The prevailing discriminatory practices during the
sixties, whose targets were working people, women, and people of
color, were atrocious. Thus, an *enforceable* race-based—and later
gender-based—affirmative action policy was the best possible
compromise and concession.

Progressives should view affirmative action as neither a major
solution to poverty nor a sufficient means to equality. We should
see it as primarily playing a negative role—namely, to ensure that
discriminatory practices against women and people of color are
abated. Given the history of this country, it is a virtual certainty
that without affirmative action racial and sexual discrimination
would return with a vengeance. Even if affirmative action fails significantly to reduce black poverty or contributes to the persistence
of racist perceptions in the workplace, without affirmative action
black access to America's prosperity would be even more difficult
to obtain and racism in the workplace would persist anyway.

This claim is not based on any cynicism toward my white
fellow citizens; rather, it rests upon America's historically weak
will toward racial justice and substantive redistributive measures.
This is why an attack on affirmative action is an attack on redistributive efforts by progressives unless there is a real possibility of
enacting and enforcing a more wide-reaching class-based affirmative action policy.

In American politics, progressives must not only cling to redistributive ideals, but must also fight for those policies that—out of
compromise and concession—imperfectly conform to those ideals.
Liberals who give only lip service to these ideals, trash the policies
in the name of *realpolitik*, or reject the policies as they perceive a

shift in the racial bellwether give up precious ground too easily. And they do so even as the sand is disappearing under our feet on such issues as regressive taxation, layoffs or takebacks from workers, and cutbacks in health and child care.

Affirmative action is not the most important issue for black progress in America, but it is part of a redistributive chain that must be strengthened if we are to confront and eliminate black poverty. If there were social democratic redistributive measures that wiped out black poverty, and if racial and sexual discrimination could be abated through the good will and meritorious judgments of those in power, affirmative action would be unnecessary. Although many of my liberal and progressive citizens view affirmative action as a redistributive measure whose time is over or whose life is no longer worth preserving, I question their view because of the persistence of discriminatory practices that increase black social misery, and the warranted suspicion that good will and fair judgment among the powerful does not loom as large toward women and people of color. . . .

8

AFFIRMATIVE ACTION:
THE PRICE OF PREFERENCE

Shelby Steele

In a few short years, when my two children will be applying to college, the affirmative action policies by which most universities offer black students some form of preferential treatment will present me with a dilemma. I am a middle-class black, a college professor, far from wealthy, but also well-removed from the kind of deprivation that would qualify my children for the label "disadvantaged." Both of them have endured racial insensitivity from whites. They have been called names, have suffered slights, and have experienced firsthand the peculiar malevolence that racism brings out in people. Yet, they have never experienced racial discrimination, have never been stopped by their race on any path they have chosen to follow. Still, their society now tells them that if they will only designate themselves as black on their college applications, they will likely do better in the college lottery than if they conceal this fact. I think there is something of a Faustian bargain in this.

Of course, many blacks and a considerable number of whites would say that I was sanctimoniously making affirmative action into a test of character. They would say that this small preference is the meagerest recompense for centuries of unrelieved oppression. And to these arguments other very obvious facts must be added. In

America, many marginally competent or flatly incompetent whites are hired everyday—some because their white skin suits the conscious or unconscious racial preference of their employer. The white children of alumni are often grandfathered into elite universities in what can only be seen as a residual benefit of historic white privilege. Worse, white incompetence is always an individual matter, while for blacks it is often confirmation of ugly stereotypes. The Peter Principle was not conceived with only blacks in mind. Given that unfairness cuts both ways, doesn't it only balance the scales of history that my children now receive a slight preference over whites? Doesn't this repay, in a small way, the systematic denial under which their grandfather lived out his days?

So, in theory, affirmative action certainly has all the moral symmetry that fairness requires—the injustice of historical and even contemporary white advantage is offset with black advantage; preference replaces prejudice, inclusion answers exclusion. It is reformist and corrective, even repentant and redemptive. And I would never sneer at these good intentions. Born in the late forties in Chicago, I started my education (a charitable term in this case) in a segregated school and suffered all the indignities that come to blacks in a segregated society. My father, born in the South, only made it to the third grade before the white man's fields took permanent priority over his formal education. And though he educated himself into an advanced reader with an almost professorial authority, he could only drive a truck for a living and never earned more than ninety dollars a week in his entire life. So yes, it is crucial to my sense of citizenship, to my ability to identify with the spirit and the interests of America, to know that this country, however imperfectly, recognizes its past sins and wishes to correct them.

Yet good intentions, because of the opportunity for innocence they offer us, are very seductive and can blind us to the effects they generate when implemented. In our society, affirmative action is, among other things, a testament to white goodwill and to black power, and in the midst of these heavy investments, its effects can be hard to see. But after twenty years of implementation, I think affirmative action has shown itself to be more bad than good and that blacks—whom I will focus on in this essay—now stand to lose more from it than they gain.

In talking with affirmative action administrators and with blacks and whites in general, it is clear that supporters of affirmative action focus on its good intentions while detractors emphasize its negative effects. Proponents talk about "diversity" and "pluralism"; opponents speak of "reverse discrimination," the unfairness of quotas and set-asides. It was virtually impossible to find people outside either camp. The closest I came was a white male manager at a large computer company who said, "I think it amounts to reverse discrimination, but I'll put up with a little of that for a little more diversity." I'll live with a little of the effect to gain a little of the intention, he seemed to be saying. But this only makes him a halfhearted supporter of affirmative action. I think many people who don't really like affirmative action support it to one degree or another anyway.

I believe they do this because of what happened to white and black Americans in the crucible of the sixties when whites were confronted with their racial guilt and blacks listed their first real power. In this stormy time white absolution and black power coalesced into virtual mandates for society. Affirmative action became a meeting ground for these mandates in the law, and in the late sixties and early seventies it underwent a remarkable escalation of its mission from simple antidiscrimination enforcement to social engineering by means of quotas, goals, timetables, set-asides and other forms of preferential treatment.

Legally, this was achieved through a series of executive orders and EEOC guidelines that allowed racial imbalances in the workplace to stand as proof of racial discrimination. Once it could be assumed that discrimination explained racial imbalances, it became easy to justify group remedies to presumed discrimination, rather than the normal case-by-case redress for proven discrimination. Preferential treatment through quotas, goals, and so on is designed to correct imbalances based on the assumption that they always indicate discrimination. This expansion of what constitutes discrimination allowed affirmative action to escalate into the business of social engineering in the name of anti-discrimination, to push society toward statistically proportionate racial representation, without any obligation of proving actual discrimination.

What accounted for this shift, I believe, was the white mandate to achieve a new racial innocence and the black mandate to gain power. Even though blacks had made great advances during the sixties without quotas, these mandates, which came to a head in the very late sixties, could no longer be satisfied by anything less than racial preferences. I don't think these mandates in themselves were wrong, since whites clearly needed to do better by blacks and blacks needed more real power in society. But, as they came together in affirmative action, their effect was to distort our understanding of racial discrimination in a way that allowed us to offer the remediation of preference on the basis of mere color rather than actual injury. By making black the color of preference, these mandates have reburdened society with the very marriage of color and preference (in reverse) that we set out to eradicate. The old sin is reaffirmed in a new guise.

But the essential problem with this form of affirmative action is the way it leaps over the hard business of developing a formerly oppressed people to the point where they can achieve proportionate representation on their own (given equal opportunity) and goes straight for the proportionate representation. This may satisfy some whites of their innocence and some blacks of their power, but it does very little to truly uplift blacks.

A white female affirmative action officer at an Ivy League university told me what many supporters of affirmative action now say: "We're after diversity. We ideally want a student body where racial and ethnic groups are represented according to their proportion in society." When affirmative action escalated into social engineering, diversity became a golden word. It grants whites an egalitarian fairness (innocence) and blacks an entitlement to proportionate representation (power). *Diversity* is a term that applies democratic principles to races and cultures rather than to citizens, despite the fact that there is nothing to indicate that real diversity is the same thing as proportionate representation. Too often the result of this on campuses (for example) has been a democracy of colors rather than of people, an artificial diversity that gives the appearance of an educational parity between black and white students that has not yet been achieved in reality. Here again, racial preferences allow society to leapfrog over the difficult problem of developing blacks to parity with whites and into a cosmetic diversity that covers the blemish of disparity—a full six years after admission, only about 26 percent of black students graduate from college.

Racial representation is not the same thing as racial development, yet affirmative action fosters a confusion of these very different needs. Representation can be manufactured; development is always hard-earned. However, it is the music of innocence and power that we hear in affirmative action that causes us to cling to it and to its distracting emphasis on representation. The fact is that after twenty years of racial preferences, the gap between white and black median income is greater than it was in the seventies. None of this is to say that blacks don't need policies that ensure our right to equal opportunity, but what we need more is the development that will let us take advantage of society's efforts to include us.

I think that one of the most troubling effects of racial preferences for blacks is a kind of demoralization, or put another way, an enlargement of self-doubt. Under affirmative action the quality that earns us preferential treatment is an implied inferiority. however this inferiority is explained—and it is easily enough explained by the myriad deprivations that grew out of our oppression—it is still inferiority. There are explanations, and then there is the fact. And the fact must be borne by the individual as a condition apart from the explanation, apart even from the fact that others like himself also bear this condition. In integrated situations where blacks must compete with whites who may be better prepared, these explanations may quickly wear thin and expose the individual to racial as well as personal self-doubt.

All of this is compounded by the cultural myth of black inferiority that blacks have always lived with. What this means in practical terms is that when blacks deliver themselves into integrated situations, they encounter a nasty little reflex in whites, a mindless, atavistic reflex that responds to the color black with alarm. Attributions may follow this alarm if the white cares to indulge them, and if they do, they will most likely be negative—one such attribution is intellectual ineptness. I think this reflex and the attributions that may follow it embarrass most whites today, therefore, it is usually quickly repressed. Nevertheless, on an equally atavistic level, the black will be aware of the reflex his color triggers and will feel a stab of horror at seeing himself reflected in this way. He, too, will do a quick repression, but a lifetime of such stabbings is what constitutes his inner realm of racial doubt.

The effects of this may be a subject for another essay. The point here is that the implication of inferiority that racial preferences engender in both the white and black mind expands rather than contracts this doubt. Even when the black sees no implication of inferiority in racial preferences, he knows that whites do, so that—consciously or unconsciously—the result is virtually the same. The effect of preferential treatment—the lowering of normal standards to increase black representation—puts blacks at war with an expanded realm of debilitating doubt, so that the doubt itself becomes an unrecognized preoccupation that undermines their ability to perform, especially in integrated situations. On largely white campuses, blacks are five times more likely to drop out than whites. Preferential treatment, no matter how it is justified in the light of day, subjects blacks to a midnight of self-doubt, and so often transforms their advantage into a revolving door.

Another liability of affirmative action comes from the fact that it indirectly encourages blacks to exploit their own past victimization as a source of power and privilege. Victimization, like implied inferiority, is what justifies preference, so that to receive the benefits of preferential treatment one must, to some extent, become invested in the view of one's self as a victim. In this way, affirmative action nurtures a victim-focused identity in blacks. The obvious irony here is that we become inadvertently invested in the very condition we are trying to overcome. Racial preferences send us the message that there is more power in our past suffering than our present achievements—none of which could bring us a *preference* over others.

When power itself grows out of suffering, then blacks are encouraged to expand the boundaries of what qualifies as racial oppression, a situation that can lead us to paint our victimization in vivid colors, even as we receive the benefits of preference. The same corporations and institutions that give us preference are also seen as our oppressors. At Stanford University minority students—some of whom enjoy as much as $15,000 a year in financial aid—recently took over the president's office demanding, among other things, more financial aid. The power to be found in victimization, like any power, is intoxicating and can lend itself to the creation of a new class of super-victims who can feel the pea of victimization under twenty mattresses. Preferential treatment rewards us for being underdogs rather than for moving beyond that status—a misplacement of incentives that, along with its deepening of our doubt, is more a yoke than a spur.

But, I think, one of the worst prices that blacks pay for preference has to do with an illusion. I saw this illusion at work recently in the mother of a middle-class black student who was going off to his first semester of college. "They owe us this, so don't think for a minute that you don't belong there." This is the logic by which many blacks, and some whites, justify affirmative action—it is something "owed," a form of reparation. But this logic overlooks a much harder and less digestible reality, that it is impossible to repay blacks living today for the historic suffering of the race. If all blacks were given a million dollars tomorrow morning it would not amount to a dime on the dollar of three centuries of oppression, nor would it obviate the residues of that oppression that we still carry today. The concept of historic reparation grows out of man's need to impose a degree of justice on the world that simply does not exist. Suffering can be endured and overcome, it cannot be repaid. Blacks cannot be repaid for the injustice done to the race, but we can be corrupted by society's guilty gestures of repayment.

Affirmative action is such a gesture. It tells us that racial preferences can do for us what we cannot do for ourselves. The corruption here is in the hidden incentive *not* to do what we believe preferences will do. This is an incentive to be reliant on others just as we are struggling for self-reliance. And it keeps alive the illusion that we can find some deliverance in repayment. The hardest thing for any sufferer to accept is that his suffering excuses him from very little and never has enough currency to restore him. To think otherwise is to prolong the suffering.

Several blacks I spoke with said they were still in favor of affirmative action because of the "subtle" discrimination blacks were subject to once on the job. One photojournalist said, "They have ways of ignoring you." A black female television producer said, "You can't file a lawsuit when your boss doesn't invite you to the insider meetings without ruining your career. So we still need affirmative action." Others mentioned the infamous "glass ceiling" through which blacks can see the top positions of authority but never reach them. But I don't think racial preferences are a protection against this subtle discrimination; I think they contribute to it.

In any workplace, racial preferences will always create two-tiered populations composed of preferreds and unpreferreds. This division makes automatic a perception of enhanced competence for the unpreferreds and of questionable competence for the preferreds—the former earned his way, even though others were given preference, while the latter made it by color as much as by competence. Racial preferences implicitly mark whites with an exaggerated superiority just as they mark blacks with an exaggerated inferiority. They not only reinforce America's oldest racial myth but, for blacks, they have the effect of stigmatizing the already stigmatized.

I think that much of the "subtle" discrimination that blacks talk about is often (not always) discrimination against the stigma of questionable competence that affirmative action delivers to blacks. In this sense, preferences scapegoat the very people they seek to help. And it may be that at a certain level employers impose a glass ceiling, but this may not be against the race so much as against the race's reputation for having advanced by color as much as by competence. Affirmative action makes a glass ceiling virtually necessary as a protection against the corruptions of preferential treatment. This ceiling is the point at which corporations shift the emphasis from color to competency and stop playing the affirmative action game. Here preference backfires for blacks and becomes a taint that holds them back. Of course, one could argue that this taint, which is, after all, in the minds of whites, becomes nothing more than an excuse to discriminate against blacks. And certainly the result is the same in either case—blacks don't get past the glass ceiling. But this argument does not get around the fact that racial preferences now taint this color with a new theme of suspicion that makes it even more vulnerable to the impulse in others to discriminate. In this crucial yet gray area of perceived competence, preferences make whites look better than they are and blacks worse, while doing nothing whatever to stop the very real discrimination that blacks may encounter. I don't wish to justify the glass ceiling here, but only to suggest the very subtle ways that affirmative action revives rather than extinguishes the old rationalizations for racial discrimination.

In education, a revolving door; in employment, a glass ceiling.

I believe affirmative action is problematic in our society because it tries to function like a social program. Rather than ask it to ensure equal opportunity we have demanded that it create parity between the races. But preferential treatment does not teach skills, or educate, or instill motivation. It only passes out entitlement by color, a situation that in my profession has created an unrealistically high demand for black professors. The social engineer's assumption is that this high demand will inspire more blacks to earn Ph.D.s and join the profession. In fact, the number of blacks earning Ph.D.s has declined in recent years. A Ph.D. must be developed from preschool on. He requires family and community support. He must acquire an entire system of values that enables him to work hard while delaying gratification. There are social programs, I believe, that can (and should) help blacks *develop* in all these areas, but entitlement by color is not a social program; it is a dubious reward for being black.

It now seems clear that the Supreme Court, in a series of recent decisions, is moving away from racial preferences. It has disallowed preferences except in instances of "identified discrimination," eroded the precedent that statistical racial imbalances are *prima facie* evidence of discrimination, and in effect granted white males the right to challenge consent degrees that use preference to achieve racial balances in the workplace. One civil rights leader said, "Night has fallen on civil rights." But I am not so sure. The effect of these decisions is to protect the constitutional rights of everyone rather than take rights away from blacks. What they do take away from blacks is the special entitlement to more rights than others that preferences always grant. Night has fallen on racial preferences, not on the fundamental rights of black Americans. The reason for this shift, I believe, is that the white mandate for absolution from past racial sins has weakened considerably during the eighties. Whites are now less willing to endure unfairness to themselves in order to grant special entitlements to blacks, even when these entitlements are justified in the name of past suffering. Yet the black mandate for more power in society has remained unchanged. And I think part of the anxiety that many blacks feel over these decisions has to do with the loss of black power they may signal. We had won a certain specialness and now we are losing it.

But the power we've lost by these decisions is really only the power that grows out of our victimization—the power to claim special entitlements under the law because of past oppression. This is not a very substantial or reliable power, and it is important that we know this so we can focus more exclusively on the kind of development that will bring enduring power. There is talk now that Congress will pass new legislation to compensate for these new limits on affirmative action. If this happens, I hope that their focus will be on development and antidiscrimination rather than entitlement, on achieving racial parity rather than jerry-building racial diversity.

I would also like to see affirmative action go back to its original purpose of enforcing equal opportunity—a purpose that in itself disallows racial preferences. We cannot be sure that the discriminatory impulse in America has yet been shamed into extinction, and I believe affirmative action can make its greatest contribution by providing a rigorous vigilance in this area. It can guard constitutional rather than racial rights, and help institutions evolve standards of merit and selection that are appropriate to the institution's needs yet as free of racial bias as possible (again, with the understanding that racial imbalances are not always an indication of racial bias). One of the most important things affirmative action can do is to define exactly what racial discrimination is and how it might manifest itself within a specific institution. The impulse to discriminate is subtle and cannot be ferreted out unless its many guises are made clear to people. Along with this there should be monitoring of institutions and heavy sanctions brought to bear when actual discrimination is found. This is the sort of affirmative action that America owes to blacks and to itself. It goes after the evil of discrimination itself, while preferences only sidestep the evil and grant entitlement to its *presumed* victims.

But if not preferences, then what? I think we need social policies that are committed to two goals: the educational and economic development of disadvantaged people, regardless of race, and the eradication from our society—through close monitoring and severe sanctions—of racial, ethnic, or gender discrimination. Preferences will not deliver us to either of these goals, since they tend to benefit those who are not disadvantaged—middle-class white women and middle-class blacks—and attack one form of discrimination with another. Preferences are inexpensive and carry the glamour of good intentions—change the numbers and the good deed is done. To be against them is to be unkind. But I think the unkindest cut is to bestow on children like my own an undeserved advantage while neglecting the development of those disadvantaged children on the East Side of my city who will likely never be in a position to benefit from a preference. Give my children fairness; give disadvantaged children a better shot at development—better elementary and secondary schools, job training, safer neighborhoods, better financial assistance for college, and so on. Fewer blacks go to college today than ten years ago; more black males of college age are in prison or under the control of the criminal justice system than in college. This despite racial preferences.

The mandates of black power and white absolution out of which preferences emerged were not wrong in themselves. What was wrong was that both races focused more on the goals of these mandates than on the means to the goals. Blacks can have no real power without taking responsibility for their own educational and economic development. Whites can have no racial innocence without earning it by eradicating discrimination and helping the disadvantaged to develop. Because we ignored the means, the goals have not been reached, and the real work remains to be done.

9

REVERSE RACISM, OR HOW THE POT GOT TO CALL THE KETTLE BLACK

Stanley Fish

I take my text from George Bush, who, in an address to the United Nations on September 23, 1991, said this of the UN resolution equating Zionism with racism: "Zionism . . . is the idea that led to the creation of a home for the Jewish people. . . . And to equate Zionism with the intolerable sin of racism is to twist history and forget the terrible plight of Jews in World War II and indeed throughout history." What happened in the Second World War was that six million Jews were exterminated by people who regarded them as racially inferior and a danger to Aryan purity. What happened after the Second World War was that the survivors of that Holocaust established a Jewish state—that is, a state centered on Jewish history, Jewish values, and Jewish traditions: in short, a Jewocentric state. What President Bush objected to was the logical sleight of hand by which these two actions were declared equivalent because they were both expressions of racial exclusiveness. Ignored, as Bush said, was the *historical* difference between them—the difference between a program of genocide and the determination of those who escaped it to establish a community in which they would be the makers, not the victims, of the laws.

Only if racism is thought of as something that occurs principally in the mind, a falling-away from proper notions of universal

---

equality, can the desire of a victimized and terrorized people to band together be declared morally identical to the actions of their would-be executioners. Only when the actions of the two groups are detached from the historical conditions of their emergence and given a purely abstract description can they be made interchangeable. Bush was saying to the United Nations, "Look, the Nazis' conviction of racial superiority generated a policy of systematic genocide; the Jews' experience of centuries of persecution in almost every country on earth generated a desire for a homeland of their own. If you manage somehow to convince yourself that these are the same, it is you, not the Zionists, who are morally confused, and the reason you are morally confused is that you have forgotten history."

A KEY DISTINCTION

What I want to say, following Bush's reasoning, is that a similar forgetting of history has in recent years allowed some people to argue, and argue persuasively, that affirmative action is reverse racism. The very phrase "reverse racism" contains the argument in exactly the form to which Bush objected: In this country whites once set themselves apart from blacks and claimed privileges for themselves while denying them to others. Now, on the basis of race, blacks are claiming special status and reserving for themselves privileges they deny to others. Isn't one as bad as the other? The answer is no. One can see why by imagining that it is not 1993 but 1955, and that we are in a town in the South with two more or less distinct communities, one white and one black. No doubt each community would have a ready store of dismissive epithets, ridiculing stories, self-serving folk myths, and expressions of plain hatred, all directed at the other community, and all based in racial hostility. Yet to regard their respective racisms—if that is the word—as equivalent would be bizarre, for the hostility of one group stems not from any wrong done to it but from its wish to protect its ability to deprive citizens of their voting rights, to limit access to educational institutions, to prevent entry into the economy except at the lowest and most menial levels, and to force members of the stigmatized group to ride in the back of the bus. The hostility of the other group is the result of these actions, and whereas hostility and racial anger are unhappy facts wherever

they are found, a distinction must surely be made between the ideological hostility of the oppressors and the experience-based hostility of those who have been oppressed.

Not to make that distinction is, adapting George Bush's words,
to twist history and forget the terrible plight of African-Americans
in the more than 200 years of this country's existence. Moreover, to
equate the efforts to remedy that plight with the actions that produced it is to twist history even further. Those efforts, designed to
redress the imbalances caused by long-standing discrimination, are
called affirmative action; to argue that affirmative action, which
gives preferential treatment to disadvantaged minorities as part of
a plan to achieve social equality, is no different from the policies
that created the disadvantages in the first place is a travesty of reasoning. "Reverse racism" is a cogent description of affirmative
action only if one considers the cancer of racism to be morally and
medically indistinguishable from the therapy we apply to it. A
cancer is an invasion of the body's equilibrium, and so is
chemotherapy; but we do not decline to fight the disease because
the medicine we employ is also disruptive of nominal functioning.
Strong illness, strong remedy: the formula is as appropriate to the
health of the body politic as it is to that of the body proper.

At this point someone will always say, "But two wrongs don't
make a right; if it was wrong to treat blacks unfairly, it is wrong to
give blacks preference and thereby treat whites unfairly." This
objection is just another version of the forgetting and rewriting of
history. The work is done by the adverb "unfairly," which suggests
two more or less equal parties, one of whom has been unjustly
penalized by an incompetent umpire. But blacks have not simply
been treated unfairly; they have been subjected first to decades of
slavery, and then to decades of second-class citizenship, widespread legalized discrimination, economic persecution, educational deprivation, and cultural stigmatization. They have been
bought, sold, killed, beaten, raped, excluded, exploited, shamed,
and scorned for a very long time. The word "unfair" is hardly an
adequate description of their experience, and the belated gift of
"fairness" in the form of a resolution no longer to discriminate
against them legally is hardly an adequate remedy for the deep
disadvantages that the prior discrimination has produced. When
the deck is stacked against you in more ways than you can even
count, it is small consolation to hear that you are now free to enter
the game and take your chances.

A TILTED FIELD

The same insincerity and hollowness of promise infect another formula that is popular with the anti-affirmative-action crowd: the formula of the level playing field. Here the argument usually takes the form of saying "It is undemocratic to give one class of citizens advantages at the expense of other citizens; the truly democratic way is to have a level playing field to which everyone has access and where everyone has a fair and equal chance to succeed on the basis of his or her merit." Fine words—but they conceal the facts of the situation as it has been given to us by history: the playing field is already tilted in favor of those by whom and for whom it was constructed in the first place. If mastery of the requirements for entry depends upon immersion in the cultural experiences of the mainstream majority, if the skills that make for success are nurtured by institutions and cultural practices from which the disadvantaged minority has been systematically excluded, if the language and ways of comporting oneself that identify a player as "one of us" are alien to the lives minorities are forced to live, then words like "fair" and "equal" are cruel jokes, for what they promote and celebrate is an institutionalized unfairness and a perpetuated inequality. The playing field is already tilted, and the resistance to altering it by the mechanisms of affirmative action is in fact a determination to make sure that the present imbalances persist as long as possible.

One way of tilting the field is the Scholastic Aptitude Test. This test figures prominently in Dinesh D'Souza's book *Illiberal Education* (1991), in which one finds many examples of white or Asian students denied admission to colleges and universities even though their SAT scores were higher than the scores of some others—often African-Americans—who were admitted to the same institution. This, D'Souza says, is evidence that as a result of affirmative-action policies colleges and universities tend "to depreciate the importance of merit criteria in admissions." D'Souza's assumption—and it is one that many would share—is that the test does in fact measure *merit*, with merit understood as a quality objectively determined in the same way that body temperature can be objectively determined.

In fact, however, the test is nothing of the kind. Statistical studies have suggested that test scores reflect income and socioeconomic status. It has been demonstrated again and again that scores vary in relation to cultural background; the test's questions assume a certain uniformity in educational experience and lifestyle and penalize those who, for whatever reason, have had a different experience and lived different kinds of lives. In short, what is being measured by the SAT is not absolutes like native ability and merit but accidents like birth, social position, access to libraries, and the opportunity to take vacations or to take SAT prep courses.

Furthermore, as David Owen notes in *None of the Above: Behind the Myth of Scholastic Aptitude* (1985), the "correlation between SAT scores and college grades . . . is lower than the correlation between weight and height; in other words you would have a better chance of predicting a person's height by looking at his weight than you would of predicting his freshman grades by looking only at his SAT scores." Everywhere you look in the SAT story, the claims of fairness, objectivity, and neutrality fall away, to be replaced by suspicions of specialized measures and unfair advantages.

Against this background a point that in isolation might have a questionable force takes on a special and even explanatory resonance: the principal deviser of the test was an out-and-out racist. In 1923 Carl Campbell Brigham published a book called *A Study of American Intelligence,* in which, as Owen notes, he declared, among other things, that we faced in America "a possibility of racial admixture . . . infinitely worse than that faced by any European country today, for we are incorporating the Negro into our racial stock, while all of Europe is comparatively free of this taint." Brigham had earlier analyzed the Army Mental Tests using classifications drawn from another racist text, Madison Grant's *The Passing of the Great Race,* which divided American society into four distinct racial strains, with Nordic, blue-eyed, blond people at the pinnacle and the American Negro at the bottom. Nevertheless, in 1925 Brigham became a director of testing for the College Board, and developed the SAT. So here is the great SAT test, devised by a racist in order to confirm racist assumptions, measuring not native ability but cultural advantage, an uncertain indicator of performance, an indicator of very little except what money and social privilege can buy. And it is in the name of this mechanism that we are asked to reject affirmative action and reaffirm "the importance of merit criteria in admissions."

THE REALITY OF DISCRIMINATION

Nevertheless, there is at least one more card to play against affirmative action, and it is a strong one. Granted that the playing field is not level and that access to it is reserved for an already advantaged elite, the disadvantages suffered by others are less racial—at least in 1993—than socioeconomic. Therefore shouldn't, as D'Souza urges, "universities . . . retain their policies of preferential treatment, but alter their criteria of application from race to socioeconomic disadvantage," and thus avoid the unfairness of current policies that reward middle-class or affluent blacks at the expense of poor whites? One answer to this question is given by D'Souza himself when he acknowledges that the overlap between minority groups and the poor is very large—a point underscored by the former Secretary of Education Lamar Alexander, who said, in response to a question about funds targeted for black students, "Ninety-eight percent of race-specific scholarships do not involve constitutional problems." He meant, I take it, that 98 percent of race-specific scholarships were also scholarships to the economically disadvantaged.

Still, the other two percent—nonpoor, middle-class, economically favored blacks—are receiving special attention on the basis of disadvantages they do not experience. What about them? The force of the question depends on the assumption that in this day and age race could not possibly be a serious disadvantage to those who are otherwise well positioned in the society. But the lie was given dramatically to this assumption in a 1991 broadcast of the ABC program "PrimeTime Live." In a stunning fifteen-minute segment reporters and a camera crew followed two young men of equal education, cultural sophistication, level of apparent affluence, and so forth around St. Louis, a city where neither was known. The two differed in only a single respect: one was white, the other black. But that small difference turned out to mean everything. In a series of encounters with shoe salesmen, record-store employees, rental agents, landlords, employment agencies, taxicab drivers, and ordinary citizens, the black member of the pair was either ignored or given a special and suspicious attention. He was asked to pay more for the same goods or come up with a larger down payment for the same car, was turned away as a prospective tenant, was rejected as a prospective taxicab fare, was treated with contempt and irritation by clerks and bureaucrats,

and in every way possible was made to feel inferior and un-
wanted.

The inescapable conclusion was that alike though they may
have been in almost all respects, one of these young men, because
he was black, would lead a significantly lesser life than his white
counterpart: he would be housed less well and at greater expense;
he would pay more for services and products when and if he was
given the opportunity to buy them; he would have difficulty establishing credit; the first emotions he would inspire on the part of
many people he met would be distrust and fear; his abilities would
be discounted even before he had a chance to display them; and,
above all, the treatment he received from minute to minute would
chip away at his self-esteem and self-confidence with consequences that most of us could not even imagine. As the young man
in question said at the conclusion of the broadcast, "You walk
down the street with a suit and tie and it doesn't matter. Someone
will make determinations about you, determinations that affect the
quality of your life."

Of course, the same determinations are being made quite early
on by kindergarten teachers, grade school principals, high school
guidance counselors, and the like, with results that cut across
socioeconomic lines and place young black men and women in the
ranks of the disadvantaged no matter what the bank accounts of
their parents happen to show. Racism is a cultural fact, and
although its effects may to some extent be diminished by socioeconomic variables, those effects will still be sufficiently great to
warrant the nation's attention and thus the continuation of affirmative-action policies. This is true even of the field thought to be
dominated by blacks and often cited as evidence of the equal
opportunities society now affords them. I refer, of course, to professional athletics. But national self-congratulation on this score
might pause in the face of a few facts: A minuscule number of
African-Americans ever receive a paycheck from a professional
team. Even though nearly 1,600 daily newspapers report on the
exploits of black athletes, they employ only seven full-time black
sports columnists. Despite repeated pledges and resolutions,
major-league teams have managed to put only a handful of blacks
and Hispanics in executive positions.

Why Me?

When all is said and done, however, one objection to affirmative action is unanswerable on its own terms, and that is the objection of the individual who says, "Why me? Sure, discrimination has persisted for many years, and I acknowledge that the damage done has not been removed by changes in the law. But why me? I didn't own slaves; I didn't vote to keep people on the back of the bus; I didn't turn water hoses on civil-rights marchers. Why, then, should I be the one who doesn't get the job or who doesn't get the scholarship or who gets bumped back to the waiting list?"

I sympathize with this feeling, if only because in a small way I have had the experience that produces it. I was recently nominated for an administrative post at a large university. Early signs were encouraging, but after an interval I received official notice that I would not be included at the next level of consideration, and subsequently I was told unofficially that at some point a decision had been made to look only in the direction of women and minorities. Although I was disappointed, I did not conclude that the situation was "unfair," because the policy was obviously not directed at me—at no point in the proceedings did someone say, "Let's find a way to rule out Stanley Fish." Nor was it directed even at persons of my race and sex—the policy was not intended to disenfranchise white males. Rather, the policy was driven by other considerations, and it was only as a by-product of those considerations—not as the main goal—that white males like me were rejected. Given that the institution in question has a high percentage of minority students, a very low percentage of minority faculty, and an even lower percentage of minority administrators, it made perfect sense to focus on women and minority candidates, and within that sense, not as the result of prejudice, my whiteness and maleness became disqualifications.

I can hear the objection in advance: "What's the difference? Unfair is unfair: you didn't get the job; you didn't even get on the short list." The difference is not in the outcome but in the ways of thinking that led up to the outcome. It is the difference between an unfairness that befalls one as the unintended effect of a policy rationally conceived and an unfairness that is pursued as an end in itself. It is the difference between the awful unfairness of Nazi extermination camps and the unfairness to Palestinian Arabs that arose from, but was not the chief purpose of, the founding of a Jewish state.

THE NEW BIGOTRY

The point is not a difficult one, but it is difficult to see when the unfairness scenarios are presented as simple contrasts between two decontextualized persons who emerge from nowhere to contend for a job or a place in a freshman class. Here is student A; he has a board score of 1,300. And here is student B; her board score is only 1,200, yet she is admitted and A is rejected. Is that fair? Given the minimal information provided, the answer is of course no. But if we expand our horizons and consider fairness in relation to the cultural and institutional histories that have brought the two students to this point, histories that weigh on them even if they are not the histories' authors, then both the question and the answer suddenly grow more complicated.

The sleight-of-hand logic that first abstracts events from history and then assesses them from behind a veil of willed ignorance gains some of its plausibility from another key word in the anti-affirmative-action lexicon. That word is "individual," as in "The American way is to focus on the rights of individuals rather than groups." Now, "individual" and "individualism" have been honorable words in the American political vocabulary, and they have often been well employed in the fight against various tyrannies. But like any other word or concept, individualism can be perverted to serve ends the opposite of those it originally served, and this is what has happened when in the name of individual rights, millions of individuals are enjoined from redressing historically documented wrongs. How is this managed? Largely in the same way that the invocation of fairness is used to legitimize an institutionalized inequality. First one says, in the most solemn of tones, that the protection of individual rights is the chief obligation of society. Then one defines individuals as souls sent into the world with equal entitlements as guaranteed either by their Creator or by the Constitution. Then one pretends that nothing has happened to them since they stepped onto the world's stage. And then one says of these carefully denatured souls that they will all be treated in the same way, irrespective of any of the differences that history has produced. Bizarre as it may seem, individualism in this argument turns out to mean that everyone is or should be the same. This dismissal of individual difference in the name of the individual would be funny were its consequences not so serious: it is the mechanism by which imbalances and inequities suffered by millions of people through no fault of their own can be sanitized and even celebrated as the natural workings of unfettered democracy.

"Individualism," "fairness," "merit"—these three words are continually misappropriated by bigots who have learned that they need not put on a white hood or bar access to the ballot box in order to secure their ends. Rather, they need only clothe themselves in a vocabulary plucked from its historical context and made into the justification for attitudes and policies they would not acknowledge if frankly named.

10

RACE-NEUTRAL PROGRAMS AND THE DEMOCRATIC COALITION

William Julius Wilson

The election of Ron Brown as the first black chairman of the Democratic National Committee triggered a new round of soul-searching among Democrats. Was the party committing political suicide by becoming too strongly identified with the aspirations of minority voters? Had America become so mired in racism that whites would desert the Democrats because blacks seemed to be running things?

My answer to these questions is an emphatic "No." Many white Americans have turned, not against blacks, but against a strategy that emphasizes programs perceived to benefit only racial minorities. In the 1990s the party needs to promote new policies to fight inequality that differ from court-ordered busing, affirmative action programs, and antidiscrimination lawsuits of the recent past. By stressing coalition politics and race-neutral programs such as full employment strategies, job skills training, comprehensive health care, reforms in the public schools, child care legislation, and prevention of crime and drug abuse, the Democrats can significantly strengthen their position. As Chairman Brown himself has emphasized, reinforcing Democratic loyalty among minorities and reaching out to reclaim white support are not mutually exclusive.

Such a change of emphasis is overdue. In the 1960s efforts to raise the public's awareness and conscience about the plight of black Americans helped to enact civil rights legislation and affirmative action programs. However, by the 1980s the civil rights strategy of dramatizing black disadvantage was backfiring. The "myth of black progress" theme, frequently invoked to reinforce arguments for stronger race-specific programs, played easily into the hands of conservative critics of antibias policies. The strategy reinforced the erroneous impression that federal antidiscrimination efforts had largely failed, and it overlooked the significance of complex racial changes since the mid-1960s. It also aroused concern that Democratic politicians' sensitivity to black complaints had come at the expense of the white majority.

The tortuous struggles of the 1960s produced real gains. To deny those achievements only invites demoralization among both black and white advocates of racial justice. Yet the movement for racial equality needs a new political strategy for the 1990s that appeals to a broader coalition and addresses many problems afflicting minorities that originated in racist practices but will not be solved by race-specific remedies.

DIFFERENTIAL RATES OF BLACK PROGRESS

As we entered the 1980s, the accomplishments of the civil rights struggle were clearly registered in the rising number of blacks in professional, technical, managerial, and administrative positions. Progress was evident also in the increasing enrollment of blacks in colleges and universities and the growing number of black homeowners. These increases were proportionately greater than those for whites. On the other hand, among the disadvantaged segments of the black population, especially the ghetto underclass, many dire problems—poverty, joblessness, family breakup, educational retardation in inner-city public schools, increased welfare dependence, and drug addiction—were getting even worse.

The differential rates of progress in the black community persisted through the 1980s. Family incomes among the poorest of the poor reveal the pattern. From 1978 to 1987, the number of blacks with incomes under half the poverty line (below $4,528 for a three-person family in 1987, adjusting for inflation) increased by 69 percent. In 1978 only one of every three poor blacks fell below half the poverty fine, but by 1987 the proportion rose to 45 percent. The average poor black family in 1986 and 1987 slipped further below the poverty level than in any year since the Census Bureau started collecting such data in 1967. While the average income of the lowest fifth of black families in the United States was dropping 24 percent, the average income of the highest fifth of black families was climbing by more than $3,000 and that of the top 5 percent by almost $9,000. Upper-income whites are considerably wealthier than upper-income blacks, but in 1987 the highest fifth of black families secured a record 47.4 percent of the total black income, compared to the 42.9 percent share of total white family income received by the highest fifth of white families.

So while income inequality widened generally in America during the 1980s, it widened even more dramatically among black Americans. If we are to fashion remedies for black poverty, we need to understand the origins and dynamics of inequality in the black community. Without disavowing the accomplishments of the civil rights movement, black leaders and liberal policy makers now need to focus on remedies that will make a difference to the poor.

PROGRESS AND PROTEST

Before the emergence of activist black protest, the professionals of the National Association for the Advancement of Colored People (NAACP), working mainly through the courts, achieved important victories in the drive for civil rights. Prior to 1960, the NAACP publicly defined the racial problem as legal segregation in the South and set as its major goal the end of all state-enforced segregation—as the civil rights slogan then had it, "free by 1963." In landmark Supreme Court decisions, the NAACP won legal mandates to improve the conditions of black Americans. Most important, of course, was the 1954 Supreme Court ruling against mandatory school segregation, which overturned the "separate but equal" doctrine and authoritatively defined blacks as first-class citizens.

Important and necessary as these victories were, it soon became apparent that they were not sufficient. Jim Crow regimes in the South ingeniously circumvented the new rulings and made it apparent to black leaders that they had defined both the problem and the goal too narrowly. The problem, as they now saw it, was token compliance with the newly created mandates; the goal they now set was the end of both de jure and de facto segregation.

Despite Southern white resistance, black expectations of continued racial progress continued rising. Not only had the Supreme Court ruled in favor of desegregation; the federal government was growing more sensitive to the condition of black America for two reasons.

The first was international. When the new African regimes broke up the old colonial empires, both the West and the Soviet bloc began competing for influence in the new states. Racial violence and animosities in the United States were now more embarrassing to federal officials than in the past. As a result, Southerners, who had enjoyed significant autonomy in handling racial matters prior to World War II, came under closer national scrutiny.

The increased voting power of blacks in national elections was also a factor. Since the elections of the 1920s, civil lights advocates had monitored the voting records of congressmen and policies of presidents. The lure of the black vote sometimes prompted politicians to support racial equality, as did the Democratic and Progressive candidates of 1928. At other times, politicians granted token concessions in the hope of preserving or gaining black support, as did President Franklin D. Roosevelt in 1940 when he increased black participation in the armed forces, though still within segregated units.

As early as the forties, the black vote was substantial enough in pivotal Northern states to decide close national elections. In 1948 President Truman recognized that to defeat his favored Republican opponent, Thomas E. Dewey, he needed strong black support. For the first time since Reconstruction, the status of blacks emerged as a central presidential campaign issue. Much to the chagrin of its Southern members, the Democratic party adopted a civil rights plank as part of its 1948 platform. That same year, satisfying a demand black leaders introduced eight years earlier, President Truman issued an executive order banning racial segregation in the armed forces. Despite a Dixiecrat walkout from the party, the strategy worked: black voters helped Truman narrowly defeat Dewey. The black vote also provided the margin of victory for Kennedy in 1960, and it almost defeated Nixon again in 1968.

*   *   *

In the 1960s, as blacks increased their political resources, white resistance to complete desegregation intensified and black support for protest action mushroomed. For a brief period, the nonviolent resistance strategy proved highly effective, particularly in forcing local governments and private agencies to integrate facilities in Southern cities and towns. The nonviolent demonstrations also pressed the federal government into passage of civil rights legislation in 1964 and voting rights legislation in 1965.

Nonviolent protest was successful for several reasons. The demands accompanying the protests—for example, end discrimination in voting"—tended to be fairly specific and hard to oppose in principle. The remedies were also relatively straightforward and did not require immediate sacrifices by most whites, which reduced white political backlash in areas outside the South. Federal officials were receptive not only because they saw the international attention these developments were receiving. They recognized the political resources blacks had developed, including the growing army of Northern whites sympathetic to the civil rights movement and to direct action protests.

The demands of the civil rights movement reflected a general assumption by black leaders in the 1960s that the government could best protect the rights of minority groups not by formally bestowing rewards and punishments based on group membership, but by using antidiscrimination measures to enhance individual freedom. The movement was particularly concerned about access to education, employment, voting, and public accommodations. So from the 1950s to 1970, the emphasis was on freedom of choice; the role of the state was to prevent the formal categorization of people on the basis of race. Antibias legislation was designed to eliminate racial discrimination without considering the proportion of minorities in certain positions. The underlying principle was that individual merit should be the sole determining factor in choosing among candidates for positions. Because civil rights protests clearly upheld this basic American principle, they carried a degree of moral authority that leaders such as Martin Luther King Jr. repeatedly and effectively invoked.

It would have been ideal if programs based on the principle of freedom of individual opportunity were sufficient to remedy racial inequality. Long periods of racial oppression can result, however, in a system of inequality that lingers even after racial barriers come down. The most disadvantaged minority individuals, crippled by the cumulative effects of both race and class subjugation, disproportionately lack the resources to compete effectively in a free and open market. Conversely, the members of a minority group who stand to benefit most from the removal of racial barriers are the ones who least need extra help.

Eliminating racial barriers creates the greatest opportunities for the better trained, talented, and educated members of minority groups because they possess the most resources to compete. Those resources reflect a variety of advantages—family stability, financial means, peer groups, and schooling—provided or made possible by their parents.

By the late 1960s a number of black leaders began to recognize this dilemma. In November 1967, for example, Kenneth B. Clark said, "The masses of Negroes are now starkly aware of the fact that recent civil lights victories benefited a very small percentage of middle-class Negroes while their predicament remained the same or worsened." Simply eliminating racial barriers was not going to be enough. As the late black economist Vivian Henderson put it in the NAACP journal *The Crisis,* "If all racial prejudice and discrimination and all racism were erased today, all the ills brought by the process of economic class distinction and economic depression of the masses of black people would remain."

Accordingly, black leaders and liberal policy makers began to emphasize the need not only to eliminate active discrimination, but also to counteract the effects of past racial oppression. Instead of seeking remedies only for individual complaints of discrimination, they sought government-mandated affirmative action programs to ensure adequate minority representation in employment, education, and public programs.

However, as the political scientist James Fishkin has argued, if the more advantaged members of minority groups benefit disproportionately from policies that embody the principle of equality of individual opportunity, they also profit disproportionately from policies of preferential treatment based solely on their racial group membership. Why? Again simply because minority individuals from the most advantaged families tend to be disproportionately represented among those of their racial group most qualified for preferred status, such as college admissions, higher-paying jobs, and promotions. Thus policies of preferential treatment are likely to improve further the socioeconomic positions of the more advantaged without adequately remedying the problems of the disadvantaged.

To be sure, affirmative action was not intended solely to benefit the more advantaged minority individuals. As William L. Taylor, the former director of the U.S. Civil Rights Commission, has stated, "The focus of much of the [affirmative action] effort has been not just on white collar jobs, but also on law enforcement, construction work, and craft and production in large companies—all areas in which the extension of new opportunities has provided upward mobility for less advantaged minority workers." Taylor also notes that studies show that many minority students entering medical schools during the 1970s were from families of low income.

Affirmative action policies, however, did not really open up broad avenues of upward mobility for the masses of disadvantaged blacks. Like other forms of "creaming," they provided opportunities for those individuals from low socioeconomic backgrounds with the greatest educational and social resources. Recent data on income, employment opportunities, and educational attainment confirm that relatively few individuals who reside in the inner-city ghettos have benefited from affirmative action.

During the past two decades, as I have argued previously in *The Truly Disadvantaged* (1987), urban minorities have been highly vulnerable to structural changes in the economy, such as the shift from goods-producing to service-producing industries, the increasing polarization of the labor market into low-wage and high-wage sectors, innovations in technology, and the relocation of manufacturing industries out of the central city. These shifts have led to sharp increases in joblessness and the related problems of highly concentrated poverty, welfare dependency, and family breakup, despite the passage of antidiscrimination legislation and the creation of affirmative action programs. In 1974, for example, 47 percent of all employed black males ages twenty to twenty-four held blue-collar, semiskilled operative and skilled-craft positions, which typically earned wages adequate to support a family. By 1986 that figure plummeted to 25 percent. A survey I have directed, randomly sampling residents from poor Chicago neighborhoods, revealed that Puerto Rican men up to age forty-five and black men under age thirty-six have borne the brunt of job losses due to deindustrialization.

However, I do not advance the foregoing arguments to suggest that race-specific programs were inefficacious. They clearly helped to bring about a sharp increase in the number of blacks entering higher education and gaining professional and managerial positions. But neither policies based on the principle of equality of individual opportunity, nor policies that call for preferential group treatment, such as affirmative action, will do much for less advantaged blacks because of the combined effects of past discrimination and current structural changes in the economy. Now more than ever we need broader solutions than those we have employed in the past.

TOWARD A NEW POLITICAL STRATEGY

Full employment policies, job skills training, comprehensive health-care legislation, educational reforms in the public schools, child care legislation, and crime and drug abuse prevention programs—these are the race-neutral policies likely to begin making a difference for the poor, black and white.

When presenting this argument to academic audiences, I am frequently told that such programs would face general opposition not only because of their cost, but also because many whites have become disenchanted with the black movement and its calls for intensified affirmative action.

These programs should be presented, however, not as ways to address the plight of poor minorities (though they would greatly benefit from them), but as strategies to help all groups, regardless of race or economic class. After all, Americans across racial and class lines continue to be concerned about unemployment and job security, declining real wages, escalating medical costs, the sharp decline in the quality of public education, the lack of good child care, and crime and drug trafficking in their neighborhoods.

Public opinion surveys reflect these concerns. For the last several years national opinion polls consistently reveal strong public backing for government labor market strategies, including training efforts to enhance employment. A 1988 Harris poll indicated that almost three quarters of the respondents would support a tax increase to pay for child care. A 1989 Harris poll reports that almost nine out of ten Americans would like to see fundamental change in the U.S. health-care system. And recent surveys conducted by the National Opinion Research Center at the University of Chicago reveal that a substantial majority of Americans want more money spent to improve the nation's schools and to halt rising crime and drug addiction.

Programs that expand employment opportunities and job skills training, improve public education, provide adequate child and health care, and reduce neighborhood crime and drug abuse could alleviate many problems of poor minorities that cannot be successfully attacked by race-specific measures alone. In the 1990s the best political strategy for those committed to racial justice is to promote these programs for all groups in America, not just minorities.

RACE-NEUTRAL PROGRAMS AND COALITION POLITICS

"The economic future of blacks in the United States," Vivian Henderson argued in 1975, "is bound up with that of the rest of the nation. Policies, programs, and politics designed in the future to cope with the problems of the poor and victimized will also yield benefits to blacks. In contrast, any efforts to treat blacks separately from the rest of the nation are likely to lead to frustration, heightened racial animosities, and a waste of the country's resources and the precious resources of black people."

Henderson's warning seems to be especially appropriate in periods of economic stagnation, when public support of programs targeted for minorities—or associated with real or imagined material sacrifice on the part of whites—seems to wane. The economy was strong when affirmative action programs were introduced during the Johnson administration. When the economy turned down in the 1970s, the public's view of affirmative action turned increasingly sour.

Furthermore, as Joseph A. Califano, Johnson's staff assistant for domestic affairs, observed in 1988, such programs were generally acceptable to whites "only as a temporary expedient to speed blacks' entry into the social and economic mainstream." But as years passed, many whites "saw continuing such preferences as an unjust insistence by Democrats that they do penance for an era of slavery and discrimination they had nothing to do with." They also associated the decline in public schools, not with broader changes in society, but with "forced integration."

The Democrats also came under fire for their support for Great Society programs that increasingly and incorrectly acquired the stigma of being intended for poor blacks alone. Virtually separate medical and legal systems developed in many cities. Public services became identified mainly with blacks, private services mainly with whites. In an era of ostensible racial justice, many public programs ironically seemed to develop into a new and cost-lier form of segregation. White taxpayers saw themselves as being forced to pay for medical and legal services for minorities that many of them could not afford to purchase for their own families.

From the New Deal to the 1960s, the Democrats were able to link Keynesian economics and middle-class prosperity with programs for integrating racial minorities and the poor into the American mainstream. "In periods of great economic progress when [the incomes of the middle classes] are rising rapidly," argues Lester Thurow, "they are willing to share some of their income and jobs with those less fortunate than themselves, but they are not willing to reduce their real standard of living to help either minorities or the poor."

As the economic situation worsened, Ronald Reagan was able to convince many working- and middle-class Americans that the decline in their living standards was attributable to expensive and wasteful programs for the poor (and implicitly for minorities). When Reagan was elected to office in 1980, the New Deal coalition collapsed; the principal groups supporting the Democratic ticket with wide majorities were blacks, Hispanics, and the poor, who represent only a quarter of the American population.

What are the implications for the Democratic party? After losing three straight presidential elections, the Democrats are reex-amining their programs and approaches to voters, partly in the hope of recapturing support from disaffected whites who voted for Reagan and Bush. Those steps ought to involve the develop-ment of race-neutral programs. Consider, for example, one issue likely to be at the core of new domestic programs—the future of the American work force.

Social scientists, corporate leaders, and government officials have all expressed concerns about the potential weakening of America's competitive position if we fail to confront the growing shortage of skilled workers. These concerns have led to a height-ened awareness of the consequences of poverty, poor education, and joblessness. Many of the new jobs will require higher levels of training and education at the very time when our public schools are graduating too many students who can barely read or write. The 1987 U.S. Department of Labor Study, "Workforce 2000," pointed out that for demographic reasons members of minority groups will necessarily fill a majority of the new jobs in the next decade.

A major policy initiative to improve the quality of the work force would open up opportunities for the minorities who are heavily represented among the educational have-nots. But such an initiative would also open opportunities for others, and it should draw general support because of concerns over the devastating effects a poorly trained work force will have on the entire economy.

NONRACIAL AFFIRMATIVE ACTION

However, even if minorities would benefit disproportionately from new race-neutral initiatives to combat the problems and consequences of social inequality, are there not severe problems in the inner-city ghetto that can only be effectively addressed by creative programs targeted on the basis of race? For example, Roger Wilkins has argued persuasively that the cumulative effects of racial isolation and subjugation have made the plight of the black poor unique. Many inner-city children have a solo parent and lack educational support and stability in their home; Wilkins contends that they need assistance to enable them to become capable adults who can provide their children with emotional and educational support. Accordingly, he maintains that special social service programs are needed for inner-city (presumably, minority) schools.

No serious initiative to improve the quality of the work force could ignore problems such as poverty, social isolation, and family instability, which impede the formal education of children and ultimately affect their job performance. Service programs to meet these needs could easily fit into an overall race-neutral initiative to improve America's work force. To be sure, this component of the larger initiative would be introduced only in the most disadvantaged neighborhoods, but the neighborhoods would not have to be racially defined. Poor minorities need not be treated separately from the rest of the nation in a national effort to enhance the skill levels of the labor force.

It is particularly important for blacks and other minorities to recognize that they have a stake in the formation of a Democratic coalition that would develop race-neutral initiatives. Only with multiracial support could programs of social and economic reform get approved in Congress. Black voters who are dubious about this approach ought to be reminded of the success of the Jesse Jackson presidential campaign. By highlighting problems plaguing all groups in America, the Jackson campaign drew far more support from white working- and middle-class voters than most political observers thought possible.

THE POSITIVE EFFECTS OF RACE-NEUTRAL POLICIES

My emphasis on race-neutral programs should be clearly distinguished from the neoconservative critique of affirmative action that attacks both racial preference and activist social welfare policies. The former is said to be antidemocratic, the latter economically counterproductive to minorities. My approach, in contrast, supports the alliance between activist government and racial justice in three key respects—as guarantor of civil rights, as custodian of coalition politics, and as sponsor of race-neutral strategies that advance the well-being of America's neediest along with that of America as a whole. For those who came of age in the 1970s, it seems paradoxical that this goal is now best achieved via race-neutral approaches. Yet, a society without racial preference has, of course, always been the long-term goal of the civil rights movement.

An emphasis on coalition politics that features progressive, race-neutral policies could have two positive effects. It could help the Democratic party regain lost political support, and it could lead to programs that would especially benefit the more disadvantaged members of minority groups—without being minority policies.

PART TWO

PHILOSOPHICAL DISCUSSIONS OF AFFIRMATIVE ACTION

INTRODUCTION TO PART II

While the public debate about affirmative action has been going on in America's streets, courts, and boardrooms, a quieter, though no less intense debate about the status of affirmative action has been going on among the nation's philosophers. For them, the issues surrounding affirmative action have not been framed primarily in terms of widespread American ideals, peoples' public hopes and resentments, or the proper interpretation of the constitution, but of what our fundamental moral intuitions tell us is right and wrong.

For philosophers, the moral status of affirmative action is problematic because many different moral intuitions are involved, which seem to pull in different directions. Considerations of fairness and justice, for example, seem to demand that everyone be treated the same as everyone else in a hiring decision. At the same time, considerations of social utility suggest that it is important to give preferential treatment to minorities in order to help give minority youth role models to aspire to. To make matters even more complicated, sometimes the same fundamental principles seem to point in two or more directions. While increasing social utility suggests we should try to select people for positions who can serve as role models, (suggesting affirmative action as a moral imperative), social utility and public good considerations also suggest we should strive for an efficient consumer-satisfying society, which may require that only the very best qualified people are given certain positions (suggesting it is morally imperative that we avoid affirmative action). Similarly, considerations of justice may seem to require that every qualified person be given equal consideration, regardless of race, when applying for a position, yet our conception of justice also entails that people be compensated for deprivations they've suffered in the past.

In the following essays, several philosophers try to clarify our intuitions regarding affirmative action, and to single out which ones we consider most important and fundamental. In most of the essays that follow, the philosophers look at our ordinary moral judgments, and try to carefully tease out the different underlying moral principles we appeal to in making those judgments. They then examine what these underlying moral principles ultimately do and don't commit us to. Does a commitment to not denying people positions of power on the basis of race commit one to to a color-blind ideal? Does an ideal of compensation for past deprivations commit one to a set of obligations that are intrinsically impossible to fulfill? These are the sorts of questions the philosophers in the following essays discuss in order to try to come to some solutions about the precise moral status of affirmative action.

In "The Moral Status of Affirmative Action," Louis P. Pojman nicely sets out what he considers to be the major arguments in favor of affirmative action, and the major arguments against it. The seven arguments for affirmative action are (1) the need for role models; (2) the need to break stereotypes; (3) the "unequal results reveals discrimination" argument, (4) the compensation argument; (5) compensation from those who have innocently benefitted from past injustice; (6) the diversity argument; and (7) antimeritocratic desert arguments to justify reverse discrimination: "no one deserves his talents." The seven arguments against affirmative action are (1) affirmative action requires discrimination against a different group: (2) affirmative action perpetuates victimization syndrome; (3) affirmative action encourages mediocrity and incompetence; (4) affirmative action policies unjustly shift the burden of proof; (5) and argument from merit; (6) the slippery slope, and (7) the mounting evidence against the success of affirmative action. Pojman ultimately argues that arguments for affirmative action, as it is now practiced, are unpersuasive, compared to the arguments against it. He argues that we can morally justify what he calls "weak affirmative action." This includes "such measures as the elimination of segregation, widespread advertisement to groups not previous represented in certain privileged positions, special scholarships for the disadvantaged classes (e.g., all the poor), using underrepresentation or a history of past discrimination as a tiebreaker when candidates are relatively equal, and the like." More vigorous "strong affirmative" action, on the other hand, e.g. overlooking more qualified people in order to achieve proportionate representation, violates our most important moral intuitions.

In "A Defense of Programs of Preferential Treatment," Richard Wasserstrom directly confronts and argues against what many people consider the strongest argument against affirmative action. In the eyes of many, it is just plain immoral to use color as a consideration in determining whether or not to offer someone an educational or employment position. The entire civil rights movements was an attempt to get people to judge each other, in the words of Martin Luther King Jr., "not by the color of their skin, but the content of their character." When one uses skin color as part of the criteria for deciding, say, who should be hired, then we are stepping away from this dream. When we award positions to people, in part, because they belong to a certain race, we must end up denying other qualified people positions because of the color of their skin. This, in the eyes, of many is precisely the sort of racial discrimination that the civil rights movement aimed to combat.

Wasserstrom argues that the sort of discrimination against white males that may result from affirmative action programs *just isn't* the same sort of discrimination that as often been practiced against blacks and women. What was wrong with previous discrimination is not that an irrelevant criterion, such as race, was employed, but that such discrimination ended up denying minorities positions of social and political power in society. However, while affirmative action programs may sometimes cause a white male to lose a job to a minority applicant, "there is simply no way in which all of these programs taken together could plausibly be viewed as capable of relegating white males to the kind of genuinely oppressive status characteristically bestowed upon women and blacks by the dominant social institutions and ideology." Reverse discrimination is different from traditional discrimination because it just does not have the same pernicious results.

Wasserstrom goes on to argue against what is probably the next most popular argument against affirmative action—that it prevents our society from being the meritocracy that we expect it to be, where positions are held by the people most skilled at and qualified for holding them. To this he responds, "We do not live in a society in which there is even the serious pretense of a qualification requirement for many jobs of substantial power and authority. . . . Would anyone claim that Henry Ford II is the head of the Ford Motor Company because he was the most qualified person for the job?" Affirmative action does not prevent us from having a desirable meritocracy—we never had one to begin with. Furthermore, argues Wasserstrom, we don't have any idea of what it means to be most qualified. Having the best grades in law school or prelaw, for example, does not result in one becoming the best lawyer. Without really knowing what it means for someone to be "most qualified," having race or sex be part of a hiring criterion can't mean that we are being unfair to the most qualified people. Finally, even if we did know what it meant to be "the most qualified," that, by itself, doesn't mean those people should be the ones selected. Wasserstrom brings up the analogy of a community with only one tennis court. Why should we automatically assume that the best players ought to be the ones permitted to use it most? "Why not those who were there first, Or those who will enjoy playing the most? Or those who are the worst, and therefore in need of the greatest opportunity to practice? Or those who have the chance to play the least frequently?" he asks. One might argue on some sort of utilitarian grounds, that giving preference to the most qualified is the most economically efficient. Wasserstrom believes, however, that, if one shifts the ground to worrying about good consequences, rather than pure justice, we are led back to considering all the good consequences that might come from affirmative action. We cannot argue against affirmative action on meritocratic grounds unless a more thorough defense of meritocracy in theory and in practice is given.

If Wasserstrom's essay seeks to counter the most common argument against affirmative action, Michael E. Levin in "Is Racial Discrimination Special?" goes after one of the most common arguments *in favor* of affirmative action. Many people believe that affirmative action is needed as a compensation for past discrimination. Giving preferential treatment for jobs and education to minorities might be viewed as compensation for past discrimination as a type of "payback" or as raising up a person to the level she *would have been* had the discrimination not occurred. Levin's arguments against such compensation are very simple and straightforward.

Racial discrimination, Levin argues, may indeed keep people from competing on an equal basis with others—but so do innumerable other harms. What is so special about this harm that we should try to rectify it, as opposed to any of the others? Person P may be harmed and rendered less able to compete because his parents were discriminated against. But Person Q might be harmed by his parents being killed; Person R, because her parents were defrauded. (Indeed, argues, Levin, those harms are more likely to have an adverse long-term affect on a person than someone's parents having been discriminated against). If it is right to compensate for the harmful effects of discrimination, it is right to compensate for the lingering effects of other past harms. To make such compensations, in all cases, however, would simply be impossible to do. What's more, it is impossible even to know what one could have achieved had the past harm not have occurred. How much better off would a person have been? Would he even have been better off? What about a person who would have been an African famine victim had not his ancestors been dragged to America as slaves?

If we set ourselves the task of finding past wrongs and rectifying them, "we will find ourselves with obligations that cannot be discharged," writes Levin. "And an undischargible obligation is no obligation at all." The popular compensation argument for affirmative action, Levin believes, cannot be persuasive, because it proves too much. The underlying principle appealed to commits us to far more than could ever be achieved.

In "Goals and Quotas in Hiring and Promotion" Tom L. Beauchamp seeks to reply to critics who see affirmative action as unjust, or as a denial of equal opportunity. Beauchamp admits that reverse discrimination is prima facie unethical. But there may be cases in which certain situations and moral principles justify reverse discrimination in the same way that certain circumstances may justify the *prima facie* unethical act of taking a human life (our example). Other utilitarian or justice interests may be served in affirmative action even if equal opportunity is being denied.

Beauchamp argues that lots of evidence indicates that our important goal of ending discrimination *simply cannot* be achieved by weaker forms of affirmative action, such as by prosecuting proven discriminators in the courts. Far too often discrimination occurs through numerous subtle, often unconscious patterns, as it was alleged to occur in a famous case at Smith College in which several women were denied tenure while "any deficiencies in the women candidates were also found in male candidates promoted and given tenure in the same period." Beauchamp writes that such evidence convincingly indicates that discrimination will not be overcome without "quotas, goals, or strong court-backed measures. . . ." Such measures, which can be seen as lessening opportunities for white males, are, nevertheless, what is needed to achieve other equally important social goals.

Furthermore, Beauchamp argues that since there are numerous ways in which corporations would actually benefit from very stringent and rigorous affirmative actions policies, such policies should be welcomed by the corporate world. Among these benefits would be a company's easy ability to show various minority groups and government regulators that they are not discriminating, by simply showing that the pre-approved goals or quotas had been met. Paradoxically, reverse discrimination lawsuits would also be lessened, as disgruntled white prospective employees could be told that, rather than race being given an undue consideration in any a particular hiring decision, a required policy was merely being fulfilled. Even though there are counter-considerations against preferential treatment, Beauchamp writes, "they are not strong enough to overcome the even more powerful case against them."

In "Justifying Reverse Discrimination in Employment," George Sher looks at various considerations for and against affirmative action and ultimately takes a mixed position. Sher begins by arguing against the notion that affirmative action is a just compensation for past privations. For one thing, there is no reason that groups that have suffered in some way in the past should be given preferential treatment for jobs now (as opposed to some other compensation—like cash payments, which don't end up discriminating against others). For another, reverse discrimination seems to require that compensation, for all intents and purposes, come *only* from those people who would have gotten the jobs had no preferential treatment policies had been in place. No one else is required to contribute any compensation. This form of affirmative action seems an unfair way to distribute the burden of compensation.

But while it may not be just or fair to give preferential treatment to certain group members to remedy past discrimination, there is another way of conceptualizing and justifying preferential treatment. "It is, I think, the key to an adequate justification of reverse discrimination," writes Sher, " to see that practice, not as the redressing of past privations, but rather as a way of neutralizing the *present* competitive disadvantage caused by those past privations and thus as a way of restoring equal access to those goods which society distributes competitively." Thinking of the practice this way, reverse discrimination makes sense as a form of compensation. If past discrimination led to peoples' families being in low-paying jobs, to their having a poor diet, and to their having an inadequate education, then what past discrimination has done is to lower a person's present ability to compete in a free market. In that case, argues Sher, "If the lost good is just the ability to compete on equal terms for first-level goods like desirable jobs, then surely the most appropriate (and so preferable) way of substituting for what has been lost is just to remove the necessity of competing on equal terms for these goods—which, of course, is precisely what reverse discrimination does." This also gives a rationale for requiring present nonminority job applicants to shoulder the burden of compensation. Without affirmative action, argues, Sher, white male job applicants, "will benefit more than others from its effect on their competitors." "They will benefit more," writes Sher, " because unless they are restrained, they, but not the others will use their competitive edge to claim jobs which their competitors would otherwise have gotten." Because they are the ones who stand to unfairly gain the most without preferential treatment, it is fair that preferential treatment be aimed at preventing their unfair gain.

With affirmative action policies being justified that way, however, the exact types of practices that are and aren't seen as morally legitimate are somewhat different than what's typically prescribed by strong affirmative action. On the "present competitive disadvantage" justification, middle class blacks who have *not* lost the ability to compete because of discrimination-based privations in education, housing, heath and intellectual stimulation should *not* be eligible for preferential treatment. Poor whites, however, may have suffered these same sorts of deprivations, and should thereby be counted as morally entitled to preferential treatment in the same way that most blacks are. Sher thus ends up giving a fairness-based moral argument that reaches a very similar conclusion to the one reached by Wilson on largely political grounds. Affirmative action, in his view, is morally justified, but it is a different sort of affirmative action than that in current practice.

As can be seen in the differing views of these philosophers, just as in the public debate, there are a number of different considerations at work here, all of which need to be carefully weighted and balanced against each other. In reading these different viewpoints, it is hoped that the person interested in affirmative action will react in a manner other than throwing up her hands and considering the topic a muddled mess. The hope is that he or she will clearly see which different considerations and principles are involved—and which ones appear to be ultimately untenable. After getting clear on what the principles involved are, a person is in a position to see which ones he or she is willing to give the most weight to, and why. With a list of the carefully weighted principles involved at one's disposal, one should arrive at a clear notion of which interests and concerns need to be satisfied, primarily and secondarily. It should also be clear which concerns and interests must ultimately be sacrificed to act in accordance with principles of more fundamental importance. Coming up with a list of the moral principles that are the most important to adhere to should then provide us with something to help guide us in formulating our publicly stated opinions, our national policies, and our laws.

Ultimately, Michael E. Levin may be right. Racial discrimination may be just one of many problems beguiling us as well as preventing some people from adequately competing with others for society's prestige, power, and influence. But the very existence of affirmative action programs and policies indicates that, special or not, it is an area of social concern we as a people believed that *it was possible to actually do something about.* Just what should be done is still something about which we have not reached a consensus. It may ultimately be that gender- and race-based affirmative action is the only workable solution, as Beauchamp suggests, or perhaps what will work best and be the most morally justified is a vigorous affirmative action policy that is not centered around race, as Sher and Wilson suggest. Or it may be that our racial problems are best dealt with by something entirely different, like various types of educational policies or training. In this next section, as in this volume as a whole, we present the views of many thinkers on this subject in the hope that the reader will be able to make up his or her mind about what sorts of gender or racial policies will ultimately make America as just, fair, and equal as it can be.

11

THE MORAL STATUS OF AFFIRMATIVE ACTION

Louis P. Pojman

A ruler who appoints any man to an office, when there is in his dominion another man better qualified for it, sins against God and against the State.

—The Koran

[Affirmative Action] is the meagerest recompense for centuries of unrelieved oppression.

—quoted by Shelby Steele as the justification for Affirmative Action

Hardly a week goes by but that the subject of affirmative action does not come up. Whether in the guise of reverse discrimination, preferential hiring, nontraditional casting, quotas, goals and time tables, minority scholarships, or race-norming, the issue confronts us as a terribly perplexing problem. Last summer's Actor's Equity debacle over the casting of the British actor, Jonathan Pryce, as a Eurasian in *Miss Saigon*; Assistant Secretary of Education Michael Williams' judgment that minority scholarships are unconstitutional; the "Civil Rights Bill of 1991," reversing recent decisions of the Supreme Court which constrain preferential hiring practices; the demand that Harvard Law School hire a black female professor; grade stipends for black students at Pennsyl-

Reprinted by permission from *Public Affairs Quarterly* (1992). Copyright © 1992 *Public Affairs Quarterly*, Bowling Green State University, Philosophy Documentation Center, Bowling Green, OH 43403.

vania State University and other schools; the revelations of race norming in state employment agencies; as well as debates over quotas, underutilization guidelines, and diversity in employment; all testify to the importance of this subject for contemporary society.

There is something salutary as well as terribly tragic inherent in this problem. The salutary aspect is the fact that our society has shown itself committed to eliminating unjust discrimination. Even in the heart of Dixie there is a recognition of the injustice of racial discrimination. Both sides of the affirmative action debate have good will and appeal to moral principles. Both sides are attempting to bring about a better society, one which is color blind, but they differ profoundly on the morally proper means to accomplish that goal.

And this is just the tragedy of the situation: good people on both sides of the issue are ready to tear each other to pieces over a problem that has no easy or obvious solution. And so the voices become shrill and the rhetoric hyperbolic. The same spirit which divides the pro-choice movement from the right to life movement on abortion divides liberal pro-affirmative action advocates from liberal anti-affirmative action advocates. This problem, more than any other, threatens to destroy the traditional liberal consensus in our society. I have seen family members and close friends who until recently fought on the same side of the barricades against racial injustice divide in enmity over this issue. The anti-affirmative liberals ("liberals who've been mugged") have tended towards a form of neoconservatism and the pro-affirmative liberals have tended to side with the radical left to form the "politically correct ideology" movement.

In this paper I will confine myself primarily to affirmative action policies with regard to race, but much of what I say can be applied to the areas of gender and ethnic minorities.

I. DEFINITIONS

First let me define my terms:

Discrimination is simply judging one thing to differ from another on the basis of some criterion. "Discrimination" is essentially a good quality, having reference to our ability to make distinctions. As rational and moral agents we need to make proper distinctions. To be rational is to discriminate between good and bad arguments, and to think morally is to discriminate between reasons based on valid principles and those based on invalid ones. What needs to be distinguished is the difference between rational and moral discrimination, on the one hand, and irrational and immoral discrimination, on the other hand.

Prejudice is a discrimination based on irrelevant grounds. It may simply be an attitude which never surfaces in action, or it may cause prejudicial actions. A prejudicial discrimination in action is immoral if it denies someone a fair deal. So discrimination on the basis of race or sex where these are not relevant for job performance is unfair. Likewise, one may act prejudicially in applying a relevant criterion on insufficient grounds, as in the case where I apply the criterion of being a hard worker but then assume, on insufficient evidence, that the black man who applies for the job is not a hard worker.

There is a difference between *prejudice* and *bias*. Bias signifies a tendency towards one thing rather than another where the evidence is incomplete or based on nonmoral factors. For example, you may have a bias towards blondes and I towards redheads. But prejudice is an attitude (or action) where unfairness is present— where one *should* know or do better, as in the case where I give people jobs simply because they are redheads. Bias implies ignorance or incomplete knowledge, whereas prejudice is deeper, involving a moral failure—usually a failure to pay attention to the evidence. But note that calling people racist or sexist without good evidence is also an act of prejudice. I call this form of prejudice "defamism," for it unfairly defames the victim. It is a contemporary version of McCarthyism.

Equal opportunity is offering everyone a fair chance at the best positions that society has at its disposal. Only native aptitude and effort should be decisive in the outcome, not factors of race, sex or special favors.

Affirmative action is the effort to rectify the injustice of the past by special policies. Put this way, it is Janus-faced or ambiguous, having both a backward-looking and a forward-looking feature. The backward-looking feature is its attempt to correct and compensate for past injustice. This aspect of affirmative action is strictly deontological. The forward-looking feature is its implicit ideal of a society free from prejudice; this is both deontological and utilitarian.

When we look at a social problem from a backward-looking perspective we need to determine who has committed or benefited from a wrongful or prejudicial act and to determine who deserves compensation for that act.

When we look at a social problem from a forward-looking perspective we need to determine what a just society (one free from prejudice) would look like and how to obtain that kind of society. The forward-looking aspect of affirmative action is paradoxically race-conscious, since it uses race to bring about a society which is not race-conscious, which is color-blind (in the morally relevant sense of this term).

It is also useful to distinguish two versions of affirmative action. *Weak affirmative action* involves such measures as the elimination of segregation (namely the idea of "separate but equal"), widespread advertisement to groups not previously represented in certain privileged positions, special scholarships for the disadvantaged classes (e.g., all the poor), using underrepresentation or a history of past discrimination as a tie breaker when candidates are relatively equal, and the like.

Strong affirmative action involves more positive steps to eliminate past injustice, such as reverse discrimination, hiring candidates on the basis of race and gender in order to reach equal or near equal results, proportionate representation in each area of society. . . .

[II.] Arguments for Affirmative Action

Let us now survey the main arguments typically cited in the debate over Affirmative Action. I will briefly discuss seven arguments on each side of the issue.

1. Need for Role Models

This argument is straightforward. We all have need for role models, and it helps to know that others like us can be successful. We learn and are encouraged to strive for excellence by emulating our heroes and role models.

However, it is doubtful whether role models of one's own racial or sexual type are necessary for success. One of my heroes was Gandhi, an Indian Hindu, another was my grade school science teacher, one Miss DeVoe, and another was Martin Luther King. More important than having role models of one's own type is having genuinely good people, of whatever race or gender, to emulate. Furthermore, even if it is of some help to people with low self-esteem to gain encouragement from seeing others of their particular kind in leadership roles, it is doubtful whether this need is a sufficient condition to justify preferential hiring or reverse discrimination. What good is a role model who is inferior to other professors or business personnel? Excellence will rise to the top in a system of fair opportunity. Natural development of role models will come more slowly and more surely. Proponents of preferential policies simply lack the patience to let history take its own course.

2. The Need of Breaking the Stereotypes

Society may simply need to know that there are talented blacks and women, so that it does not automatically assign them lesser respect or status. We need to have unjustified stereotype beliefs replaced with more accurate ones about the talents of blacks and women. So we need to engage in preferential hiring of qualified minorities even when they are not the most qualified.

Again, the response is that hiring the less qualified is neither fair to those better qualified who are passed over nor an effective way of removing inaccurate stereotypes. If competence is accepted as the criterion for hiring, then it is unjust to override it for purposes of social engineering. Furthermore, if blacks or women are known to hold high positions simply because of reverse discrimination, then they will still lack the respect due to those of their rank. In New York City there is a saying among doctors, "Never go to a black physician under 40," referring to the fact that affirmative action has affected the medical system during the past fifteen years. The police use "Quota Cops" and "Welfare Sergeants" to refer to those hired without passing the standardized tests. (In 1985, 180 black and Hispanic policemen, who had failed a promotion test, were promoted anyway to the rank of sergeant.) The destruction of false stereotypes will come naturally as qualified blacks rise naturally in fair competition (or if it does not—then the stereotypes may be justified). Reverse discrimination sends the message home that the stereotypes are deserved—otherwise, why do these minorities need so much extra help? RACISM

3. Equal Results Argument

Some philosophers and social scientists hold that human nature is roughly identical, so that on a fair playing field the same proportion from every race and gender and ethnic group would attain to the highest positions in every area of endeavor. It would follow that any inequality of results itself is evidence for inequality of opportunity. John Arthur, in discussing an intelligence test, Test 21, puts the case this way.

> History is important when considering governmental rules like Test 21 because low scores by blacks can be traced in large measure to the legacy of slavery and racism: segregation, poor schooling, exclusion from trade unions, malnutrition, and poverty have all played their roles. Unless one assumes that blacks are naturally less able to pass the test, the conclusion must be that the results are themselves socially and legally constructed, not a mere given for which law and society can claim no responsibility.
>
> The conclusion seems to be that genuine equality eventually requires equal results. Obviously blacks have been treated unequally throughout US history, and just as obviously the economic and psychological effects of that inequality linger to this day, showing up in lower income and poorer performance in school and on tests than whites achieve. Since we have no reason to believe that differences in performance can be explained by factors other than history, equal results are a good benchmark by which to measure progress made toward genuine equality.[1]

The result of a just society should be equal numbers in proportion to each group in the work force.

However, Arthur fails even to consider studies that suggest that there are innate differences between races, sexes, and groups. If there are genetic differences in intelligence and temperament within families, why should we not expect such differences between racial groups and the two genders? Why should the evidence for this be completely discounted?

Perhaps some race or one gender is more intelligent in one way than another. At present we have only limited knowledge about genetic differences, but what we do have suggests some difference besides the obvious physiological traits.[2] The proper use of this evidence is not to promote discriminatory policies but to be *open* to

the possibility that innate difference may have led to an overrepresentation of certain groups in certain areas of endeavor. It seems
that on average blacks have genetic endowments favoring them in
the development of skills necessary for excellence in basketball.

Furthermore, on Arthur's logic, we should take aggressive
affirmative action against Asians and Jews since they are over-represented in science, technology, and medicine. So that each group
receives its fair share, we should ensure that 12% of the philosophers in the United States are black, reduce the percentage of Jews
from an estimated 15% to 2%—firing about 1,300 jewish philosophers. The fact that Asians are producing 50% of Ph.D.'s in science
and math and blacks less than 1% clearly shows, on this reasoning,
that we are providing special secret advantages to Asians.

But why does society have to enter into this results game in the
first place? Why do we have to decide whether all difference is
environmental or genetic? Perhaps we should simply admit that
we lack sufficient evidence to pronounce on these issues with any
certainty—but if so, should we not be more modest in insisting on
equal results? Here is a thought experiment. Take two families of
different racial groups, Green and Blue. The Greens decide to have
only two children, to spend all their resources on them, to give
them the best education. The two Green kids respond well and end
up with achievement test scores in the 99th percentile. The Blues
fail to practice family planning. They have 15 children. They can
only afford 2 children, but lack of ability or whatever prevents
them from keeping their family down. Now they need help for
their large family. Why does society have to step in and help them?
Society did not force them to have 15 children. Suppose that the
achievement test scores of the 15 children fall below the 25th percentile. They cannot compete with the Greens. But now enters AA.
It says that it is society's fault that the Blue children are not as able
as the Greens and that the Greens must pay extra taxes to enable
the Blues to compete. No restraints are put on the Blues regarding
family size. This seems unfair to the Greens. Should the Green children be made to bear responsibility for the consequences of the
Blues' voluntary behavior?

My point is simply that Arthur needs to cast his net wider and
recognize that demographics and childbearing and -rearing practices are crucial factors in achievement. People have to take some
responsibility for their actions. The equal results argument (or
axiom) misses a greater part of the picture.

4. The Compensation Argument

The argument goes like this: blacks have been wronged and severely harmed by whites. Therefore white society should compensate blacks for the injury caused them. Reverse discrimination in terms of preferential hiring, contracts, and scholarships is a fitting way to compensate for the past wrongs.

This argument actually involves a distorted notion of compensation. Normally, we think of compensation as owed by a specific person A to another person B whom A has wronged in a specific way C. For example, if I have stolen your car and used it for a period of time to make business profits that would have gone to you, it is not enough that I return your car. I must pay you an amount reflecting your loss and my ability to pay. If I have only made $5,000 and only have $10,000 in assets, it would not be possible for you to collect $20,000 in damages—even though that is the amount of loss you have incurred.

Sometimes compensation is extended to groups of people who have been unjustly harmed by the greater society. For example, the United States government has compensated the Japanese-Americans who were interred during the Second World War, and the West German government has paid reparations to the survivors of Nazi concentration camps. But here a specific people have been identified who were wronged in an identifiable way by the government of the nation in question.

On the face of it the demand by blacks for compensation does not fit the usual pattern. Perhaps Southern states with Jim Crow laws could be accused of unjustly harming blacks, but it is hard to see that the United States government was involved in doing so. Furthermore, it is not clear that all blacks were harmed in the same way or whether some were *unjustly* harmed or harmed more than poor whites and others (e.g., short people). Finally, even if identifiable blacks were harmed by identifiable social practices, it is not clear that most forms of Affirmative Action are appropriate to restore the situation. The usual practice of a financial payment seems more appropriate than giving a high level job to someone unqualified or only minimally qualified, who, speculatively, might have been better qualified had he not been subject to racial discrimination. If John is the star tailback of our college team with a promising professional future and I accidentally (but culpably) drive my pick-up truck over his legs, and so cripple him, John may be due compensation, but he is not due the tailback spot on the football team.

Still, there may be something intuitively compelling about compensating members of an oppressed group who are minimally qualified. Suppose that the Hatfields and the McCoys are enemy clans and some youths from the Hatfields go over and steal diamonds and gold from the McCoys, distributing it within the Hatfield economy. Even though we do not know which Hatfield youths did the stealing, we would want to restore the wealth, as far as possible, to the McCoys. One way might be to tax the Hatfields, but another might be to give preferential treatment in terms of scholarships and training programs and hiring to the McCoys.[3]

This is perhaps the strongest argument for affirmative action, and it may well justify some weak versions of affirmative action, but it is doubtful whether it is sufficient to justify strong versions with quotas and goals and time tables in skilled positions. There are at least two reasons for this. First, we have no way of knowing how many people of group G would have been at competence level L had the world been different. Secondly, the normal criterion of competence is a strong prima facie consideration when the most important positions are at stake. There are two reasons for this: (1) society has given people expectations that if they attain certain levels of excellence they will be awarded appropriately and (2) filling the most important positions with the best-qualified is the best way to insure efficiency in job-related areas and in society in general. These reasons are not absolutes. They can be overridden. But there is a strong presumption in their favor so that a burden of proof rests with those who would override them.

At this point we get into the problem of whether innocent non-blacks should have to pay a penalty in terms of preferential hiring of blacks. We turn to that argument.

5. Compensation from Those Who Innocently Benefited from Past Injustice

White males as innocent beneficiaries of unjust discrimination of blacks and women have no grounds for complaint when society seeks to rectify the tilted field. White males may be innocent of oppressing blacks and minorities (and women), but they have unjustly benefited from that oppression or discrimination. So it is perfectly proper that less qualified women and blacks be hired before them.

The operative principle is: He who knowingly and willingly benefits from a wrong must help pay for the wrong. Judith Jarvis Thomson puts it this way. "Many [white males] have been direct beneficiaries of policies which have down-graded blacks and women . . . and even those who did not directly benefit . . . had, at any rate, the advantage in the competition which comes of the confidence in one's full membership [in the community], and of one's right being recognized as a matter of course."[4] That is, white males obtain advantages in self-respect and self-confidence deriving from a racist system which denies these to blacks and women.

Objection. As I noted in the previous section, compensation is normally individual and specific. If *A* harms *B* regarding *x*, *B* has a right to compensation from *A* in regards to x. If *A* steals *B*'s car and wrecks it, *A* has an obligation to compensate *B* for the stolen car, but *A*'s son has no obligation to compensate *B*. Furthermore, if *A* dies or disappears, *B* has no moral right to claim that society compensate him for the stolen car—though if he has insurance, he can make such a claim to the insurance company. Sometimes a wrong cannot be compensated, and we just have to make the best of an imperfect world.

Suppose my parents, divining that I would grow up to have an unsurpassable desire to be a basketball player, bought an expensive growth hormone for me. Unfortunately, a neighbor stole it and gave it to little Lew Alcindor, who gained the extra 18 inches—my 18 inches—and shot up to an enviable 7 feet 2 inches. Alias Kareem Abdul Jabbar, he excelled in basketball, as I would have done had I had my proper dose.

Do I have a right to the millions of dollars that Jabbar made as a professional basketball player—the unjustly innocent beneficiary of my growth hormone? I have a right to something from the neighbor who stole the hormone, and it might be kind of Jabbar to give me free tickets to the Laker basketball games, and perhaps I should be remembered in his will. As far as I can see, however, he does not owe me anything, either legally or morally.

Suppose further that Lew Alcindor and I are in high school together and we are both qualified to play basketball, only he is far better than I. Do I deserve to start in his position because I would have been as good as he is had someone not cheated me as a child? Again, I think not. But if being the lucky beneficiary of wrongdoing does not entail that Alcindor (or the coach) owes me anything in regards to basketball, why should it be a reason to engage in preferential hiring in academic positions or highly coveted jobs? If minimal qualifications are not adequate to override excellence in basketball, even when the minimality is a consequence of wrongdoing, why should they be adequate in other areas?

6. The Diversity Argument

It is important that we learn to live in a pluralistic world, learning to get along with those of other races and cultures, so we should have fully integrated schools and employment situations. Diversity is an important symbol and educative device. Thus preferential treatment is warranted to perform this role in society.

But, again, while we can admit the value of diversity, it hardly seems adequate to override considerations of merit and efficiency. Diversity for diversity's sake is moral promiscuity, since it obfuscates rational distinctions, and unless those hired are highly qualified the diversity factor threatens to become a fetish. At least at the higher levels of business and the professions, competence far outweighs considerations of diversity. I do not care whether the group of surgeons operating on me reflect racial or gender balance, but I do care that they are highly qualified. And likewise with airplane pilots, military leaders, business executives, and, may I say it, teachers and professors. Moreover, there are other ways of learning about other cultures besides engaging in reverse discrimination.

7. Anti-Meritocratic (Desert) Argument to Justify Reverse Discrimination: "No One Deserves His Talents"

According to this argument, the competent do not deserve their intelligence, their superior character, their industriousness, or their discipline; therefore they have no right to the best positions in society; therefore society is not unjust in giving these positions to less (but still minimally) qualified blacks and women. In one form this argument holds that since no one deserves anything, society may use any criteria it pleases to distribute goods. The criterion most often designated is social utility. Versions of this argument are found in the writings of John Arthur, John Rawls, Bernard Boxill, Michael Kinsley, Ronald Dworkin, and Richard Wasserstrom. Rawls writes, "No one deserves his place in the distribution of native endowments, any more than one deserves one's initial starting place in society. The assertion that a man deserves the superior character that enables him to make the effort to cultivate his abilities is equally problematic; for his character depends in large part upon fortunate family and social circumstances for which he can claim no credit. The notion of desert seems not to apply to these cases."[5] Michael Kinsley is even more adamant:

> Opponents of affirmative action are hung up on a distinction that seems more profoundly irrelevant: treating individuals versus treating groups. What is the moral difference between dispensing favors to people on their "merits" as individuals and passing out society's benefits on the basis of group identification?
>
> Group identifications like race and sex are, of course, immutable. They have nothing to do with a person's moral worth. But the same is true of most of what comes under the label "merit." The tools you need for getting ahead in a meritocratic society—not all of them but most: talent, education, instilled cultural values such as ambition—are distributed just as arbitrarily as skin color. They are fate. The notion that people somehow "deserve" the advantages of these characteristics in a way they don't "deserve" the advantage of their race is powerful, but illogical.[6]

It will help to put the argument in outline form.

1. Society may award jobs and positions as it sees fit as long as individuals have no claim to these positions.
2. To have a claim to something means that one has earned it or deserves it.
3. But no one has earned or deserves his intelligence, talent, education, or cultural values which produce superior qualifications.
4. If a person does not deserve what produces something, he does not deserve its products.
5. Therefore better qualified people do not deserve their qualifications.
6. Therefore, society may override their qualifications in awarding jobs and positions as it sees fit (for social utility or to compensate for previous wrongs).

So it is permissible if a minimally qualified black or woman is admitted to law or medical school ahead of a white male with excellent credentials or if a less qualified person from an "under-utilized" group gets a professorship ahead of a far better qualified white male. Sufficiency and underutilization together outweigh excellence.

Objection. Premise 4 is false. To see this, reflect that just because I do not deserve the money that I have been given as a gift (for instance) does not mean that I am not entitled to what I get with that money. If you and I both get a gift of $100 and I bury mine in the sand for five years while you invest yours wisely and double its value at the end of five years, I cannot complain that you should split the increase 50/50 since neither of us deserved the original gift. If we accept the notion of responsibility at all, we must hold that persons deserve the fruits of their labor and conscious choices. Of course, we might want to distinguish moral from legal desert and argue that, morally speaking, effort is more important than outcome, whereas, legally speaking, outcome may be more important. Nevertheless, there are good reasons in terms of efficiency, motivation, and rough justice for holding a strong prima facie principle of giving scarce high positions to those most competent.

The attack on moral desert is perhaps the most radical move that egalitarians like Rawls and company have made against meritocracy, but the ramifications of their attack are far-reaching. The following are some of its implications. Since I do not deserve my two good eyes or two good kidneys, the social engineers may take one of each from me to give to those needing an eye or a kidney—even if they have damaged their organs by their own voluntary actions. Since no one deserves anything, we do not deserve pay for our labors or praise for a job well done or first prize in the race we win. The notion of moral responsibility vanishes in a system of levelling.

But there is no good reason to accept the argument against desert. We do act freely and, as such, we are responsible for our actions. We deserve the fruits of our labor, reward for our noble feats and punishment for our misbehavior.

We have considered seven arguments for affirmative action and have found no compelling case for strong affirmative action and only one plausible argument (a version of the compensation argument) for weak affirmative action. We must now turn to the arguments against affirmative action to see whether they fare any better.[7]

[III.] ARGUMENTS AGAINST AFFIRMATIVE ACTION

1. Affirmative Action Requires Discrimination against a Different Group

Weak affirmative action weakly discriminates against new minorities, mostly innocent young white males, and strong affirmative action strongly discriminates against these new minorities. As I argued in II.5, this discrimination is unwarranted, since, even if some compensation to blacks were indicated, it would be unfair to make innocent white males bear the whole brunt of the payments. In fact, it is poor white youth who become the new pariahs on the job market. The children of the wealthy have no trouble getting into the best private grammar schools and, on the basis of superior early education, into the best universities, graduate schools, managerial and professional positions. Affirmative action simply shifts injustice, setting blacks and women against young white males, especially ethnic and poor white males. It does little to rectify the goal of providing equal opportunity to all. If the goal is a society where everyone has a fair chance, then it would be better to concentrate on support for families and early education and decide the matter of university admissions and job hiring on the basis of traditional standards of competence.

2. Affirmative Action Perpetuates the Victimization Syndrome

Shelby Steele admits that affirmative action may seem "the meagerest recompense for centuries of unrelieved oppression" and that it helps promote diversity. At the same time, though, notes Steele, affirmative action reinforces the spirit of victimization by telling blacks that they can gain more by emphasizing their suffering, degradation, and helplessness than by discipline and work. This message holds the danger of blacks becoming permanently handicapped by a need for special treatment. It also sends to society at large the message that blacks cannot make it on their own.

Leon Wieseltier sums up the problem this way.

> The memory of oppression is a pillar and a strut of the identity of every people oppressed. It is no ordinary marker of difference. It is unusually stiffening. It instructs the individual and the group

about what to expect of the world, imparts an isolating sense of aptness. . . . Don't be fooled, it teaches, there is only repetition. For that reason, the collective memory of an oppressed people is not only a treasure but a trap.

In the memory of oppression, oppression outlives itself. The scar does the work of the wound. That is the real tragedy: that injustice retains the power to distort long after it has ceased to be real. It is a posthumous victory for the oppressors, when pain becomes a tradition. And yet the atrocities of the past must never be forgotten. This is the unfairly difficult dilemma of the newly emancipated and the newly enfranchised: an honorable life is not possible if they remember too little and a normal life is not possible if they remember too much.[8]

With the eye of recollection, which does not "remember too much," Steele recommends a policy which offers "educational and economic development of disadvantaged people regardless of race and the eradication from our society—through close monitoring and severe sanctions—of racial and gender discrimination.[9]

3. Affirmative Action Encourages Mediocrity and Incompetence

Last Spring Jesse Jackson joined protesters at Harvard Law School in demanding that the Law School faculty hire black women. Jackson dismissed Dean of the Law School Robert C. Clark's standard of choosing the best qualified person for the job as "cultural anemia." "We cannot just define who is qualified in the most narrow vertical academic terms," he said. "Most people in the world are yellow, brown, black, poor, non-Christian and don't speak English, and they can't wait for some white male with archaic rules to appraise them."[10] It might be noted that if Jackson is correct about the depth of cultural decadence at Harvard, blacks might be well advised to form and support their own more vital law schools and leave places like Harvard to their archaism.

At several universities, the administration has forced departments to hire members of minorities even when far superior candidates were available. Shortly after obtaining my Ph.D. in the late '70s I was mistakenly identified as a black philosopher (I had a civil rights record and was once a black studies major) and was flown to a major university, only to be rejected for a more qualified candidate when it discovered that I was white.

Stories of the bad effects of affirmative action abound. The philosopher Sidney Hook writes that "At one Ivy League university, representatives of the Regional HEW demanded an explanation of why there were no women or minority students in the Graduate Department of Religious Studies. They were told that a reading knowledge of Hebrew and Greek was presupposed. Whereupon the representatives of HEW advised orally: 'Then end those old-fashioned programs that require irrelevant languages. And start up programs on relevant things which minority group students can study without learning languages.' "[11]

Nicholas Capaldi notes that the staff of HEW itself was one-half women, three-fifths members of minorities, and one-half black —a clear case of racial overrepresentation.

In 1972 officials at Stanford University discovered a proposal for the government to monitor curriculum in higher education: the "Summary Statement . . . Sex Discrimination Proposed HEW Regulation to Effectuate Title IX of the Education Amendment of 1972" to "establish and use internal procedure for reviewing curricula, designed both to ensure that they do not reflect discrimination on the basis of sex and to resolve complaints concerning allegations of such discrimination, pursuant to procedural standards to be prescribed by the Director of the office of Civil Rights." Fortunately, Secretary of HEW Caspar Weinberger, when alerted to the intrusion, assured Stanford University that he would never approve of it.[12]

Government programs of enforced preferential treatment tend to appeal to the lowest possible common denominator. Witness the 1974 HEW Revised Order No. 14 on affirmative action expectations for preferential hiring: "Neither minorities nor female employees should be required to possess higher qualifications than those of the lowest qualified incumbents."

Furthermore, no test may be given to candidates unless it is *proved* to be relevant to the job.

> No standard or criteria which have, by intent or effect, worked to exclude women or minorities as a class can be utilized, unless the institution can demonstrate the necessity of such standard to the performance of the job in question.
>
> Whenever a validity study is called for . . . the user should include . . . an investigation of suitable alternative selection procedures and suitable alternative methods of using the selection procedure which have as little adverse impact as possible. . . .

Whenever the user is shown an alternative selection procedure with evidence of less adverse impact and substantial evidence of validity for the same job in similar circumstances, the user should investigate it to determine the appropriateness of using or validating it in accord with these guidelines.[13]

At the same time Americans are wondering why standards in our country are falling and the Japanese are getting ahead. Affirmative action with its twin idols, Sufficiency and Diversity, is the enemy of excellence. I will develop this thought below (IV.6).

4. Affirmative Action Policies Unjustly Shift the Burden of Proof

Affirmative action legislation tends to place the burden of proof on the employer who does not have an "adequate"representation of "underutilized"groups in his work force. He is guilty until proven innocent. I have already recounted how in the mid-eighties the Supreme Court shifted the burden of proof back onto the plaintiff, while Congress is now attempting to shift the burden back to the employer. Those in favor of deeming disproportional representation "guilty until proven innocent" argue that it is easy for employers to discriminate against minorities by various subterfuges, and I agree that steps should be taken to monitor against prejudicial treatment. But being prejudiced against employers is not the way to attain a just solution to discrimination. The principle: innocent until proven guilty, applies to employers as well as criminals. Indeed, it is clearly special pleading to reject this basic principle of Anglo-American law in this case of discrimination while adhering to it everywhere else.

5. An Argument from Merit

Traditionally, we have believed that the highest positions in society should be awarded to those who are best qualified—as the Koran states in the quotation at the beginning of this paper. Rewarding excellence both seems just to the individuals in the competition and makes for efficiency. Note that one of the most successful acts of integration, the recruitment of Jackie Robinson in the late 40s, was done in just this way, according to merit. If Robinson had been brought into the major league as a mediocre player or had batted

.200, he would have been scorned and sent back to the minors where he belonged.

Merit is not an absolute value. There are times when it may be overridden for social goals, but there is a strong prima facie reason for awarding positions on its basis, and it should enjoy a weighty presumption in our social practices.

In a celebrated article Ronald Dworkin says that "Bakke had no case" because society did not owe Bakke anything. That may be, but then why does it owe anyone anything? Dworkin puts the matter in Utility terms, but if that is the case, society may owe Bakke a place at the University of California/Davis, for it seems a reasonable rule-utilitarian principle that achievement should be rewarded in society. We generally want the best to have the best positions, the best qualified candidate to win the political office, the most brilliant and competent scientist to be chosen for the most challenging research project, the best qualified pilots to become commercial pilots, only the best soldiers to become generals. Only when little is at stake do we weaken the standards and content ourselves with sufficiency (rather than excellence)—there are plenty of jobs where "sufficiency" rather than excellence is required. Perhaps we now feel that medicine or law or university professorships are so routine that they can be performed by minimally qualified people—in which case affirmative action has a place.

But note, no one is calling for quotas or proportional representation of *underutilized* groups in the National Basketball Association where blacks make up 80 percent of the players. But if merit and merit alone reigns in sports, should it not be valued at least as much in education and industry?

6. The Slippery Slope

Even if strong affirmative action or reverse discrimination could meet the other objections, it would face a tough question: once you embark on this project, how do you limit it? Who should be excluded from reverse discrimination? Asians and Jews are over-represented, so if we give blacks positive quotas, should we place negative quotas to these other groups? Since white males, "WMs," are a minority which is suffering from reverse discrimination, will we need a new affirmative action policy in the twenty-first century to compensate for the discrimination against WMs in the late twentieth century?

Furthermore, affirmative action has stigmatized the *young* white male. Assuming that we accept reverse discrimination, the fair way to make sacrifices would be to retire *older* white males who are more likely to have benefited from a favored status. Probably the least guilty of any harm to minority groups is the young white male—usually a liberal who has been required to bear the brunt of ages of past injustice. Justice Brennan's announcement that the Civil Rights Act did not apply to discrimination against whites shows how the clearest language can be bent to serve the ideology of the moment.[14]

7. The Mounting Evidence against the Success of Affirmative Action

Thomas Sowell of the Hoover Institute has shown in his book *Preferential Policies: An International Perspective* that preferential hiring almost never solves social problems. It generally builds in mediocrity or incompetence and causes deep resentment. It is a short-term solution which lacks serious grounding in social realities.

For instance, Sowell cites some disturbing statistics on education. Although twice as many blacks as Asian students took the nationwide Scholastic Aptitude Test in 1983, approximately fifteen times as many Asian students scored above 700 (out of a possible 800) on the mathematics half of the SAT. The percentage of Asians who scored above 700 in math was also more than six times higher than the percentage of American Indians and more than ten times higher than that of Mexican Americans—as well as more than double the percentage of whites. As Sowell points out, in all countries studied, "intergroup performance disparities are huge."

> There are dozens of American colleges and universities where the median combined verbal SAT score and mathematics SAT score total 1200 or above. As of 1983 there were less than 600 black students in the entire United States with combined SAT scores of 1200. This meant that, despite widespread attempts to get a black student "representation" comparable to the black percentage of the population (about 11 percent), there were not enough black students in the entire country for the Ivy League alone to have such a "representation without going beyond this pool—even if the entire pool went to the eight Ivy League colleges.[15]

Often it is claimed that a cultural bias is the cause of the poor performance of blacks on SAT (or IQ tests), but Sowell shows that these test scores are actually a a better predictor of college performance for blacks than for Asians and whites. He also shows the harmfulness of the effect on blacks of preferential acceptance. At the University of California, Berkeley, where the freshman class closely reflects the actual ethnic distribution of California high school students, more than 70 percent of blacks fail to graduate. All 312 black students entering Berkeley in 1987 were admitted under "affirmative action" criteria rather than by meeting standard academic criteria. So were 480 out of 507 Hispanic students. In 1986 the median SAT score for blacks at Berkeley was 952, for Mexican Americans 1014, for American Indians 1082 and for Asian Americans 1254. (The average SAT for all students was 1181.)

The result of this mismatching is that blacks who might do well if they went to a second tier or third tier school where their test scores would indicate they belong, actually are harmed by preferential treatment. They cannot compete in the institutions where high abilities are necessary.

Sowell also points out that affirmative action policies have mainly assisted the middle class black, those who have suffered least from discrimination. "Black couples in which both husband and wife are college-educated overtook white couples of the same description back in the early 1970s and continued to at least hold their own in the 1980s."

Sowell's conclusion is that similar patterns of results obtained from India to the United States wherever preferential policies exist. "In education, preferential admissions policies have led to high attrition rates and substandard performances for those preferred students . . . who survived to graduate." In all countries the preferred tended to concentrate in less difficult subjects which lead to less remunerative careers. "In the employment market, both blacks and untouchables at the higher levels have advanced substantially while those at the lower levels show no such advancement and even some signs of retrogression. These patterns are also broadly consistent with patterns found in countries in which majorities have created preferences for themselves. . . ."

The tendency has been to focus at the high level end of education and employment rather than on the lower level of family structure and early education. But if we really want to help the worst off improve, we need to concentrate on the family and early education. It is foolish to expect equal results when we begin with grossly unequal starting points—and discriminating against young white males is no more just than discriminating against women, blacks, or anyone else.

CONCLUSION

Let me sum up. The goal of the civil rights movement and of moral people everywhere has been equal opportunity. The question is: how best to get there. Civil rights legislation removed the legal barriers to equal opportunity, but did not tackle the deeper causes that produced differential results. Weak affirmative action aims at encouraging minorities in striving for the highest positions without unduly jeopardizing the rights of majorities, but the problem of weak affirmative action is that it easily slides into strong affirmative action where quotas, "goals," and equal results are forced into groups, thus promoting mediocrity, inefficiency, and resentment. Furthermore affirmative action aims at the higher levels of society—universities and skilled jobs—yet if we want to improve our society, the best way to do it is to concentrate on families, children, early education, and the like. Affirmative action is, on the one hand, too much, too soon and on the other hand, too little, too late.

Martin Luther said that humanity is like a man mounting a horse who always tends to fall off on the other side of the horse. This seems to be the case with affirmative action. Attempting to redress the discriminatory iniquities of our history, our well-intentioned social engineers engage in new forms of discriminatory iniquity and thereby think that they have successfully mounted the horse of racial harmony. They have only fallen off on the other side of the issue.[16]

NOTES

1. John Arthur, *The Unfinished Constitution* (Belmont, Calif., 1990), p. 238.

2. See Phillip E. Vernon's excellent summary of the literature in *Intelligence: Heredity and Environment* (New York, 1979) and Yves Christen "Sex Differences in the Human Brain" in Nicholas Davidson (ed.), *Gender*

Sanity (Lanham, 1989), and T. Bouchard et al., "Sources of Human Psychological Differences: The Minnesota Studies of Twins Reared Apart," *Science,* vol. 250 (1990).

3. See Michael Levin, "Is Racial Discrimination Special?" *Policy Review,* Fall issue (1982).

4. Judith Jarvis Thomson, "Preferential Hiring" in Marshall Cohen, Thomas Nagel and Thomas Scanlon (eds.), *Equality and Preferential Treatment* (Princeton, 1977).

5. John Rawls, *A Theory of Justice* (Cambridge, 1971), p. 104; See Richard Wasserstrom "A Defense of Programs of Preferential Treatment," *National Forum* (Phi Kappa Phi Journal), vol. 58 (1978). See also Bernard Boxill, "The Morality of Preferential Hiring," *Philosophy and Public Affairs,* vol. 7 (1978).

6. Michael Kinsley, "Equal Lack of Opportunity," *Harper's,* June issue (1983).

7. There is one other argument which I have omitted. It is from precedence and has been stated by Judith Jarvis Thomson in the article cited earlier:

> Suppose two candidates for a civil service job have equally good test scores, but there is only one job available. We could decide between them by coin-tossing. But in fact we do allow for declaring for *A* straightaway, where *A* is a veteran, and *B* is not. It may be that *B* is a non-veteran through no fault of his own. . . . Yet the fact is that *B* is not a veteran and *A* is. On the assumption that the veteran has served his country, the country owes him something. And it is plain that giving him preference is not an unjust way in which part of that debt of gratitude can be paid (p. 379f).

The two forms of preferential hiring are analogous. Veteran's preference is justified as a way of paying a debt of gratitude, preferential hiring is a way of paying a debt of compensation. In both cases innocent parties bear the burden of the community's debt, but it is justified.

My response to this argument is that veterans should not be hired in place of better qualified candidates, but that benefits like the GI scholarships are part of the contract with veterans who serve their country in the armed services. The notion of compensation only applies to individuals who have been injured by identifiable entities. So the analogy between veterans and minority groups seems weak.

8. Quoted in Jim Sleeper, *The Closest of Strangers* (New York, 1990), p. 209.

9. Shelby Steele, "A Negative Vote on Affirmative Action," *New York Times,* May 13,1990.

10. *New York Times,* May 10, 1990.

11. Nicholas Capaldi, *Out of Order: Affirmative Action and the Crisis of Doctrinaire Liberalism* (Amherst, N.Y.: Prometheus Books, 1985), p. 85.

12. Ibid., p. 95.

13. Ibid.

14. The extreme form of this New Speak is incarnate in the Politically Correct Movement ("PC" ideology) where a new orthodoxy has emerged, condemning white, European culture and seeing African culture as the new savior of us all. Perhaps the clearest example of this is Paula Rothenberg's book *Racism and Sexism* (New York, 1987) which asserts that there is no such thing as black racism; only whites are capable of racism (p. 6). Ms. Rothenberg's book has been scheduled as required reading for all freshmen at the University of Texas. See Joseph Salemi, "Lone Star Academic Politics," no. 87 (1990).

15. Thomas Sowell, *Preferential Policies: An International Perspective* (New York: Morrow, 1990), p. 108.

16. I am indebted to Jim Landesman, Michael Levin, and Abigail Rosenthal for comments on a previous draft of this paper. I am also indebted to Nicholas Capaldi's *Out of Order* for first making me aware of the extent of the problem of affirmative action.

12

A DEFENSE OF PROGRAMS
OF PREFERENTIAL TREATMENT

Richard Wasserstrom

Many justifications of programs of preferential treatment depend upon the claim that in one respect or another such programs have good consequences or that they are effective means by which to bring about some desirable end, e.g., an integrated, equalitarian society. I mean by "programs of preferential treatment" to refer to programs such as those at issue in the *Bakke* case —programs which set aside a certain number of places (for example, in a law school) as to which members of minority groups (for example, persons who are non-white or female) who possess certain minimum qualifications (in terms of grades and test scores) may be preferred for admission to those places over some members of the majority group who possess higher qualifications (in terms of grades and test scores).

Many criticisms of programs of preferential treatment claim that such programs, even if effective, are unjustifiable because they are in some important sense unfair or unjust. In this paper I present a limited defense of such programs by showing that two of the chief arguments offered for the unfairness or injustice of these programs do not work in the way or to the degree supposed by critics of these programs.

The first argument is this. Opponents of preferential treatment

Reprinted from *National Forum: The Phi Kappa Phi Journal* 58, no. 1 (Winter 1978): 15–18. Copyright ©1978 by Richard Wasserstrom. By permission of the publishers.

programs sometimes assert that proponents of these programs are guilty of intellectual inconsistency, if not racism or sexism. For, as is now readily acknowledged, at times past employers, universities, and many other social institutions did have racial or sexual quotas (when they did not practice overt racial or sexual exclusion), and many of those who were most concerned to bring about the eradication of those racial quotas are now untroubled by the new programs which reinstitute them. And this, it is claimed, is inconsistent. If it was wrong to take race or sex into account when blacks and women were the objects of racial and sexual policies and practices of exclusion, then it is wrong to take race or sex into account when the objects of the policies have their race or sex reversed. Simple considerations of intellectual consistency—of what it means to give racism or sexism as a reason for condemning these social policies and practices—require that what was a good reason then is still a good reason now.

The problem with this argument is that despite appearances, there is no inconsistency involved in holding both views. Even if contemporary preferential treatment programs which contain quotas are wrong, they are not wrong for the reasons that made quotas against blacks and women pernicious. The reason why is that the social realities do make an enormous difference. The fundamental evil of programs that discriminated against blacks or women was that these programs were a part of a larger social universe which systematically maintained a network of institutions which unjustifiably concentrated power, authority, and goods in the hands of white male individuals, and which systematically consigned blacks and women to subordinate positions in the society.

Whatever may be wrong with today's affirmative action programs and quota systems, it should be clear that the evil, if any, is just not the same. Racial and sexual minorities do not constitute the dominant social group. Nor is the conception of who is a fully developed member of the moral and social community one of an individual who is either female or black. Quotas which prefer women or blacks do not add to an already relatively overabundant supply of resources and opportunities at the disposal of members of these groups in the way in which the quotas of the past did maintain and augment the overabundant supply of resources and opportunities already available to white males.

The same point can be made in a somewhat different way. Sometimes people say that what was wrong, for example, with the system of racial discrimination in the South was that it took an irrelevant characteristic, namely race, and used it systematically to allocate social benefits and burdens of various sorts. The defect was the irrelevance of the characteristic used—race—for that meant that individuals ended up being treated in a manner that was arbitrary and capricious.

I do not think that was the central flaw at all. Take, for instance, the most hideous of the practices, human slavery. The primary thing that was wrong with the institution was not that the particular individuals who were assigned the place of slaves were assigned there arbitrarily because the assignment was made in virtue of an irrelevant characteristic, their race. Rather, it seems to me that the primary thing that was and is wrong with slavery is the practice itself—the fact of some individuals being able to own other individuals and all that goes with that practice. It would not matter by what criterion individuals were assigned; human slavery would still be wrong. And the same can be said for most if not all of the other discrete practices and institutions which comprised the system of racial discrimination even after human slavery was abolished. The practices were unjustifiable—they were oppressive—and they would have been so no matter how the assignment of victims had been made. What made it worse, still, was that the institutions and the supporting ideology all interlocked to create a system of human oppression whose effects on those living under it were as devastating as they were unjustifiable.

Again, if there is anything wrong with the programs of preferential treatment that have begun to flourish within the past ten years, it should be evident that the social realities in respect to the distribution of resources and opportunities make the difference. Apart from everything else, there is simply no way in which all of these programs taken together could plausibly be viewed as capable of relegating white males to the kind of genuinely oppressive status characteristically bestowed upon women and blacks by the dominant social institutions and ideology.

The second objection is that preferential treatment programs are wrong because they take race or sex into account rather than the only thing that does matter—that is, an individual's qualifications. What all such programs have in common and what makes them all objectionable, so this argument goes, is that they ignore the persons who are more qualified by bestowing a preference on those who are less qualified in virtue of their being either black or female.

There are, I think, a number of things wrong with this objection based on qualifications, and not the least of them is that we do not live in a society in which there is even the serious pretense of a qualification requirement for many jobs of substantial power and authority. Would anyone claim, for example, that the persons who comprise the judiciary are there because they are the most qualified lawyers or the most qualified persons to be judges? Would anyone claim that Henry Ford II is the head of the Ford Motor Company because he is the most qualified person for the job? Part of what is wrong with even talking about qualifications and merit is that the argument derives some of its force from the erroneous notion that we would have a meritocracy were it not for programs of preferential treatment. In fact, the higher one goes in terms of prestige, power and the like, the less qualifications seem ever to be decisive. It is only for certain jobs and certain places that qualifications are used to do more than establish the possession of certain minimum competencies.

But difficulties such as these to one side, there are theoretical difficulties as well which cut much more deeply into the argument about qualifications. To begin with, it is important to see that there is a serious inconsistency present if the person who favors "pure qualifications" does so on the ground that the most qualified ought to be selected because this promotes maximum efficiency. Let us suppose that the argument is that if we have the most qualified performing the relevant tasks we will get those tasks done in the most economical and efficient manner. There is nothing wrong in principle with arguments based upon the good consequences that will flow from maintaining a social practice in a certain way. But it is inconsistent for the opponent of preferential treatment to attach much weight to qualifications on this ground, because it was an analogous appeal to the good consequences that the opponent of preferential treatment thought was wrong in the first place. That is to say, if the chief thing to be said in favor of strict qualifications and preferring the most qualified is that it is the most efficient way of getting things done, then we are right back to an assessment of the different consequences that will flow from different programs, and we are far removed from the considerations of justice or fairness that were thought to weigh so heavily against these programs.

It is important to note, too, that qualifications—at least in the educational context—are often not connected at all closely with any plausible conception of social effectiveness. To admit the most qualified students to law school, for example—given the way qualifications are now determined—is primarily to admit those who have the greatest chance of scoring the highest grades at law school. This says little about efficiency except perhaps that these students are the easiest for the faculty to teach. However, since we know so little about what constitutes being a good, or even successful lawyer, and even less about the correlation between being a very good law student and being a very good lawyer, we can hardly claim very confidently that the legal system will operate most effectively if we admit only the most qualified students to law school.

To be at all decisive, the argument for qualifications must be that those who are the most qualified deserve to receive the benefits (the job, the place in law school, etc.) because they are the most qualified. The introduction of the concept of desert now makes it an objection as to justice or fairness of the sort promised by the original criticism of the programs. But now the problem is that there is no reason to think that there is any strong sense of "desert" in which it is correct that the most qualified deserve anything.

Let us consider more closely one case, that of preferential treatment in respect to admission to college or graduate school. There is a logical gap in the inference from the claim that a person is most qualified to perform a task, e.g., to be a good student, to the conclusion that he or she deserves to be admitted as a student. Of course, those who deserve to be admitted should be admitted. But why do the most qualified deserve anything? There is simply no necessary connection between academic merit (in the sense of being the most qualified) and deserving to be a member of a student body. Suppose, for instance, that there is only one tennis court in the community. Is it clear that the two best tennis players ought to be the ones permitted to use it? Why not those who were there first? Or those who will enjoy playing the most? Or those who are the worst and, therefore, need the greatest opportunity to practice? Or those who have the chance to play least frequently?

We might, of course, have a rule that says that the best tennis players get to use the court before the others. Under such a rule the best players would deserve the court more than the poorer ones. But that is just to push the inquiry back one stage. Is there any reason to think that we ought to have a rule giving good tennis players such a preference? Indeed, the arguments that might be given for or against such a rule are many and varied. And few if any of the arguments that might support the rule would depend upon a connection between ability and desert.

Someone might reply, however, that the most able students deserve to be admitted to the university because all of their earlier schooling was a kind of competition, with university admission being the prize awarded to the winners. They deserve to be admitted because that is what the rule of the competition provides. In addition, it might be argued, it would be unfair now to exclude them in favor of others, given the reasonable expectations they developed about the way in which their industry and performance would be rewarded. Minority-admission programs, which inevitably prefer some who are less qualified over some who are more qualified, all possess this flaw.

There are several problems with this argument. The most substantial of them is that it is an empirically implausible picture of our social world. Most of what are regarded as the decisive characteristics for higher education have a great deal to do with things over which the individual has neither control nor responsibility: such things as home environment, socioeconomic class of parents, and, of course, the quality of the primary and secondary schools attended. Since individuals do not deserve having had any of these things vis-à-vis other individuals, they do not, for the most part, deserve their qualifications. And since they do not deserve their abilities they do not in any strong sense deserve to be admitted because of their abilities.

To be sure, if there has been a rule which connects, say, performance at high school with admission to college, then there is a weak sense in which those who do well at high school deserve, for that reason alone, to be admitted to college. In addition, if persons have built up or relied upon their reasonable expectations concerning performance and admission, they have a claim to be admitted on this ground as well. But it is certainly not obvious that these claims of desert are any stronger or more compelling than the competing claims based upon the needs of or advantages to women or blacks from programs of preferential treatment. And as I have indicated, all rule-based claims of desert are very weak unless and until the rule which creates the claim is itself shown to be a justified one. Unless one has a strong preference for the status quo, and unless one can defend that preference, the practice within a system of allocating places in a certain way does not go very far at all in showing that that is the right or the just way to allocate those places in the future.

A proponent of programs of preferential treatment is not at all committed to the view that qualifications ought to be wholly irrelevant. He or she can agree that, given the existing structure of any institution, there is probably some minimal set of qualifications without which one cannot participate meaningfully within the institution. In addition, it can be granted that the qualifications of those involved will affect the way the institution works and the way it affects others in the society. And the consequences will vary depending upon the particular institution. But all of this only establishes that qualifications, in this sense, are relevant, not that they are decisive. This is wholly consistent with the claim that race or sex should today also be relevant when it comes to matters such as admission to college or law school. And that is all that any preferential treatment program—even one with the kind of quote used in the *Bakke* case—has ever tried to do.

I have not attempted to establish that programs of preferential treatment are right and desirable. There are empirical issues concerning the consequences of these programs that I have not discussed, and certainly not settled. Nor, for that matter, have I considered the argument that justice may permit, if not require, these programs as a way to provide compensation or reparation for injuries suffered in the recent as well as distant past, or as a way to remove benefits that are undeservedly enjoyed by those of the dominant group. What I have tried to do is show that it is wrong to think that programs of preferential treatment are objectionable in the centrally important sense in which many past and present discriminatory features of our society have been and are racist and sexist. The social realities as to power and opportunity do make a fundamental difference. It is also wrong to think that programs of preferential treatment are in any strong sense either unjust or unprincipled. The case for programs of preferential treatment could, therefore, plausibly rest both on the view that such programs are not unfair to white males (except in the weak, rule-dependent sense described above) and on the view that it is unfair to continue the present set of unjust—often racist and sexist—institutions that comprise the social reality. And the case for these programs could rest as well on the proposition that, given the distribution of power and influence in the United States today, such programs may reasonably be viewed as potentially valuable, effective means by which to achieve admirable and significant social ideals of equality and integration.

13

IS RACIAL DISCRIMINATION SPECIAL?

Michael E. Levin

I take "reverse discrimination" to be the policy of favoring members of certain groups (usually racial), in situations in which merit has been at least ideally the criterion, on the grounds that *past* members of these groups have suffered discrimination. I do not include giving someone a job he was denied because *he* was discriminated against, since such redress is justified by ordinary canons of justice, in particular that of giving someone what he is owed. I am referring, rather, to the practice of hiring or admitting a present number of (e.g.) blacks regardless of whether the blacks so hired have be wronged, and regardless of the qualifications of competing whites. The difference between the two policies is that between restoring a robbery victim's property to him, and hunting up the descendants of robbery victims and giving them goods at the expense of people who themselves robbed no one. I have no quarrel with the former, many quarrels with the latter: I believe reverse discrimination is as ill-advised a course of action as any undertaken by this country in at least a century. It cannot be justified by its social benefits, since experience suggests that the consequences of this policy are proving disastrous. It cannot be justified as giving particular members of the chosen group what they would have gotten if they had not been discriminated against,

From *Journal of Value Inquiry* 15 (1981): 225–32. "Is Racial Discrimination Special?" by Michael E. Levin. Copyright © 1981 Martinus Nijhoff Publishers, The Hague, with kind permission from Kluwer Academic Publishers and the author.

since by stipulation "affirmative action" goes beyond such an appeal to ordinary ideas of justice and compensation. It penalizes a group of present-day whites—those who are at least as well qualified but passed over—without proof that they have discriminated or directly benefited from discrimination; whites no more responsible for past discrimination than anyone else.

But such frontal assaults on reverse discrimination (or "affirmative action," in bureaucratese) usually accomplish nothing, so I will not attempt one here. I will try instead to focus on a clear-cut issue which is central to the debate but which has, surprisingly, been almost completely ignored. It is this: what is so special about racial discrimination? Let me put the question more exactly. I will be arguing shortly that the only possible defense of reverse discrimination represents it as an attempt to rectify the consequences of past racial discrimination. But why has society selected one kind of wrong—discrimination—as particularly deserving or demanding rectification? Other past wrongs have left their traces—acts of theft, despoliation, fraud, anti-Semitism—yet society has no organized policy of rectifying those wrongs. It surely seems that if the consequences of one kind of wrong should not be allowed to unfold, neither should those of any other. And this is what I want to convince you of: acts of racial discrimination have no morally special status. Important consequences flow from this. For reasons I will propose, it seems to me clear that society—and in particular the employer—has no general standing obligation to block the consequences of past wrongs. So if discriminatory acts are no more deserving of rectification than wrong acts generally, no one is under any obligation at all to rectify them, or to be deprived so that these acts may be rectified.

With these preliminary points as background, let us look at the issue again. I noted that reverse discrimination discriminates against whites in a way which cannot be justified by ordinary notions of justice. Thus, if it is justifiable at all, it must be because we owe something to present-day blacks in some extraordinary sense. And the standard reason offered is that the blacks to be hired today bear the burdens of past discrimination. Had there been no racial discrimination, they would have been able to get those jobs; their qualifications would have been as good as those of the better-qualified whites they are displacing. (It is sometimes added that all whites benefit in some way from past discrimination, so all whites owe blacks something, namely a more advantageous position.) Affirmative action is supposed to rectify the consequences of past discrimination, to draw the sting from acts so bad that their consequences cannot be permitted to unfold.

But if our aim is to undo the consequences of past discrimination, the issue I raised becomes very pressing. If there is nothing morally special about discrimination, nothing which makes it especially deserving of rectification, any policy which treats discrimination as if it were morally special is arbitrary and irrational. Consider: Mr. X, a black of today, is supposedly owed special treatment. But surely if you owe Mr. X special treatment because his ancestors were the target of one wrong—discrimination—it would seem you owe Mr. Y special treatment if his ancestors were the target of some other wrong—theft, say. Racial discrimination is not the *only* wrong that can be committed against someone, and indeed it is far from the worst. I would rather be denied a job because I am Jewish than be murdered. My murderer violates my rights and handicaps my children much more seriously than someone who keeps me out of medical school. So the question is: if I owe Mr. X a job because his ancestors were discriminated against, don't I owe Mr. Y the same if his ancestors were defrauded? I believe the answer must be yes: there is nothing special about acts of discrimination. And even if you think I have misrepresented affirmative action or its rationale, the question and its answer are important. Other justifications for reverse discrimination also tend to treat racial discrimination as somehow special. Indeed, a quarter-century's preoccupation with race has created a sense that racial prejudice is not just a wrong but a sin, an inexpungeable blot on the soul. Whether this attitude is rational is an issue worth considering.

Let me start with a truism. Discrimination deserves to be halted where it exists, and redressed where it can be, because it is *wrong*. Discrimination is worth doing something about because wrongs are worth doing something about and discrimination is wrong. Once we grant this, we start to see that there is nothing *sui generis* about discrimination. It competes with other wrongs for righting. And I take it as obvious that some wrongs demand righting more urgently than others. If I pass a negative comment on Jones's tie in private but defame Robinson's ancestry on national television. I had better apologize to Robinson before I do so to Jones. And if I have embezzled the funds of an orphanage, top priority goes to seeing that I give the money back. Finally, if

Smith is destitute because I defrauded Smith's father, I had better make amends before I worry about the sons of men I insulted. So: denying a man a job on grounds of color is evidently just one among many ways of wronging him. It is far less egregious than assault or murder.

It is frequently but mistakenly claimed that racial discrimination is special because it involves a group. Certainly, an act of racial discrimination involves a whole group in the sense that it involves treating an individual not in his own right but insofar as he belongs to a group. But racial discrimination is not the only kind of act that is thus group-related. Many wrongs having nothing to do with race are discriminatory in the precise sense that they base the treatment of an individual on membership in a morally irrelevant group. Nepotism is discrimination against nonrelatives. When I make my lazy nephew district manager, I am disqualifying more able competitors because they belong to a group—nonfamily—membership in which should not count in the matter at hand. Discrimination need not be racial: any time you make a moral distinction on morally irrelevant grounds, you discriminate invidiously. In a society in which racial discrimination was unknown but capricious nepotism was the norm, denial of due process on grounds of family would provoke as much indignation as racial discrimination does now.

It would be sheer confusion to argue that acts of racial discrimination are special because they insult a whole race as well as wrong an individual. When I assault you, assault no one else—and when I discriminate against you, I discriminate against no one else. True, my discrimination may indicate a readiness to discriminate against others and may create widespread anxiety—but my assaulting you may indicate a readiness to assault others and create even greater general anxiety. If I bypass Mr. X because he is black, only Mr. X and his dependents suffer thereby. Perhaps because color is so salient a trait, we tend in uncritical moments to think of the black race as an entity existing in and of itself, above and beyond the particular blacks who make it up. Philosophers call this "reification." We then think that an insult to this reified race is particularly malign, either in itself or because this entity somehow transmits to all blacks the harm done by single acts of discrimination. Some such reasoning must underlie the oft-heard ideas that the harm done to a single black man "hurts blacks everywhere" and that the appointment of a black to the Supreme Court

is "a victory for blacks everywhere," remarks which make no literal sense. This tendency to reify is especially pernicious in the
context of compensation. Why are we willing to contemplate special treatment for blacks now, when we would not contemplate
special treatment for someone whose ancestors were defrauded by
a man who left no descendants? Because, I suspect, we think that
by benefiting today's black we will apologize for the long-ago
insult to the race, and that this apology and benefit will somehow
be transmitted back to the blacks who endured the original discrimination. Were this picture accurate, it might justify supposing
that past discriminatory acts cast longer shadows than other
wrongs. But it is just a myth. A racial grouping no more deserves
reification than does the class of people whose ancestors were
defrauded. We resist the impulse in the latter case only because the
trait in question is not visually salient and has no especially
coherent history.

(Some slight sense can be made of "injury to a group," as when
we say that a traitor endangers the security of a nation. But even
here the harm done is to individuals, the particular citizens. The
traitor deserves punishment because of the harm he has done to
each citizen, not to "the nation" as a thing apart.)

Perhaps the main reason for thinking of acts of racial discrimination as morally distinctive is that each is an instance of a pattern.
My discriminating against Mr. X is part of a self-sustaining pattern
of wrongs. And, indeed, we do find wrong acts that together form
a pattern more disturbing than each wrong act taken singly: Jack
the Ripper's legacy is more appalling than eleven isolated murders. Wrongs seem to be like notes, which have different musical
values when part of a melody than when heard in isolation. But
this intuition must be carefully assessed. A single wrong act cannot
be made *more wrong* because there is some other wrong act which
it resembles. If I discriminate against you, my act has a certain
amount of wrongness. If I then discriminate against someone else,
my previous act against you does not take on more wrongness.
This is so even with Jack the Ripper. His murder of the first prostitute did not become more wrong when he murdered his second. If
he had died before committing his second murder, his first murder
would still have been as bad as it actually was. If, say, he owed the
family of the first prostitute some compensation for his action, he
did not suddenly owe them more after his second. So the fact that
acts of discrimination come in groups does not show that a single

act of discrimination is any worse, any more deserving of rectification, than it would have been had it occurred alone.

Two factors account for our feeling that patterned wrongs are worse than isolated ones. The first is that the *perpetrator* of a patterned wrong is worse. Jack the Ripper is worse than a man who kills once from passion. But this does not mean that what he did, in each case, is worse than a single act of murder. Similarly, the most we can say of bigotry is that a habitual bigot is worse than a one-shot bigot, not that an act of bigotry is in itself worse than an act of caprice. The second reason patterned wrongs seem especially malign is that they create anxiety through their promise of repetition. Jack the Ripper's actions create more anxiety than eleven unconnected murders because we believe he will strike again. But this shows only that it is especially important to *halt patterns*, be they of murder or discrimination. It does not mean that a particular act in a discriminatory pattern is worse than it would have been in isolation. And it is worth repeating that antidiscrimination laws without benefit of affirmative action suffice to halt patterns of discrimination.

Granted, racial wrongs have gone beyond discrimination in hiring or the use of public facilities, extending all the way to lynching. But to acknowledge this is to bring racial wrongs under independent headings—denial of due process, assault, murder. Lynching Emmet Till was wrong not because Emmet Till was black, but because lynching is murder. So if blacks deserve special treatment because of (say) this country's history of lynching, it is because descendants of murder victims deserve special treatment. But this concedes my point: what was wrong about especially egregious acts of racial discrimination is what is wrong about parallel nonracial acts; and if we treat the former as special, we must treat the latter as special as well. I also deny that past discriminations were special because they were state-approved and in some case state-mandated. State sanction in itself can make no difference. Even if "the state" is an entity over and above its citizens and their legal relations, the wrongness of an act (although not the blameworthiness of an agent) is independent of who performs it. So if discriminating is wrong, it is wrong, and to the same extent, no matter who performs it. Therefore, state-sanctioned past discrimination is no stronger a candidate for rectification than any other discrimination. In any case, even if we did consider state sanction to be morally significant, to be consistent we would have to apply this to all other state-sanctioned wrongs. We would have to say, for example, that we ought to give special treatment now to descendants of people who were harmed under the terms of a statute repealed decades ago. But I take it that no one would support affirmative action for the grandchildren of brewmasters bankrupted by the Volstead Act.

Finally, it has been suggested that grave discriminatory wrongs, such as the lynching of Negroes, were special because done with the intention of intimidating the other members of the terrorized group. Quite so: but again this makes my very point. To call an act of lynching wrong for this reason is to bring it under the umbrella of *intimidation*: a precisely parallel nonracial act of intimidation is just as wrong (although we might have reason to think the perpetrator is not as vicious). Many years ago, unions were in the habit of wrecking restaurants that refused to be unionized as a warning to other restaurants. Even today, Mob enforcers will kill an informer, or a retailer who refuses to pay protection, in order to intimidate other potential informers or defaulters. So if we treat blacks as special because they belong to a class other members of which were terrorized, so must we treat restaurateurs as special, and indeed all small businessmen in businesses once victimized by the protection racket. And I take it that no one would suggest affirmative action for restaurateurs. Nor will it do to say that this is because today no restaurateur is in danger from union or Mob goons. In fact, a restaurateur is in considerably more danger than a black. The last lynching occurred in 1954, while union vandalism and criminal extortion are the stuff of today's sensational press.

A subsidiary point. I have so far let pass one peculiarity of affirmative action programs: they award jobs (or placement) to rectify past wrongs. Yet normally when we compensate someone for wrongful deprivation, we give him the equivalent of what he lost, giving him the thing itself only when feasible. If a pianist loses his hands through your negligence, you are not obliged to hire him to do a concert. The whole thrust of his complaint, after all, is that he is no longer competent to undertake such an enterprise. You owe him the money he would have made from concertizing, plus some monetary equivalent of the satisfaction your negligence has cost him. So *even if* past racial discrimination has wrongfully cost Mr. X a job, it does not follow that proper compensation is a job. What he is owed is the job or the monetary equivalent thereof. If the job is unavailable—where this normally includes Mr. X's not being the best-qualified applicant—all he is owed is its monetary equivalent. Why, then, is it assumed without question in so many quarters that if past discrimination has cost present-day blacks jobs, they deserve *jobs* rather than the monetary equivalent of the jobs they would have gotten? Only, I believe, because we think there is something *special* about discrimination, that its consequences deserve amelioration in a way that the consequences of other wrongs do not. Discrimination is so bad that not only must we compensate for it, we must so change the world that things will become as if the wrong had never been. Only by attributing such reasoning can I make sense of the special form "affirmative action" programs invariably take. And if indeed racial discrimination is not especially wrong, such special compensation starts to appear morally arbitrary and even bizarre.

It is obvious that no employer has a general obligation to rectify wrongful acts, to offer extraordinary compensation. I am not speaking, again, of righting wrongs he perpetrates or directly benefits from. I mean that if, as a result of some wrong once done—not necessarily to an ancestor—I am worse off than I would have been, you, an arbitrarily chosen employer, have no obligation whatever to neutralize the consequences of that wrong. No one has any obligation to make me as well off as I would have been had that wrong not been committed. Why? Basically because it is *impossible* to rectify the consequences of all past wrongs. Consider how we might decide on compensatory payments. We trace the world back to the moment at which the wrong was done, suppose the wrong not done, and hypothetically trace forward the history of the world. Where I end up under this hypothetical reconstruction is where I deserve to be. I am owed the net difference between where I am now and where I would have been had the wrong not been done. But for most wrongs, it would take omniscience to say how the world would have turned out had the wrong not been done. If you wanted to make up to me for the theft of my grandfather's watch in 1900, how on Earth do you propose to reckon the position I would have been in had my grandfather's watch not been stolen? I might have been richer by a watch. I might have been poorer— since, being in fact deprived of a watch, I have worked harder than I otherwise would have. I might not have existed—if my grandfather met my grandmother while hunting for his stolen watch. Indeed, if you suppose yourself under a general ameliorative obligation, you will have to calculate simultaneously how well off each and every one of us would have been had all past wrongs not occurred. There is more: I am supposedly owed a certain something, but who owes it to me? Surely not you—you don't owe me *all* of it. Do all employers owe me an equal proportion? Or is their proportion dependent on how much they have benefited from the initial theft? If the latter, how is one to calculate their debt, if the theft was in another country another century?

14

GOALS AND QUOTAS IN HIRING AND PROMOTION

Tom L. Beauchamp

Since the 1960s, government and corporate policies that set goals for hiring women and minorities have been sharply criticized. Their opponents maintain that many policies establish indefensible quotas and discriminate in reverse against sometimes more qualified white males. In 1991, President George Bush referred to the word "quota" as the "dreaded q-word." Quotas, he said, had "finally" been eliminated from government policies. Such opposition is understandable. No worker wants to lose a job to a less qualified person, and no employer wants to be restricted in its hiring and promotion by a quota.

Although some policies that set target goals and adopt quotas sometimes violate rules of fair and equal treatment, such policies can be justified. My objective in this paper is to defend policies that set goals and quotas. I argue that goals and quotas, rightly conceived, are congenial to management—not hostile as they are often depicted. Both the long-range interest of corporations and the public interest are served by carefully selected preferential policies.

Two Polar Positions

In 1965, President Lyndon Johnson issued an executive order that announced a toughened federal initiative requiring goals and timetables for equal employment opportunity.[1] This initiative was the prevailing regulatory approach for many years. But recently two competing schools of thought on the justifiability of preferential programs have come into sharp conflict, one mirroring the views of Bush, and the other mirroring those of Johnson.

The first school, like Bush, stands in opposition to quotas, accepting the view that all persons are entitled to an equal opportunity and to constitutional guarantees of equal protection in a color-blind, nonsexist society. Civil rights laws, in this approach, should offer protection only to individuals who have been victimized by forms of discrimination, not groups. Hiring goals, timetables, and quotas only work to create new victims of discrimination.

The second school, like Johnson, supports strong affirmative action policies. The justification of affirmative action programs is viewed as the correction of discriminatory employment practices, not group compensation for prior injustice. This second school views the first school as construing "equal opportunity" and "civil rights" so narrowly that persons affected by discrimination do not receive adequate aid in overcoming the effects of prejudice. This second school believes that mandated hiring protects minorities and erodes discrimination, whereas the identification of individual victims of discrimination would be, as the editors of the *New York Times* once put it, the "project of a century and [would] leave most victims of discrimination with only empty legal rights."[2]

These two schools may not be as far apart morally as they first appear. If legal enforcement of civil rights law could efficiently and comprehensively identify discriminatory treatment and could protect its victims, both schools would agree that the legal-enforcement strategy is preferable. But there are at least two reasons why this solution will not be accepted by the second school. First, there is the unresolved issue of whether those in contemporary society who have been advantaged by *past* discrimination (for example, wealthy owners of family businesses) deserve their advantages. Second, there is the issue of whether *present*, ongoing discrimination can be successfully, comprehensively, and fairly combatted by identifying and prosecuting violators without resorting to quotas.

This second issue is the more pivotal and is closely related to the justification of quotas.

A "quota," as used here, does not mean that fixed numbers of employees should be hired regardless of an individual's qualification for a position. Quotas are simply target employment percentages. In some cases a less qualified person may be hired or promoted; but it has never been a part of affirmative action to hire below the threshold of "basically qualified,"[3] and often significant questions exist in the employment situation about the exact qualifications needed for positions.[4] Quotas, then, are numerically expressible goals that one is obligated to pursue with good faith and due diligence. If it is impossible to hire the basically qualified persons called for by the goals in a given time frame, the schedule can be relaxed, as long as the target goals, the due diligence, and the good faith continue. The word *quota* does not mean "fixed number" in any stronger sense.

DATA ON DISCRIMINATION

Discrimination affecting hiring and promotion is not present everywhere in our society, but it is pervasive. An impressive body of statistics constituting prima facie evidence of discrimination has been assembled in recent years. It indicates that (1) women with identical credentials are promoted at approximately one-half the rate of their male counterparts; (2) 69% or more of the white-collar positions in the United States are held by women, but only approximately 10% of the management positions are held by women; (3) 87% of all professionals in the private business sector are of oriental origin, but they constitute only 1.3% of the management positions; (4) in the total U.S. population, 3 out of 7 employees hold white-collar positions, whereas the ratio is only 1 of 7 for blacks; (5) blacks occupy over 50% of the nation's jobs as garbage collectors and maids, but only 4% of the nation's management positions.[5]

Such statistics are not decisive indicators of discrimination, but additional facts also support the conclusion that racist and sexist biases powerfully influence the marketplace. Consider prevailing biases in real estate rentals and sales. Studies have shown that there is an 85% probability that blacks will encounter discrimination in rental housing and a 50% probability that blacks will suffer discrimination in purchasing a house and in applying for a mortgage; that blacks suffer more discrimination than other economically comparable minority groups; and that there may be as many as two million instances of discrimination in the housing market each year in the United States. One study indicates that approximately 80% of American residential neighborhoods in the largest 29 metropolitan areas remained entirely segregated from 1960 to 1980. Not socioeconomic status, but race, is the difference in real estate sales and loans.[6]

If we shift from housing to jobs, a similar pattern is found, especially for black males, for whom employment has become steadily more difficult in almost every sector from the mid-1970s through the early 1990s.[7] In 1985 the Grier Partnership and the Urban League produced independent studies that reveal striking disparities in the employment levels of college-trained blacks and whites in Washington, D.C., one of the best markets for blacks. Both studies found that college-trained blacks have much more difficulty than their white counterparts in securing employment. Both cite discrimination as the major underlying factor.[8]

A 1991 study by the Urban Institute is a powerful illustration of the problem. This study examined employment practices in Washington, D.C., and Chicago. Equally qualified, identically dressed white and black applicants for jobs were used to test for bias in the job market, as presented by newspaper advertised positions. Whites and blacks were matched identically for speech patterns, age, work experience, personal characteristics, and physical build. Investigators found repeated discrimination against black male applicants. The higher the position, the higher they found the level of discrimination to be. The white men received job offers three times more often than the equally qualified blacks who interviewed for the same position. The authors of the study concluded both that discrimination against black men is "widespread and entrenched" and that fears of reverse discrimination by white males are unfounded because the effects of discrimination more than offset any effects of reverse discrimination.[9]

These statistics help frame the significance of racial discrimination in the United States. Although much is now known about patterns of discrimination, much remains to be discovered, in part because it is hidden and subtle.

PROBLEMS OF PROOF AND INTENTION

We typically conceive racism and sexism as an intentional form of favoritism or exclusion, but major problems confronting American business and government arise from *unintended* institutional practices. Employees are frequently hired through a network that, without design, excludes women or minority groups. For example, hiring may occur through personal connections or by word of mouth, and layoffs may be entirely controlled by a seniority system. The actual hiring policies themselves may be racially and sexually neutral. Nonetheless, they can have an adverse effect on the ability of minorities in securing positions. There may be no intention to discriminate against anyone: nonetheless, the system has discriminatory consequences. In some cases, past discrimination that led to unfair hiring practices and an imbalanced work force is perpetuated even when there is no desire to perpetuate them.

In 1985 the U.S. Supreme Court unanimously held that persons may be guilty of discriminating against the handicapped when there is no "invidious animus, but rather [a discriminatory effect] of thoughtlessness and indifference—of benign neglect." The Court held that discrimination would be difficult and perhaps impossible to prevent if *intentional* discrimination alone qualified as discrimination.[10] Discrimination is still invisible to many who discriminate. This, in my judgment, is the main reason quotas are an indispensable government and management tool: They are the only way to break down old patterns of discrimination and thereby change the configuration of the workplace.

Courts in the United States have on a few occasions resorted to quotas because an employer had an intractable history and a bullheaded resistance to change that necessitated strong measures. The Supreme Court has never directly supported quotas using the term "quota,"[11] but it has upheld affirmative action programs that contain numerically expressed hiring formulas that are intended to reverse the patterns of both intentional and unintentional discrimination.[12] At the same time, the Supreme Court has suggested that some programs using these formulas have gone too far.[13] Whether the formulas are excessive depends on the facts in the individual case. From this perspective, there is no inconsistency between *Fullilove* v. *Klutznick* (1980), which allowed percentage set-asides for minority contractors, and *City of Richmond* v. *J. A. Croson Co.*

(1989), which disallowed certain set-asides. The later case of *Adarand Constructors Inc.* v. *Pena* (1995) defended a standard requiring that there be a compelling governmental interest for race-based preferences in construction contracts for minority-owned companies; it continued the long line of cases that weigh and balance different interests.

I believe the Supreme Court has consistently adhered to this balancing strategy and that it is the right moral perspective as well as the proper framework for American law.[14] Numerical goals or quotas should be implemented only when necessary to overcome the discriminatory impact of insensitive institutional policies and irrelevant criteria used for employment. Proposed formulas can be excessive here just as they can elsewhere.

Although I have distinguished between intentional practices and unintentional practices that have discriminatory impact, the two often work together. For example, the practices and framework of policies in a corporation may be nondiscriminatory, but those implementing the practices and policies may have discriminatory attitudes. Fair rules can easily be exploited or evaded by both personnel officers and unions, who often use criteria for hiring and promotion such as "self-confidence," "fitting in," "collegiality," and "personal appearance," among other superficial characteristics.[15]

Issues about the breadth and depth of discrimination may divide us as a society more than any other issue about affirmative action. If one believes there is but a narrow slice of surface discrimination, one is likely to agree with what I have called the first school. But if one believes discrimination is deeply, almost invisibly entrenched in our society, one is apt to agree with the second school. I have been arguing for the perspective taken by the second school, but this perspective needs to be specified to prevent it from assuming the same bullheaded insensitivity that it pretends to locate elsewhere. Discriminatory attitudes and practices are likely to be deep-seated in some institutions, while shallow or absent in others. Society is not monolithic in the depth and breadth of discrimination. In some cases affirmative action programs are not needed, in other cases only modest good faith programs are in order, and in still others enforced quotas are necessary to break down discriminatory patterns.

Because we deeply disagree about the depth, breadth, and embeddedness of discrimination, we disagree further over the social policies that will rid us of the problem. Those who believe discrimination is relatively shallow and detectable look for formulas and remedies that center on *equal opportunity*. Those who believe discrimination is deep, camouflaged, and embedded in society look for formulas that center on *measurable outcomes*.[16]

WHY CORPORATIONS SHOULD WELCOME GOALS AND QUOTAS

Little has been said to this point about corporate policy. I shall discuss only so-called *voluntary* programs that use target goals and quotas. They stand in sharp contrast to legally enforced goals and quotas, and there are at least three reasons why it is in the interest of responsible businesses to use aggressive plans that incorporate goals and quotas: (1) an improved workforce, (2) maintenance of a bias-free corporate environment, and (3) congeniality to managerial planning.

(1) First, corporations that discriminate will fail to look at the full range of qualified persons in the market and, as a result, will employ a higher percentage of second-best employees. The U.S. workforce is projected to be 80% women, minorities, and immigrants by the year 2000, and corporations are already reporting both that they are finding fewer qualified workers for available positions and that they have profited from vigorous, internally generated rules of nonracial, nonsexist hiring.[17] Hal Johnson, a senior vice-president at Travelers Cos., noted the benefits in adopting goals and quotas: "In [the 1990s] more of the work force is going to be minorities—Hispanics, blacks—and women. The companies that started building bridges back in the 1970s will be all right. Those that didn't won't."[18]

Goals and quotas that are properly conceived should yield superior, not inferior employees. No one would argue, for example, that baseball has poorer talent for dropping its color barrier. To find the best baseball talent, bridges had to be built that extended, for example, into the population of Puerto Rico. Businesses will be analogously improved if they extend their boundaries and provide proper training and diversity programs. Bill McEwen of the Monsanto Corporation and spokesperson for the National Association of Manufacturers (NAM) notes that this extension has long been happening at NAM companies:

We have been utilizing affirmative action plans for over 20 years. We were brought into it kicking and screaming. But over the past 20 years we've learned that there's a reservoir of talent out there, of minorities and women that we hadn't been using before. We found that [affirmative action] works.[19]

Maintaining a high quality workforce is consistent with the management style already implemented in many companies. For example, James R. Houghton, Chairman of Corning Glass, has established voluntary quotas to increase the quality of employees, not merely the number of women and black employees. Corning established the following increased-percentage targets for the total employment population to be met between 1988 and 1991: women professionals to increase from 17.4% to 23.2%, black professionals to increase from 5.1% to 7.4%, the number of black senior managers to increase from 1 to 5, and the number of women senior managers to increase from 4 to 10. Corning management interpreted the targets as follows: "Those numbers were not commandments set in stone. We won't hire people just to meet a number. It will be tough to meet some of [our targets]." Corning found that it could successfully recruit in accordance with these targets, but also found severe difficulty in maintaining the desired target numbers in the workforce because of an attrition problem. The company continues to take the view that in an age in which the percentage of white males in the employment pool is constantly declining, a "total quality company" must vigorously recruit women and minorities using target goals.[20]

A diverse workforce can, additionally, create a more positive employment environment and better serve its customers. An internal U S West study found that white males were ten times more likely to be promoted than minority women (black, Hispanic, and Asian). As a result, the company designed a plan to promote its female employees and to prepare employees for more demanding positions. U S West adopted the view that a diverse group of employees is better suited to develop new and creative ideas than a homogeneous group that approaches problems from a similar perspective and that racial and sexual patterns of discrimination in hiring have to be combatted by target-driven hiring programs. They therefore targeted "Women of Color" for training and promotion.[21]

Many corporations have found that vigorous affirmative action has economic and not only social benefits. Diversity in the workforce produces diversity of ideas, different perspectives on strategic planning, and improved, more open personnel policies. As a result, as the director of personnel at Dow Chemical puts it, "If anything there is [in the corporate world] a new push on affirmative action plans because of the increasing numbers of women and minorities entering the workforce."[22]

(2) Second, pulling the foundations from beneath affirmative-action hiring would open old wounds in many municipalities and corporations that have been developing target goals and quotas through either a consent-decree process with courts or direct negotiations with representatives of minority groups and unions. These programs have, in some cases, been agonizingly difficult to develop and would disintegrate if goals and timetables were ruled impermissible. The P. Q. Corporation, for example, reports that it has invested years of training in breaking down managerial biases and stereotypes while getting managers to hire in accordance with affirmative action guidelines. The corporation is concerned that without the pressure of affirmative action programs, managers will fail to recognize their own biases and use of stereotypes. Removal of voluntary programs might additionally stigmatize a business by signalling to minorities that a return to older patterns of discrimination is permissible. Such stigmatization is a serious blow in today's competitive market.[23]

(3) Third, affirmative action programs involving quotas have been successful for the corporations that have adopted them, and there is no need to try to fix what is not broken. As the editors of *Business Week* maintained, "Over the years business and regulators have worked out rules and procedures for affirmative action, including numerical yardsticks for sizing up progress, that both sides understand. It has worked and should be left alone."[24] It has worked because of the abovementioned improved workforce and because of a businesslike approach typical of managerial planning: Managers set goals and timetables for almost everything—from profits to salary bonuses. From a manager's point of view, setting goals and timetables is simply a basic way of measuring progress.

One survey of 200 major American corporations found that the same approach has often been taken to the management of affirmative action: Over 75% of these corporations already use "voluntary internal numerical objectives to assess [equal employment opportunity] performance." Another survey of 300 top corporate executives reported that 72% believe that minority hiring improves rather than hampers productivity, while 64% said there is a need for the government to help bring women and minorities into the mainstream of the workforce. Many corporations have used their records in promotion and recruitment to present a positive image of corporate life in public reports and recruiting brochures. Such reports and brochures have been published, for example, by Schering-Plough, Philip Morris, Exxon, AT&T, IBM, Westinghouse, and Chemical Bank.[25]

Affirmative action has also worked to increase productivity and improved consumer relationships. Corporations in consumer goods and services industries report increased respect and increased sales after achieving affirmative action results. They report that they are able to target some customers they otherwise could not reach, enjoy increased competitiveness, and better understand consumer complaints as a result of a more diverse workforce. Corporations with aggressive affirmative action programs have also been shown to outperform their competitors.[26]

Conclusion

If the social circumstances of discrimination were to be substantially altered, my conclusions in this paper would be modified. I agree with critics that the introduction of preferential treatment on a large scale runs the risk of producing economic advantages to individuals who do not deserve them, protracted court battles, congressional lobbying by power groups, a lowering of admission and work standards, reduced social and economic efficiency, increased racial and minority hostility, and the continued suspicion that well-placed minorities received their positions purely on the basis of quotas. These reasons constitute a strong case against affirmative action policies that use numerical goals and quotas. However, this powerful case is not sufficient to overcome the still stronger counterarguments.

Notes

1. Executive Order 11,246. C.F.R. 339 (1964–65). This order required all federal contractors to develop affirmative action policies.

2. "Their Right to Remedy, Affirmed," *New York Times,* July 3, 1986, p. A30.

3. This standard has been recognized at least since *EEOC* v. *AT&T*, No. 73–149 (E.D. Pa 1973). See also U.S. Department of Labor, Employment Standards Administration, Office of Federal Contract Compliance Programs, "OFCCP: Making EEO and Affirmative Action Work," January 1987 OFCCP-28.

4. See Laura Purdy, "Why Do We Need Affirmative Action?" *Journal of Social Philosophy* 25 (1994): 133–43.

5. See Bron Taylor, *Affirmative Action at Work: Law, Politics, and Ethics* (Pittsburgh: University of Pittsburgh Press, 1991); National Center for Education Statistics, *Faculty in Higher Education Institutions, 1988, Contractor Survey Report*, compiled Susan H. Russell, et al. (Washington, D.C.: U.S. Dept. of Education, March 1990), pp. 5–13; Herman Schwartz, "Affirmative Action," *Minority Report*, ed. L. W. Dunbar (New York: Pantheon Books, 1984), pp. 61–62; Betty M. Vetter, ed., *Professional Women and Minorities: A Manpower Data Resource Service*, 8th ed. (Washington, D.C.: Commission on Science and Technology, 1989); Irene Pave, "A Woman's Place Is at GE, Federal Express, P&G. . . ." *Business Week*, June 23, 1986, pp. 75–76.

6. See *A Common Destiny: Blacks and American Society*, ed. Gerald D. Jaynes and Robin M. Williams Jr., Committee on the Status of Black Americans, Commission on Behavioral and Social Sciences and Education, National Research Council (Washington, D.C.: NAS Press, 1989), pp. 12–13, 138–48; Glenn B. Canner and Wayne Passmore, "Home Purchase Lending in Low-Income Neighborhoods and to Low-Income Borrowers," *Federal Reserve Bulletin* 81 (February 1995): 71–103; Yi-Hsin Chang, "Mortgage Denial Rate for Blacks in '93 Was Double the Level for Whites, Asians," July 29, 1994, p. A2; "Business Bulletin," *Wall Street Journal*, February 28, 1985, p. 1; Constance L. Hays, "Study Says Prejudice in Suburbs Is Aimed Mostly at Blacks," *New York Times*, November 23, 1988, p. A16.

7. Paul Burstein, *Discrimination, Jobs, and Politics* (Chicago: University of Chicago Press, 1985); Bureau of Labor Statistics, *Employment and Earnings* (Washington, D.C.: U.S. Dept. of Labor, January 1989); *A Common Destiny*, op. cit., pp. 16–18, 84–88.

8. As reported by Rudolf A. Pyatt Jr., "Significant Job Studies," *Washington Post*, April 30, 1985, pp. D1–D2.

9. See Margery Austin Turner, Michael Fix, and Raymond Struyk, *Opportunities Denied, Opportunities Diminished: Discrimination in Hiring* (Washington, D.C.: The Urban Institute, 1991).

10. *Alexander* v. *Choate*, 469 U.S. 287, at 295.

11. But the Court comes very close in *Local 28 of the Sheet Metal Workers' International Association* v. *Equal Employment Opportunity Commission*, 106 S.Ct. 3019—commonly known as *Sheet Metal Workers*.

12. *Fullilove* v. *Klutznick*, 448 U.S. 448 (1980); *United Steelworkers* v. *Weber*, 443 U.S. 193 (1979); *United States* v. *Paradise*, 480 U.S. 149 (1987); *Johnson* v. *Transportation Agency*, 480 U.S. 616 (1987).

13. *Firefighters* v. *Stotts*, 467 U.S. 561 (1984); *City of Richmond* v. *J. A. Croson Co.*, 109 S.Ct. 706 (1989); *Adarand Constructors Inc.* v. *Federica Pena*, 63 LW4523 (1995); *Wygant* v. *Jackson Bd. of Education*, 476 U.S. 267 (1986); *Wards Cove Packing* v. *Atonio*, 490 U.S. 642.

14. For a very different view, stressing inconsistency, see Yong S. Lee, "Affirmative Action and Judicial Standards of Review: A Search for the Elusive Consensus," *Review of Public Personnel Administration* 12 (September–December 1991): 47–69.

15. See the argument to this effect in Gertrude Ezorsky, *Racism & Justice: The Case for Affirmative Action* (Ithaca, N.Y.: Cornell University Press, 1991), chap. 1.

16. For a balanced article on this topic, see Robert K. Fullinwider, "Affirmative Action and Fairness," *Report from the Institute for Philosophy & Public Policy* 11 (University of Maryland, Winter 1991): 10–13.

17. See. L. Joseph Semien, "Opening the Utility Door for Women and Minorities," *Public Utilities Fortnightly*, July 5, 1990, pp. 29–31; Irene Pave, "A Woman's Place," p. 76.

18. As quoted in Walter Kiechel, "Living with Human Resources," *Fortune*, August 18, 1986, p. 100.

19. As quoted in Peter Perl, "Rulings Provide Hiring Direction: Employers Welcome Move," *Washington Post*, July 3, 1986, pp. A1, A11.

20. Tim Loughran, "Corning Tries to Break the Glass Ceiling," *Business & Society Review* 76 (Winter 1991): 52–55.

21. Richard Remington, "Go West, Young Woman!" in *Telephony* 215 (November 1988): 30–32; Diane Feldman, "Women of Color Build a Rainbow of Opportunity," *Management Review* 78 (August 1989): 18–21.

22. Loughran, op. cit., p. 54.

23. See Jeanne C. Poole and E. Theodore Kautz, "An EEO/AA Program that Exceeds Quotas—It Targets Biases," *Personnel Journal* 66 (January 1987): 103–105; Mary Thornton, "Justice Dept. Stance on Hiring Goals Resisted," *Washington Post*, May 25, 1985, p. A2; Pyatt, "The Basis of Job Bias," p. D2; Linda Williams, "Minorities Find Pacts with Corporations Are Hard to Come By and Enforce," *Wall Street Journal*, August 23, 1985, p. 13.

24. Editorial, "Don't Scuttle Affirmative Action," *Business Week*, April 5, 1985, p. 174.

25. "Rethinking *Weber*: The Business Response to Affirmative Action," *Harvard Law Review* 102 (January 1989): 661, note 18; Robertson, "Why Bosses Like to Be Told," p. 2.

26. See "Rethinking *Weber*," esp. pp. 668–70; Joseph Michael Pace and Zachary Smith, "Understanding Affirmative Action: From the Practitioner's Perspective," *Public Personnel Management* 24 (Summer 1995): 139–47.

15

JUSTIFYING REVERSE DISCRIMINATION IN EMPLOYMENT

George Sher

A currently favored way of compensating for past discrimina-tion is to afford preferential treatment to the members of those groups which have been discriminated against in the past. I pro-pose to examine the rationale behind this practice when it is applied in the area of employment. I want to ask whether, and if so under what conditions, past acts of discrimination against mem-bers of a particular group justify the current hiring of a member of that group who is less than the best qualified applicant for a given job. Since I am mainly concerned about exploring the relations between past discrimination and present claims to employment, I shall make the assumption that each applicant is at least minimally competent to perform the job he seeks; this will eliminate the need to consider the claims of those who are to receive the services in question. Whether it is ever justifiable to discriminate in favor of an incompetent applicant, or a less than best qualified applicant for a job such as teaching, in which almost any increase in em-ployee competence brings a real increase in services rendered, will be left to be decided elsewhere. Such questions, which turn on bal-ancing the claim of the less than best qualified applicant against the competing claims of those who are to receive his services, are not as basic as the question of whether the less than best qualified applicant ever *has* a claim to employment.[1]

From *Philosophy & Public Affairs* 4, no. 2 (Winter 1975): 159–70. © 1975 by Princeton University Press. Reprinted by permission.

I

It is sometimes argued, when members of a particular group have been barred from employment of a certain kind, that since this group has in the past received less than its fair share of the employment in question, it now deserves to receive *more* by way of compensation.[2] This argument, if sound, has the virtue of showing clearly why preferential treatment should be extended even to those current group members who have not themselves been denied employment: if the point of reverse discrimination is to compensate a wronged *group,* it will presumably hardly matter if those who are preferentially hired were not among the original victims of discrimination. However, the argument's basic presupposition, that groups as opposed to their individual members are the sorts of entities that can be wronged and deserve redress, is itself problematic.[3] Thus the defense of reverse discrimination would be convincing only if it were backed by a further argument showing that groups can indeed be wronged and have deserts of the relevant sort. No one, as far as I know, has yet produced a powerful argument to this effect, and I am not hopeful about the possibilities. Therefore I shall not try to develop a defense of reverse discrimination along these lines.

Another possible way of connecting past acts of discrimination in hiring with the claims of current group members is to argue that even if these current group members have not (yet) been denied *employment,* their membership in the group makes it very likely that they have been discriminatorily deprived of other sorts of goods. It is a commonplace, after all, that people who are forced to do menial and low-paying jobs must often endure corresponding privations in housing, diet, and other areas. These privations are apt to be distributed among young and old alike, and so to afflict even those group members who are still too young to have had their qualifications for employment bypassed. It is, moreover, generally acknowledged by both common sense and law that a person who has been deprived of a certain amount of one sort of good may sometimes reasonably be compensated by an equivalent amount of a good of another sort. (It is this principle, surely, that underlies the legal practice of awarding sums of money to compensate for pain incurred in accidents, damaged reputations, etc.) Given these facts and this principle, it appears that the preferential hiring of current members of discriminated-against groups may be justified as compensation for the other sorts of discrimination these individuals are apt to have suffered.[4]

But, although this argument seems more promising than one presupposing group deserts, it surely cannot be accepted as it stands. For one thing, insofar as the point is simply to compensate individuals for the various sorts of privations they have suffered, there is no special reason to use reverse discrimination rather than some other mechanism to effect compensation. There are, moreover, certain other mechanisms of redress which seem prima facie preferable. It seems, for instance, that it would be most appropriate to compensate for past privations simply by making preferentially available to the discriminated-against individuals equivalent amounts of the very same sorts of goods of which they have been deprived; simple cash settlements would allow a far greater precision in the adjustment of compensation to privation than reverse discriminatory hiring ever could. Insofar as it does not provide any reason to adopt reverse discrimination rather than these prima facie preferable mechanisms of redress, the suggested defense of reverse discrimination is at least incomplete.

Moreover, and even more important, if reverse discrimination is viewed simply as a form of compensation for past privations, there are serious questions about its fairness. Certainly the privations to be compensated for are not the sole responsibility of those individuals whose superior qualifications will have to be bypassed in the reverse discriminatory process. These individuals, if responsible for those privations at all, will at least be no more responsible than others with relevantly similar histories. Yet reverse discrimination will compensate for the privations in question at the expense of these individuals alone. It will have no effect at all upon those other, equally responsible persons whose qualifications are inferior to begin with, who are already entrenched in their jobs, or whose vocations are noncompetitive in nature. Surely it is unfair to distribute the burden of compensation so unequally.[5]

These considerations show, I think, that reverse discriminatory hiring of members of groups that have been denied jobs in the past cannot be justified simply by the fact that each group member has been discriminated against in other areas. If this fact is to enter into the justification of reverse discrimination at all, it must be in some more complicated way.

II

Consider again the sorts of privations that are apt to be distributed among the members of those groups restricted in large part to menial and low-paying jobs. These individuals, we said, are apt to live in substandard homes, to subsist on improper and imbalanced diets, and to receive inadequate educations. Now, it is certainly true that adequate housing, food, and education are goods in and of themselves; a life without them is certainly less pleasant and less full than one with them. But, and crucially, they are also goods in a different sense entirely. It is an obvious and well-documented fact that (at least) the sorts of nourishment and education a person receives as a child will causally affect the sorts of skills and capacities he will have as an adult—including, of course, the very skills which are needed if he is to compete on equal terms for jobs and other goods. Since this is so, a child who is deprived of adequate food and education may lose not only the immediate enjoyments which a comfortable and stimulating environment bring but also the subsequent ability to compete equally for other things of intrinsic value. But to lose this ability to compete is, in essence, to lose one's access to the goods that are being competed for; and this, surely, is itself a privation to be compensated for if possible. It is, I think, the key to an adequate justification of reverse discrimination to see that practice, not as the redressing of *past* privations, but rather as a way of neutralizing the *present* competitive disadvantage caused by those past privations and thus as a way of restoring equal access to those goods which society distributes competitively.[6] When reverse discrimination is justified in this way, many of the difficulties besetting the simpler justification of it disappear.

For whenever someone has been irrevocably deprived of a certain good and there are several alternative ways of providing him with an equivalent amount of another good, it will ceteris paribus be preferable to choose whichever substitute comes closest to actually replacing the lost good. It is this principle that makes preferential access to decent housing, food, and education especially desirable as a way of compensating for the experiential impoverishment of a deprived childhood. If, however, we are concerned to compensate not for the experiential poverty, but for the effects of childhood deprivations, then this principle tells just as heavily for reverse discrimination as the proper form of compensation. If the lost good is just the *ability* to compete on equal terms for first-level goods like desirable jobs, then surely the most appropriate (and so preferable) way of substituting for what has been lost is just to remove the *necessity* of competing on equal terms for these goods— which, of course, is precisely what reverse discrimination does.

When reverse discrimination is viewed as compensation for lost ability to compete on equal terms, a reasonable case can also be made for its fairness. Our doubts about its fairness arose because it seemed to place the entire burden of redress upon those individuals whose superior qualifications are bypassed in the reverse discriminatory process. This seemed wrong because these individuals are, of course, not apt to be any more responsible for past discrimination than others with relevantly similar histories. But, as we are now in a position to see, this objection misses the point. The crucial fact about these individuals is not that they are more *responsible* for past discrimination than others with relevantly similar histories (in fact, the dirty work may well have been done before any of their generation attained the age of responsibility), but rather that unless reverse discrimination is practiced, they will *benefit* more than the others from its effects on their competitors. They will benefit more because unless they are restrained, they, but not the others, will use their competitive edge to claim jobs which their competitors would otherwise have gotten. Thus, it is only because they stand to *gain* the most from the relevant effects of the *original* discrimination, that the bypassed individuals stand to lose the most from *reverse* discrimination.[7] This is surely a valid reply to the charge that reverse discrimination does not distribute the burden of compensation equally.

III

So far, the argument has been that reverse discrimination is justified insofar as it neutralizes competitive disadvantages caused by past privations. This may be correct, but it is also oversimplified. In actuality, there are many ways in which a person's environment may affect his ability to compete; and there may well be logical differences among these ways which affect the degree to which reverse discrimination is called for. Consider, for example, the following cases:

(1) An inadequate education prevents someone from acquiring the degree of a certain skill that he would have been able to acquire with a better education.
(2) An inadequate diet, lack of early intellectual stimulation, etc., lower an individual's ability, and thus prevent him from acquiring the degree of competence in a skill that he would otherwise have been able to acquire.
(3) The likelihood that he will not be able to use a certain skill because he belongs to a group which has been discriminated against in the past leads a person to decide, rationally, not even to try developing that skill.
(4) Some aspect of his childhood environment renders an individual incapable of putting forth the sustained effort needed to improve his skills.

These are four different ways in which past privations might adversely affect a person's skills. Ignoring for analytical purposes the fact that privation often works in more than one of these ways at a time, shall we say that reverse discrimination is equally called for in each case?

It might seem that we should say it is, since in each case a difference in the individual's environment would have been accompanied by an increase in his mastery of a certain skill (and, hence, by an improvement in his competitive position with respect to jobs requiring that skill). But this blanket counterfactual formulation conceals several important distinctions. For one thing, it suggests (and our justification of reverse discrimination seems to require) the possibility of giving *just enough* preferential treatment to the disadvantaged individual in each case to restore to him the competitive position that he would have had, had he not suffered his initial disadvantage. But in fact, this does not seem to be equally possible in all cases. We can roughly calculate the difference that a certain improvement in education or intellectual stimulation would have made in the development of a person's skills if his efforts had been held constant (cases 1 and 2); for achievement is known to be a relatively straightforward compositional function of ability, environmental factors, and effort. We cannot, however, calculate in the same way the difference that improved prospects or environment would have made in degree of *effort* expended; for although effort is affected by environmental factors, it is not a known compositional function of them (or of anything else).

Because of this, there would be no way for us to decide how much preferential treatment is just enough to make up for the efforts that a particular disadvantaged individual would have made under happier circumstances.

There is also another problem with (3) and (4). Even if there were a way to afford a disadvantaged person just enough preferential treatment to make up for the efforts he was prevented from making by his environment, it is not clear that he *ought* to be afforded that much preferential treatment. To allow this, after all, would be to concede that the effort he would have made under other conditions is worth just as much as the effort that his rival actually *did* make; and this, I think, is implausible. Surely a person who *actually has* labored long and hard to achieve a given degree of a certain skill is more deserving of a job requiring that skill than another who is equal in all other relevant respects, but who merely *would* have worked and achieved the same amount under different conditions. Because actual effort creates desert in a way that merely possible effort does not, reverse discrimination to restore precisely the competitive position that a person would have had if he had not been prevented from working harder would not be desirable even if it were possible.

There is perhaps also a further distinction to be made here. A person who is rationally persuaded by an absence of opportunities not to develop a certain skill (case 3) will typically not undergo any sort of character transformation in the process of making this decision. He will be the same person after his decision as before it, and, most often, the same person without his skill as with it. In cases such as (4), this is less clear. A person who is rendered incapable of effort by his environment does in a sense undergo a character transformation; to become truly incapable of sustained effort is to become a different (and less meritorious) person from the person one would otherwise have been. Because of this (and somewhat paradoxically, since his character change is itself apt to stem from factors beyond his control), such an individual may have less of a claim to reverse discrimination than one whose lack of effort does not flow from even an environmentally induced character fault, but rather from a justified rational decision.[8]

IV

When reverse discrimination is discussed in a nontheoretical context, it is usually assumed that the people most deserving of such treatment are blacks, members of other ethnic minorities, and women. In this last section, I shall bring the results of the foregoing discussion to bear on this assumption. Doubts will be raised both about the analogy between the claims of blacks and women to reverse discrimination and about the propriety, in absolute terms, of singling out either group as the proper recipient of such treatment.

For many people, the analogy between the claims of blacks and the claims of women to reverse discrimination rests simply upon the undoubted fact that both groups have been discriminatorily denied jobs in the past. But on the account just proposed, past discrimination justifies reverse discrimination only insofar as it has adversely affected the competitive position of present group members. When this standard is invoked, the analogy between the claims of blacks and those of women seems immediately to break down. The exclusion of blacks from good jobs in the past has been only one element in an interlocking pattern of exclusions and often has resulted in a poverty issuing in (and in turn reinforced by) such other privations as inadequate nourishment, housing, and health care, lack of time to provide adequate guidance and intellectual stimulation for the young, dependence on (often inadequate) public education, etc. It is this whole complex of privations that undermines the ability of the young to compete; and it is largely because of its central causal role in this complex that the past unavailability of good jobs for blacks justifies reverse discrimination in their favor now. In the case of women, past discrimination in employment simply has not played the same role. Because children commonly come equipped with both male *and* female parents, the inability of the female parent to get a good job need not, and usually does not, result in a poverty detracting from the quality of the nourishment, education, housing, health, or intellectual stimulation of the female child (and, of course, when such poverty does result, it affects male and female children indifferently). For this reason, the past inaccessibility of good jobs for women does not seem to create for them the same sort of claim on reverse discrimination that its counterpart does for blacks.

Many defenders of reverse discrimination in favor of women would reply at this point that although past discrimination in employment has of course not played the *same* causal role in the case of women which it has in the case of blacks, it has nevertheless played *a* causal role in both cases. In the case of women, the argument runs, that role has been mainly psychological: past discrimination in hiring has led to a scarcity of female "role-models" of suitably high achievement. This lack, together with a culture which in many other ways subtly inculcates the idea that women should not or cannot do the jobs that men do, has in turn made women psychologically less able to do these jobs. This argument is hard to assess fully, since it obviously rests on a complex and problematic psychological claim.[9] The following objections, however, are surely relevant. First, even if it is granted without question that cultural bias and absence of suitable role-models do have some direct and pervasive effect upon women, it is not clear that this effect must take the form of a reduction of women's *abilities* to do the jobs men do. A more likely outcome would seem to be a reduction of women's *inclinations* to do these jobs—a result whose proper compensation is not preferential treatment of those women who have sought the jobs in question, but rather the encouragement of others to seek those jobs as well. Of course, this disinclination to do these jobs may in turn lead some women not to develop the relevant skills; to the extent that this occurs, the competitive position of these women will indeed be affected, albeit indirectly, by the scarcity of female role-models. Even here, however, the resulting disadvantage will not be comparable to those commonly produced by the poverty syndrome. It will flow solely from lack of effort, and so will be of the sort (cases 3 and 4) that neither calls for nor admits of full equalization by reverse discrimination. Moreover, and conclusively, since there is surely the same dearth of role-models, etc., for blacks as for women, whatever psychological disadvantages accrue to women because of this will beset blacks as well. Since blacks, but not women, must also suffer the privations associated with poverty, it follows that they are the group more deserving of reverse discrimination.

Strictly speaking, however, the account offered here does not allow us to speak this way of *either* group. If the point of reverse discrimination is to compensate for competitive disadvantages caused by past discrimination, it will be justified in favor of only those group members whose abilities have actually been reduced;

and it would be most implausible to suppose that *every* black (or *every* woman) has been affected in this way. Blacks from middle-class or affluent backgrounds will surely have escaped many, if not all, of the competitive handicaps besetting those raised under less fortunate circumstances; and if they have, our account provides no reason to practice reverse discrimination in their favor. Again, whites from impoverished backgrounds may suffer many, if not all, of the competitive handicaps besetting their black counterparts; and if they do, the account provides no reason *not* to practice reverse discrimination in their favor. Generally, the proposed account allows us to view racial (and sexual) boundaries only as roughly suggesting which individuals are likely to have been disadvantaged by past discrimination. Anyone who construes these boundaries as playing a different and more decisive role must show us that a different defense of reverse discrimination is plausible.

NOTES

1. In what follows I will have nothing to say about utilitarian justifications of reverse discrimination. There are two reasons for this. First, the winds of utilitarian argumentation blow in too many directions. It is certainly socially beneficial to avoid the desperate actions to which festering resentments may lead—but so too is it socially useful to confirm the validity of qualifications of the traditional sort, to assure those who have amassed such qualifications that "the rules of the game have not been changed in the middle," that accomplishment has not been downgraded in society's eyes. How could these conflicting utilities possibly be measured against one another?

Second and even more important, to rest a defense of reverse discrimination upon utilitarian considerations would be to ignore what is surely the guiding intuition of its proponents, that this treatment is *deserved* where discrimination has been practiced in the past. It is the intuition that reverse discrimination is a matter not (only) of social good but of right which I want to try to elucidate.

2. This argument, as well as the others I shall consider, presupposes that jobs are (among other things) goods, and so ought to be distributed as fairly as possible. This presupposition seems to be amply supported by the sheer economic necessity of earning a living, as well as by the fact that some jobs carry more prestige and are more interesting and pay better than others.

3. As Robert Simon has pointed out in "Preferential Hiring: A Reply to Judith Jarvis Thomson," *Philosophy & Public Affairs* 3, no. 3 (Spring 1974): 312–20, it is also far from clear that the preferential hiring of its individual members could be a proper form of compensation for any wronged group that *did* exist.

4. A version of this argument is advanced by Judith Jarvis Thomson in "Preferential Hiring," *Philosophy & Public Affairs* 2, no. 4 (Summer 1973): 364–84.

5. Cf. Simon, "Preferential Hiring," sec. III.

6. A similar justification of reverse discrimination is suggested, but not ultimately endorsed, by Thomas Nagel in "Equal Treatment and Compensatory Discrimination," *Philosophy & Public Affairs* 2, no. 4 (Summer 1973): 348–63. Nagel rejects this justification on the grounds that a system distributing goods solely on the basis of performance determined by native ability would itself be unjust, even if not as unjust as one distributing goods on a racial or sexual basis. I shall not comment on this, except to remark that our moral intuitions surely run the other way: the average person would certainly find the latter system of distribution *far* more unjust than the former, if, indeed, he found the former unjust at all. Because of this, the burden is on Nagel to show exactly why a purely meritocratic system of distribution would be unjust.

7. It is tempting, but I think largely irrelevant, to object here that many who are now entrenched in their jobs (tenured professors, for example) have already benefited from the effects of past discrimination at least as much as the currently best qualified applicant will if reverse discrimination is not practiced. While many such individuals have undoubtedly benefited from the effects of discrimination upon their original competitors, few if any are likely to have benefited from a reduction in the abilities of the *currently best qualified applicant's* competitor. As long as none of them have so benefited, the best qualified applicant in question will still stand to gain the most from that *particular* effect of past discrimination, and so reverse discrimination against him will remain fair. Of course, there will also be cases in which an entrenched person *has* previously benefited from the reduced abilities of the currently been qualified applicant's competitor. In these cases, the best qualified applicant will *not* be the single main beneficiary of his rival's handicap, and so reverse discrimination against him will not be entirely fair. I am inclined to think there may be a case for reverse discrimination even here, however; for if it is truly impossible to dislodge the entrenched previous beneficiary of his rival's handicap, reverse discrimination against the best qualified applicant may at least be the fairest (or least unfair) of the practical alternatives.

8. A somewhat similar difference might seem to obtain between cases (1) and (2). One's ability to learn is more intimately a part of him than his actual degree of education; hence, someone whose ability to learn is lowered by his environment (case 2) is a changed person in a way in which a person who is merely denied education (case 1) is not. However, one's ability to learn is not a feature of moral character in the way ability to exert effort is, and so this difference between (1) and (2) will have little bearing an the degree to which reverse discrimination is called for in these cases.

9. The feminist movement has convincingly documented the ways in which sexual bias is built into the information received by the young; but it is one thing to show that such information is received, and quite another to show how, and to what extent, its reception is causally efficacious.

BIBLIOGRAPHY

Since the early 1970s there have been literally thousands of essays, research papers, books, anthologies, and monographs published on affirmative action and its relation to social justice. The following is a lengthy list of publications which we have compiled, though it is only the tip of the iceberg. They represent a wide range of political and philosophical positions on this issue. Some of these works are considered contemporary classics; others are less well-known, though they make an important contribution to the debate.

Abrahms, Kathryn. "Gender Discrimination and the Transformation of Workplace Norms." *Vanderbilt Law Review* 42 (1989).

Abrams, Elliot. "The Quota Commission." *Commentary* 50 (October 1972).

Adelson, Joseph. "Living With Quotas. "*Commentary* 65 (May 1987).

Amdur, Robert. "Compensatory Justice: The Question of Costs." *Political Theory* 7 (May 1979).

Arkes, Hadley. *First Things: An Inquiry into the First Principles of Morals and Justice.* Princeton, N.J.: Princeton University Press, 1986.

Askin, Helen. "The Case For Compensatory Treatment." *Rutgers Law Review* 24 (1970).

———. "Eliminating Racist Inequality in a Racist World." *Civil Liberties Review* 2 (1975).

Askin, Helen, and Carl Cohen. "Preferential Admissions in Higher Education: Should We Support Or Condemn It?" (Debate). *Civil Liberties Review* 2 (1975).

Auer, Andreas. "Public School Desegregation and the Color-Blind Constitution. " *Southwestern Law Journal* 27 (August 1973).

Axelsen, Diana. "With All Deliberate Delay: On Justifying Preferential Policies in Education and Employment." *Philosophical Forum* 9 (Winter/Spring 1977–78).

Bayles, Michael D. "Compensatory Reverse Discrimination in Hiring." *Social Theory and Practice* 2 (Spring 1973).

———. "Reparations to Wronged Groups." *Analysis* 33 (June 1973).

Beckwith, Francis J. "The Epistemology of Political Correctness." *Public Affairs Quarterly* 8 (1994).

———. *That's No White Male, That's My Husband, or Affirmative Action and the Civil Rights Vision.* Reno: Nevada Policy Research Institute, 1996.

Beckwith, Francis J., and Michael Bauman, eds. *Are You Politically Correct?: Debating America's Cultural Standards.* Amherst, N.Y.: Prometheus Books, 1993.

Beckwith, Francis J., and James Harris. *Affirmative Action: A Debate.* Crossroads Monograph Series in Faith and Public Policy. Wynnewood, Pa.: Crossroads, 1997.

Bedau, Hugo Adam. "Compensatory Justice and the Manifesto." *The Monist* 56 (January 1972).

Bell, Derrick A., Jr. "*Bakke,* Minority Admissions, and the Usual Price of Racial Remedies." *California Law Review* 67 (January 1979).

———. "In Defense of Minority Admissions Programs; A Reply to Professor Graglia." *University of Pennsylvania Law Review* 119 (1970).

———. "Racial Remediation: An Historical Perspective On Current Conditions." *Notre Dame Lawyer* 52 (October 1976).

———. "Racism in American Courts: Cause for Black Disruption or Despair?" *Califomia Law Review* 61 (1973).

Belz, Herman. *Equality Transformed: A Quarter Century of Affirmative Action.* New Brunswick, N.J.: Transaction Press, 1992.

Bennett, William J., and Terry Eastland. "Why Bakke Won't End Reverse Discrimination." *Commentary* 66 (September 1978).

Bittker, Boris I. *The Case for Black Reparations.* New York: Random House, 1973.

———. "The Case of the Checker-Board Ordinance: An Experiment in Race Relations." *Yale Law Journal* 71 (1962)

Blackstone, William T. "Compensatory Justice and Affirmative Action." *Proceedings of the American Catholic Philosophical Association* 69 (1975).

———. "Reverse Discrimination and Compensatory Justice." *Social Theory and Practice* 3 (Spring 1975).

Blackstone, William T., and Robert Heslep, eds. *Social Justice and Preferential Treatment* Athens, Ga.: University of Georgia Press, 1977.

Blasi, Vincent. "*Bakke* as Precedent: Does Mr. Justice Powell Have a Theory?" *California Law Review* 67 (January 1979).

Bork, Robert H. *Slouching Toward Gomorrah: Modern Liberalism and American Decline.* New York: Harper Collins, 1996. Chapter 12.

Bowie, Norman E. (ed.) *Equal Opportunity.* Boulder, Col.: Westview, 1988.

Boxill, Bernard. *Blacks and Social Justice.* Rev. ed. Totowa, N.J.: Rowman & Littlefield, 1993.

————. "The Morality of Preferential Hiring." *Philosophy & Public Affairs* 7 (Spring 1978).

————. "The Morality of Reparations." *Social Theory and Practice* 2 (1972).

Bracy, Warren. "The Questionable Legality of Affirmative Action: A Response to Rejoinder." *Journal of Urban Law* 52 (November 1974).

Cahn, Steven M., ed. *Affirmative Action and the University: A Philosophical Inquiry.* Philadelphia: Temple University Press, 1993.

Calabresi, Guido. "*Bakke* as Psuedo-Tragedy." *Catholic University Law Review* 28 (Spring 1979).

Capaldi, Nicholas. *Out of Order: Affirmative Action and the Crisis of Doctrinaire Liberalism.* Amherst, N.Y.: Prometheus Books, 1985.

Carter, Stephen L. *Reflections of an Affirmative Action Baby.* New York: Basic Books, 1991.

Choper, Jesse H. "The Constitutionality of Affirmative Action: Views from the Supreme Court." *Kentucky Law Journal* 79 (1981–82).

————. "Continued Uncertainty as to the Constitutionality of Remedial Racial Classifictions: Identifying the Pieces of the Puzzle." *Iowa Law Review* 72 (1987).

Cohen, Carl. "The DeFunis Case: Race and Constitution." *The Nation* (February 8, 1975).

————. "Why Racial Preference Is Illegal and Immoral." *Commentary* 67 (June 1979).

Cohen, Marshall, Thomas Nagel, and Thomas Scanlon, eds. *Equality and Preferential Treatment.* Princeton, N.J.: Princeton University Press, 1976.

Coleman, Jules L. "Justice And Preferential Hiring." *Journal of Critical Analysis* 5 (July–October 1973).

Conti, Joseph G. and Brad Stetson. *Challenging the Civil Rights Establishment, Profiles of a New Black Vanguard.* Westport, Conn.: Praeger, 1993.

Cowan, J. L. "Inverse Discrimination." *Analysis* 33 (October 1972).

Crandel, John C. "Affirmative Action: Goals and Consequences." *Philosophical Exchange* 1 (Summer 1974).

Davidson, Nicholas. *The Failure of Feminism*. Amherst, N.Y.: Prometheus Books, 1988.

D'Souza, Dinesh. *The End of Racism*. New York: The Free Press, 1995.

Dworkin, Ronald. *A Matter of Principle*. Cambridge, Mass.: Harvard University Press, 1985.

———. *Taking Rights Seriously*. Cambridge, Mass.: Harvard University Press, 1977.

———. "Why Bakke Has No Case." *New York Review of Books* (November 10, 1977).

Eastland, Terry. *Ending Affirmative Action: The Case for Colorblind Justice*. New York: Basic Books, 1996.

Ezorsky, Gertrude. *Racism And Justice: The Case for Affirmative Action*. Ithaca, N.Y.: Cornell University Press, 1991.

Flew, Antony. *The Politics of Procrustes: Contradictions of Enforced Equality*. Amherst, N.Y.: Prometheus Books, 1981.

Fuchs, Lawrence H. *The American Kaleidoscope: Race, Ethnicity, and the Civic Culture*. Hanover, N.H.: Wesleyan University Press, 1995.

Fullinwider, Robert K. *The Reverse Discrimination Controversy: A Moral And Legal Analysis*. Totowa, N.J.: Rowman & Littlefield, 1980.

Fullinwider, Robert K., and Claudia Mills. *The Moral Foundations of Civil Rights*. Totowa, N.J.: Rowman & Littlefield, 1986.

Glendon, Mary Ann. *Rights Talk: The Impoverishment of Political Discourse*. New York: The Free Press, 1991.

Goldberg, D. T., ed. *Anatomy of Racism*. Minneapolis: University of Minnesota Press, 1988.

Goldman, Alan H. *Justice and Reverse Discrimination*. Princeton, N.J.: Princeton University Press, 1979.

Greenawalt, Kent, ed. *Discrimination and Reverse Discrimination*. New York: Alfred A. Knopf, 1983.

Gross, Barry R. *Discrimination in Reverse: Is Turnabout Fair Play?* New York: State University of New York Press, 1978.

———, ed. *Reverse Discrimination*. Amherst, N.Y.: Prometheus Books, 1977.

Guinier, Lani. *The Tyranny of the Majority: Fundamental Fairness in Representative Democracy*. New York: The Free Press, 1994.

Harder, Martha B. "How They Get Us with Subtle Discrimination." *Context* 12 (Spring 1978).

Hill, James. "The New Judicial Perception of Employment Discrimination: Litigation Under Title VII of the Civil Rights Act of 1964." *University of Colorado Law Review* 43 (March 1972).

———. "What Justice Requires: Some Comments on Professor Schoeman's Views on Compensatory Justice." *Personalist* 56 (Winter 1975).

Horowitz, Donald L. "Are the Courts Going Too Far?" *Commentary* 63 (January 1977).

Jagger, Alison. "On Sexual Equality." In *Sex Equality*, edited by Jane English. Englewood Cliffs, N.J.: Prentice-Hall, 1977.

Karst, Kenneth L., and Harold W. Horowitz. "Affirmative Action and Equal Protection." *Virginia Law Review* 60 (October 1974).

———. "The *Bakke* Opinions and Equal Protection Doctrine." *Harvard Civil Rights-Civil Liberties Law Review* 14 (Spring 1979).

Katzner, Louis. "Is the Favoring of Women and Blacks in Employment and Educational Opportunities Justified?" In *Philosophy of Law*, 4th ed., edited by Joel Feinberg and Hyman Gross. Belmont, Calif.: Wadsworth, 1991.

Kennedy, Randall. "Persuasion and Distrust." In *Racial Preference and Racial Justice: The New Affirmative Action Controversy*, edited by Russell Nieli. Washington, D.C.: Ethics and Public Policy Center, 1991.

Kull, Andrew. *The Color-Blind Constitution.* Cambridge, Mass.: Harvard University Press, 1992.

Levin, Betsy, and Willis D. Hawley, eds. *The Courts, Social Science, and School Desegregation.* New Brunswick, N.J.: Transaction Books, 1977.

Levin, Michael. *Feminism and Freedom.* New Brunswick, N.J.: Transaction Books, 1987.

Livingston, John C. *Fair Game?: Inequality And Affirmative Action.* San Francisco: W. H. Freeman and Co., 1979.

Lynch, Frederick. *The Diversity Machine: The Drive to Change "The White Male Work Place."* New York: The Free Press, 1997.

———. *Invisible Victims: White Males and the Crisis of Affirmative Action.* Westport, Conn.: Praeger, 1991.

MacIntyre, Alasdair. *Whose Justice? Which Rationality?* Notre Dame, Ind.: University of Notre Dame Press, 1983.

MacKinnon, Catherine. *Feminism Unmodified: Discourses on Life and Law.* Cambridge: Harvard University Press, 1987.

Martin, Michael. "Pedagogical Arguments for Preferential Hiring and Tenuring of Women Teachers in the University." *Philosophical Forum* 5 (Fall/Winter 1973–74).

Mills, Nicholas, ed. *Debating Affirmative Action: Race, Gender, Ethnicity, and the Politics of Inclusion.* New York: Dell Publishing, 1994.

Murray, Charles, and Richard Hernstein. *The Bell Curve: Intelligence and Class Structure in American Life.* New York: The Free Press, 1994.

Nagel, Thomas. "Equal Treatment and Compensatory Discrimination." *Philosophy & Public Affairs* 2 (Summer 1973).

———. *Equality and Partiality.* New York: Oxford University Press, 1991.

Nielsen, Kai. *Equality and Liberty: A Defense of Radical Egalitarianism.* Totowa, N.J.: Rowan & Littlefield, 1985.

Newton, Lisa H. "Corruption of Thought, Word and Deed: Reflections on Affirmative Action And Its Current Defenders." *Contemporary Philosophy* 13 (January/February 1991).

———. "Reverse Discrimination as Unjustified." *Ethics* 83 (1973).

Nickel, James W. "Discrimination and Morally Relevant Characteristics." *Analysis* 32 (March 1972).

———. "Preferential Policies in Hiring and Admissions: A Jurisprudential Approach." *Columbia Law Review* 75 (April 1975).

———. Review of *The Case for Black Reparations,* by Boris Bittiker. *Ethics* 84 (1974).

———. "Should Reparations Be to Individuals or to Groups?" *Analysis* 34 (April 1974).

Novak, Michael. *The Spirit of Democratic Capitalism.* New York: Simon & Schuster, 1982.

Nozick, Robert. *Anarchy, State, and Utopia.* New York: Basic Books, 1974.

Nunn, William A. "Reverse Discrimination." *Analysis* 34 (April 1974).

Okin, Susan Moller. *Justice, Gender, and the Family.* New York: Basic Books, 1989.

O'Neil, Robert M. "*Bakke* in Balance: Some Preliminary Thoughts," *California Law Review* 67 (January 1979).

———. *Discriminating Against Discrimination: Preferential Admissions and the DeFunis Case.* Bloomington, Ind.: Indiana University Press, 1975.

———. "Racial Preference and Higher Education: The Larger Context." *Virginia Law Review* 60 (October 1974).

Pojman, Louis P. "A Critique of Contemporary Egalitarianism: A Christian Perspective." *Faith and Philosophy* 8 (October 1991).

———. "The Moral Status of Affirmative Action." *Public Affairs Quarterly* 6 (1992).

Pojman, Louis P., and Robert Westmoreland, eds. *Equality: Selected Readings.* New York: Oxford University Press, 1997.

Pollack, Louise H. "DeFunis Non Est Disputantum." *Columbia Law Review* 75 (April 1975).

Pollit, D. H. "Racial Discrimination in Employment: Proposals for Corrective Action." *Buffalo Law Review* 13 (1963).

Posner, Richard A. "The *Bakke* Case and the Future of 'Affirmative Action'." *California Law Review* 67 (January 1979).

———. "The *DeFunis* Case and the Constitutionality of Preferential Treatment of Racial Minorities." In *The Supreme Court Review,* Philip Kurland (ed.). Chicago: University of Chicago Press, 1975.

Rawls, John. *Political Liberalism.* New York: Columbia University Press, 1993.
————. *A Theory of Justice.* Cambridge, Mass.: Harvard University Press, 1971.
Raz, Joseph. "Principles of Equality." *Mind* 88 (July 1978).
Redish, Martin H. "Preferential Law School Admissions and the Equal Protection Clause: An Analysis of the Competing Arguments." *UCLA Law Review* 22 (December 1974).
Reynolds, William Bradford. "An Equal Opportunity Scorecard." *Georgia Law Review* 21 (1987).
Roberts, Paul Craig, and Lawrence M. Stratton. *The New Color Line: How Quotas and Privilege Destroy Democracy.* Washington D.C.: Regnery, 1996.
Rothbard, Murray. *For a New Liberty: The Libertarian Manifesto,* rev. ed. San Francisco: Fox & Wilkes, 1978.
St. Antoine, Theodore. "Affirmative Action: Hypocritical Euphemism or Noble Mandate?" *University of Michigan Journal of Law Reform* 10 (Fall 1976).
Samford, Frank P. "Towards a Constitutional Definition of Racial Discrimination." *Emory Law Journal* 25 (Summer 1976).
Sandel, Michael J. *Democracy's Discontent.* Cambridge, Mass.: Harvard University Press, 1996.
————. *Liberalism and the Limits of Justice.* New York: Cambridge University Press, 1982.
Sandlow, Terrance. "Judicial Protection of Minorities." *Michigan Law Review* 75 (April/May 1977).
————. "Racial Preferences in Higher Education: Political Responsibility and the Judicial Role." *University of Chicago Law Review* 42 (Summer 1975).
Scales, Ann. "The Emergence of Feminist Jurisprudence: An Essay." *Yale Law Journal* 95 (1986).
Schlesinger, Arthur M., Jr. *The Disuniting of America: Reflections on Multicultural Society.* New York: W. W. Norton, 1992.
Schoeman, Ferdinand. "When Is It Just to Discriminate?" *Personalist* 56 (Spring 1975).
Schucter, Arnold. *Reparations.* Philadelphia: Lippincott, 1970.
Schwartz, Herman. "The 1986 and 1987 Affirmative Action Cases: It's All Over but the Shouting." *Michigan Law Review* 86 (1987).
Schwerin, Kurt. "German Compensation for Victims of Nazi Persecution." *Northwestern University Law Review* 67 (September/October 1972).
Seabury, Paul. "H.E.W. And The Universities." *Commentary* 53 (February 1972).

Sedler, Robert Allen. "Beyond *Bakke*: The Consitution and Redressing the Social History of Racism." *Harvard Civil Rights-Civil Liberties Law Review* 14 (Spring 1979).

———. "Racial Preference, Reality, and the Constitution: *Bakke* v. *Regents of University of California*." *Santa Clara Law Review* 17 (1977).

Seligman, Daniel. "How 'Equal Opportunity' Turned into Employment Quotas." *Fortune* 87 (March 1973).

Sher, George. "Groups and Justice." *Ethics* 87 (January 1977).

———. "Justifying Reverse Discrimination in Employment." *Philosophy & Public Affairs* 4 (Winter 1975).

Sherain, Howard. "The Questionable Legality of Affirmative Action." *Journal of Urban Law* 51 (August 1973).

———. "The Questionable Legality of Affirmative Action: A Rejoinder." *Journal of Urban Law* 52 (November 1974).

Sherman, Malcolm, J. "Affirmative Action and the AAUP." *AAUP Bulletin* 61 (Winter 1975).

Shiner, Roger A. "Individuals, Groups and Inverse Discrimination." *Analysis* 33 (June 1973).

Silvestri, Philip. "The Justification of Inverse Discrimination." *Analysis* 34 (October 1973).

Simon, Robert L. "Equality, Merit, and the Determination of Our Gifts." *Social Research* 41 (Autumn 1974).

———. "Individual Rights and 'Benign' Discrimination." *Ethics* 90 (1979).

———. "Preferential Hiring: A Reply to Judith Jarvis Thomson."*Philosophy & Public Affairs* 3 (Spring 1974).

———. "Statistical Justification of Discrimination." *Analysis* 38 (January 1978).

Smith, James and Finis Welch. *Closing the Gap: Forty Years of Economic Progress for Blacks*. Santa Monica, Calif.: The Rand Corporation, 1986.

Solomon, Lewis D., and Judith S. Heeter. "Affirmative Action in Higher Education: Towards a Rationale for Preference." *Notre Dame Lawyer* 52 (October 1976).

Sommers, Christina Hoff. *Who Stole Feminism?* New York: Simon & Schuster, 1994.

Sowell, Thomas. " 'Affirmative Action' Reconsidered." *Public Interest* 42 (Winter 1976).

———. *Civil Rights: Rhetoric or Reality?* New York: Wilham Morrow, 1984.

———. *The Economics and Politics of Race: An International Perspective*. New York: Quill, 1983.

———. *Preferential Policies: An International Perspective*. New York: William Morrow, 1990.

Steele, Claude, and Stephen Greer. "Affirmative Action and Academic Hiring: A Case Study of a Value Conflict." *Journal of Higher Education* 47 (July/August 1976).

Steele, Shelby. *The Content of Our Character: A New Vision of Race in America.* New York: St. Martin's Press, 1990.

Sterba, James P. "Justice as Desert." *Social Theory and Practice* 3 (1974).

Strike, Kenneth A. "Justice and Reverse Discrimination." *University of Chicago School Review* 84 (August 1976).

Taylor, Paul. "Reverse Discrimination and Compensatory Justice." *Analysis* 33 (June 1973).

Thalberg, Irving. "Themes in the Reverse Discrimination Debate." *Ethics* 91 (1980).

Thomas, Clarence. "Affirmative Action Goals and Timetables: Too Tough? Not Tough Enough!" *Yale Law & Policy Review* 5 (Spring/Summer 1987).

———. "The Higher Law Background of the Privileges and Immunities Clause of the Fourteenth Amendment." *Harvard Journal of Law & Public Policy* 12 (Winter 1989).

———. "Toward a 'Plain Reading' of the Constitution—The Declaration of Independence in Constitutional Interpretation." *Howard Law Journal* 30 (1987).

Thomson, Judith Jarvis. *Rights, Restitution, and Risk: Essays in Moral Theory,* edited by William Parent. Cambridge, Mass.: Harvard University Press, 1986.

West, Cornell. "The New Cultural Politics of Difference." *October* 53 (Summer 1990).

Westen, Peter. "The Concept of Equal Opportunity." *Ethics* 95 (1985).

———. "The Empty Idea of Equality." *Harvard Law Review* 95 (1982).

Vieira, Norman. "Racial Imbalance, Black Separatism and Permissible Classification by Race." *Michigan Law Review* 67 (1969).

Wade, Francis C. "Preferential Treatment of Blacks." *Social Theory and Practice* 4 (Spring 1978).

Walzer, Michael. *Spheres of Justice: A Defense of Pluralism and Equality.* New York: Basic Books, 1983.

Warren, Mary Anne. "Secondary Sexism and Quota Hiring." *Philosophy & Public Affairs* 6 (Spring 1977).

Wilson, William Julius. *The Truly Disadvantaged.* Chicago: University of Chicago Press, 1978.

Yates, Steven. *Civil Wrongs: What Went Wrong with Affirmative Action?* San Francisco: Institute for Contemporary Studies, 1994.

———. "Multiculturalism and Epistemology." *Public Affairs Quarterly* 6 (1992).

CONTRIBUTORS

TOM L. BEAUCHAMP is professor of philosophy at Georgetown University as well as senior research scholar at Georgetown's Kennedy Institute of Ethics.

FRANCIS J. BECKWITH is associate professor of philosophy, culture, and law at the Trinity Graduate School of Trinity International University (Southern California campus) as well as senior research fellow, Nevada Policy Research Institute.

WARD CONNERLY, a member of the board of regents of the University of California system, is president and chief executive officer of Connerly and Associates Inc., a housing and association management consulting firm founded in 1973 by him and his wife, Ilene.

RONALD DWORKIN is professor of law at New York University and university professor of jurisprudence at Oxford University in England.

STANLEY FISH is professor of English and law at Duke University.

LYNDON BAINES JOHNSON was president of the United States of America between 1964 and 1969.

TODD JONES is associate professor of philosophy at the University of Nevada, Las Vegas.

NICHOLAS LEMANN is a national correspondent for the *Atlantic Monthly.*

MICHAEL E. LEVIN is professor of philosophy at the City College of New York-CUNY Graduate Center.

FREDERICK R. LYNCH is Carthage Scholar at Claremont-McKenna College in southern California.

LOUIS P. POJMAN is professor of philosophy at the United States Military Academy, West Point, New York.

GEORGE SHER is Herbert S. Autrey Professor of Philosophy at Rice University.

THOMAS SOWELL is a senior fellow at the Hoover Institution, Stanford University.

SHELBY STEELE is professor of English at San Jose State University.

RICHARD WASSERSTROM is professor of philosophy at the University of California, Santa Cruz.

CORNEL WEST is professor of Afro-American studies and philosophy of religion at Harvard University.

WILLIAM JULIUS WILSON is Lucy Flower Distinguished Service Professor of Sociology at the University of Chicago and Malcolm Wiener Professor of Social Policy at Harvard University.